(c

LUXURY AND CAPITALISM

WERNER SOMBART

Luxury and Capitalism

Introduction by Philip Siegelman

Ann Arbor

THE UNIVERSITY OF MICHIGAN PRESS

Translated by W. R. Dittmar

INTRODUCTION
by Philip Siegelman

One need not be a Marxist to grant that intellectual fashion can respond to the tug of the economic order. Some of Werner Sombart's work is being pulled back into the orbit of contemporary academic consciousness not only because of its intrinsic merits, but also because some of his concerns have reappeared in the work of contemporary students of political economy. In the last two decades the interest in economic development, nation-building, and modernization has refocused attention on the origins of modern capitalism—impelled, perhaps, by a desire to find the roots of the deep forms of many of the social and political institutions and practices of the West. For those who are interested in studying the ways in which earlier social forms may provide models for understanding their emerging contemporary analogues and for students of economic history, the sociology of religion, and political economy, Sombart's work should have considerable interest.

Sombart was born in 1863—he was Max Weber's senior by one year—and came to maturity in that period of German thought when Marxism, socialism, and the study of analytic and retrospective sociology (often dominated by economic history) had emerged or were emerging as major magnetic points on the intellectual compass. Some years before that time—starting about mid-century—a circle of German thinkers whose most distinguished representatives came to include Wilhelm Roscher at the University of Berlin and Karl Knies at the University of Heidelberg had established a school of German economic history in reaction against the orthodox economics dominated by English thinkers—especially

Adam Smith and David Ricardo. Hegelian thought, of course, covered all aspects of the life of the mind, providing one of the many touchstones for separating numerous expressions of British realism and utilitarianism from German idealism. And more immediately, these scholars felt that Englishmen and Germans confronted different kinds of problems. The economic doctrines and intellectual postures of a nation of overseas traders characterized by rapidly growing industrialism seemed to them an inappropriate guide. This was especially true for those whose attitudes were formed by intellectual alliances with the left Hegelians; they were men who were particularly sensitive to the need to escape from the conservative implications of Hegel's doctrines. They regarded English economics as overly abstract and falsely universal at the expense of the particular, as insufficiently historical, too much committed to laissez-faire, too cavalier about the rights of workers, excessively materialistic, and indifferent to the demands of culture.[1]

Max Weber and Werner Sombart were, perhaps, the two most gifted descendants of these students of economic society. While each was to struggle through to an independent position during the course of his own career, both were influenced by the earlier generation either directly or indirectly through such later historians as Gustav Schmoller (a self-acknowledged disciple of Roscher and Knies) and Karl Bücher, or the philosopher Heinrich Rickert. Weber, in fact, occupied Knies's chair at Heidelberg and subjected the work of his acknowledged masters, Roscher and Knies, to penetrating scrutiny; in a series of inquiries (carried on mainly from 1903-6) deeply important to his own development, Weber freed himself from their domination and moved on to profounder scientific studies of society characterized by far greater sweep and methodological sophistication. Sombart had been a pupil and an admirer of Schmoller's at Berlin (Weber had also referred to himself as Schmoller's disciple), and spoke of him as an important influence on his intellectual development. He was to carry on the prevailing activism of the older economic historians who were his mentors.

Sombart moved to the University of Berlin after having begun his academic training at the University of Pisa. From the beginning of his career he was concerned with social justice and reform—an awareness created by an infatuation with certain writers (". . . he

steeped himself in Marx" notes M. Epstein, his major English translator and friend) in the context of German economic development
and industrialization under Bismarck. In the Verein für Sozialpolitik, a society founded in 1873 by academics of the Roscher-Knies-
Schmoller generation, he and other young luminaries like Max
Weber could merge their intellectual interests and activist propen-
sities as they explored alternatives to Marxian ways of achieving
social justice and of liberalizing the political climate. What Benjamin Nelson has noted of Marx and Weber applies to Sombart
as well: ". . . they were haunted by the fate and hope of man in
evolving bourgeois technological society."[2] Sombart's first academic appointment (he had earlier served as counselor to the
Bremen Chamber of Commerce) came in 1890 as professor extraordinary[3] of political economy at the University of Breslau. His promotion there to the status of professor was thwarted apparently
because his avowed liberalism was regarded with hostility by the
conservative authorities of Prussia. After fifteen years at Breslau,
a period of impressive productivity during which his formal studies
of capitalism began to appear, he accepted an appointment at the
newly established Handelshochschule (Commercial College) in
Berlin as professor of political economy. Finally, in 1917, he was
invited to the University of Berlin at the highest rank, ending his
academic career as professor emeritus in 1931. He died ten years
later. His life of scholarship had been marked by an impressive
output of more than twenty books, some of which were to achieve
the status of classics, many translated into diverse languages, by a
host of articles and special studies, and by a reputation as a brilliant
and persuasive classroom teacher. His career was marked and
scarred by much controversy and polemical antagonism occasioned
by his boldness and originality, by his sometimes erratic scholarship
and frequently controversial subject matter, and by his shifting
ideological positions as he changed over the years from socialist
critic of capitalism to exponent of National Socialism.

It may be of value to isolate some of the controlling principles
of Sombart's life-long study of capitalism by briefly locating his
work in relation to the concerns of the larger body of German
social science of which it is a part.[4] We have already mentioned
some of the major intellectual landmarks that bring Sombart's work
into focus: Marx's interpretation of history especially as relevant

to the growth of capitalism, the examination of the validity of the claims of socialism, and the working out of a form of historical inquiry that abandoned the articulation of general and presumably universal laws in favor of examining the unique nature of particular social forms and epochs. Numerous commentators have noted that Sombart was one of the most powerful German students of the dynamics of capitalism to struggle against Marx while simultaneously carrying forward Marx's criticisms of capitalism—at least during the first half of his fifty-year career. Sombart noted more than once that his own work was a "continuation" and a "completion" of Marx. But even before his violent attack on Marxian socialism after World War I, he revealed the necessity of abandoning important Marxist doctrines. Thus, for example, he circumvented the materialist dialectic of Marx in favor of a form of explanation that is allied to pre-Marxian German idealism. He denied the validity of the Marxian attempt to explain the origins of capitalism by recourse to economic determinism. He stressed the unique evolution of capitalism as the expression of an interdependent cultural complex given direction by a spirit of quantifying rationality that infused the totality of culture with its special identity and purpose. A double somersault is evidenced in this aspect of Sombart's thought: Marx, as he himself made clear, had stood Hegel "right side up again" in establishing a causal logic that gave ideas their identity by virtue of the material-economic base on which they rested. In a sense Sombart now carried this acrobatic feat forward another turn, so that the spirit or the ethos of capitalism became the source of concrete social realities. One doctrinaire determinism, it would seem, generated a counterdeterminism, justified apparently by its presumed explanatory powers. Indeed, it was probably Sombart's continuing massive efforts to analyze the *spirit* of European capitalism that established the parameters and the integrating principles of his genetic studies and allowed him to subdue enormous quantities of historical data in an orderly fashion.

Another controlling perspective in Sombart's thought is his opposition to unilinear theories of historical evolution born of the Enlightenment's belief in the inevitability of human progress. Here again Sombart departs from Marx. For Marx's teleological-eschatological theory of history reveals him as a product of the Enlightenment; he looks not to the fulfillment of the promise of freedom exemplified in Hegel's Absolute Spirit, but to the actions of a material dialectic in bringing about the withering away of the state under the classless society. Thus, Marx sees capitalism as a necessary economic mode which will generate its antithesis. But Sombart regards capitalism as morally exhausted, containing no guarantee of higher forms waiting to spring with telic certainty from the womb of the dying social order. For him, each culture is unique and self-actualizing—integrated by its own spirit or ethos, not involved in preparations for realizing higher unities. It is this stress on the singular unity of the capitalist spirit that reveals the grounds for such other views of Sombart's as his antipathy toward piecemeal attempts at amelioration of social problems.

Thus far we have cited some of Sombart's differences with Marx expressed mainly during the period when Sombart was sympathetic toward socialism. But there were also positive Marxian influences at work on Sombart's thought. Some were expressed rather generally in his view of socialism as the "intellectual embodiment of the modern Social Movement" concerned with attempts to emancipate the proletariat.[5] Perhaps most fundamentally influential was Marx's analysis of capitalism as a highly complex unique social form which could be conceived as a systemic unity exerting inescapable influence on all human affairs in ways that (in Marx's words) placed men in "determined and necessary relations with one another which are independent of their wills." This idea of capitalism as an impersonal integrated economic system is important to Weber as well;[6] it allowed the student of capitalism to see its consequences as the result of overwhelmingly powerful, rationalizing forces that dwarf the merely personal choices of individuals. Readers may recall Weber's much-quoted sentence from *The Protestant Ethic and the Spirit of Capitalism:* "The Puritan wanted to work in a calling, we are forced to do so." The Puritan saint's cloak of material possessions once could be thrown off in an instant, "but fate," continued Weber, "decreed that the cloak should become an iron cage." For Sombart too, capitalism is "a system fashioned by men . . . and influencing the activities of its creator without any reference to his will. . . . The system pervades

the capitalist undertaking like some silent ghost . . . [It] dominates
the undertaker himself . . . [it] forces him to do what it requires.
. . . [It] lives a life of its own."

From the outset, we have linked Sombart's name to Weber's
in various ways, and indeed, their theories and influence have frequently come together in their own work and in the work of
others. Along with Edgar Jaffe, beginning in 1904, Weber and
Sombart reorganized and edited the most influential social science
journal of their day, *Archiv für Sozialwissenschaft und Sozialpolitik*. During their years as editors of the *Archiv*, Weber and Sombart carried in its pages numbers of discussions of their work which
—particularly in Weber's case—have proved to be classical contributions to twentieth-century social science. Within three years
after the publication of Sombart's *Der moderne Kapitalismus* in
1902, Weber published in the *Archiv* his two powerful essays on
Die protestantische Ethik und der Geist des Kapitalismus (vol. XX,
1904; vol. XXI, 1905). Both essays contain numerous references to
Sombart's work on capitalism. And when Weber reprinted the
two essays in 1920 as the first part of his series entitled *Gesammelte
Aufsätze zur Religionssoziologie* (a study interrupted by his death),
he continued in his revisions to take serious note of Sombart's work
of the intervening fifteen years. Much of what Weber had to say
about Sombart is negative; at times his comments reflect deep vexa-
tion. For example, in discussing the differences between the formal
and theoretical ethical prescriptions of the early Pietistic sects and
the psychological sanctions that were rooted in religious practice,
Weber accuses Sombart of having "badly misunderstood" his discussion of these matters:

> Especially Sombart, but also Brentano, continually cite the
> ethical writers (mostly those of whom they have heard
> through me) as codifications of rules of conduct without ever
> asking which of them were supported by psychologically
> effective religious sanctions.

Again, Weber charges that Sombart's *Der Bourgeois* (translated
into English as *The Quintessence of Capitalism*, 1915) is full of
"excesses" and describes it as "a book with a thesis in the worst
sense." Alluding to other technical references in Sombart's writings on capitalism, Weber contends that Sombart has at various

times "seriously misrepresented," brought forward "polemics" against him,[7] "maintained an untenable thesis," and so on.

But this is only one side of Weber's judgment of Sombart. For example, in commenting in the first Protestant ethic essay on the "in every respect, excellent observations of Sombart [in] *Die deutsche Volkswirtshaft im 19ten Jahrhundert" (The Economic Progress of Germany in the Nineteenth Century*, translated in 1903), Weber makes the following acknowledgment:

> In general I do not need . . . to point out, although the follow-
> ing studies go back in their most important points of view to
> much older work, how much they owe in their development
> to the mere existence of Sombart's important works, with their
> pointed formulations and this even, perhaps especially, where
> they take a different road. Even those who feel themselves
> continually and decisively disagreeing with Sombart's views,
> and who reject many of his theses, have the duty to do so only
> after a thorough study of his work.[8]

And scattered throughout Weber's numerous books are frequent references to Sombart's work—especially to particular historical data rather than to major interpretative theses—that are equally laudatory. The differences between the two theorists are not, how-ever, to be ignored; they frequently strike to the heart of their respective interpretations of the origin and nature of capitalism. Though there is not a single reference to Weber's work in Chapter XIX, "Protestantism," of Sombart's *The Quintessence of Capitalism* (1915), its opening paragraph immediately joins issue with Weber:

> Protestantism has been all along the line a foe to capitalism,
> and more especially, to the capitalist economic outlook. How
> could it be otherwise? Capitalism is something worldly, some-
> thing for this life on earth . . . But for that very reason it will
> be hated and condemned of all who regard our life here as
> only a preparation for life hereafter.

Of course, this directly opposes Weber's thesis, expounded in *The Protestant Ethic and the Spirit of Capitalism*, that Protestantism, especially Calvinism and English Puritanism, had a key role in gen-erating the ethos or "the spirit of modern capitalism." Weber par-ticularly emphasized the Protestant's ethical obligation to make money in pursuit of a "calling," thereby endowing secular and often trivial activities with religious significance. It was the pursuit of this calling that distinguished earlier forms of "capitalism" from modern capitalism. Weber argued that for Luther one's "calling" meant serving God in the day-to-day activities of one's working life; it was Calvinism that further extended the idea of a "calling" beyond its monastic origins and most decisively converted it into an ascetic pursuit of economic gain to affirm one's status as a member of God's elect.

Sombart, however, saw the development of capitalism very differently: Puritanism "had nothing to do with middle-class virtues"; "Puritan preachers were totally averse to all money-getting."[9] "Free competition Puritanism condemned utterly." "Puritanism hardly encouraged farsighted and adventurous enterprises; shopkeeping was the most it could achieve." "It would be a narrow conception of the capitalist spirit thus to see its various manifestations springing from Puritanism." "In Calvinist lands the Church was distinctly hostile to capitalism. . . ." Baxter's writings contain even more "condemnation of riches" than do those of the Scholastics. And so on. Thus, the issue seems drawn with Weber. Or does it?

We may be able to answer the question more clearly after looking at one of Sombart's most controversial books, *Der Juden und das Wirtschaftsleben* (1911).[10] Sombart concedes in a section entitled "Judaism and Puritanism" that

> Max Weber's study of the importance of Puritanism for the capitalistic system was the impetus that set me to consider the importance of the Jew, especially as I felt that the dominating ideas of Puritanism which were so powerful in capitalism were more perfectly developed in Judaism, and were also of course of much earlier date.

In various aspects of the growth of capitalism—e.g., the intensification of international trade in the sixteenth century, the increased dominance of commerce in the economic life of Western Europe —Sombart finds

> an almost unique identity of view between Judaism and Puritanism. . . . In both will be found the preponderance of reli-

gious interests, the idea of divine rewards and punishments, asceticism *within* the world, the close relationship between religion and business, the arithmetical conception of sin, and, above all, the rationalization of life.[11]

Thus Sombart is led to the conclusion: "Puritanism *is* Judaism."

With a boldness that reveals his characteristic management of detail and synoptic generalization, Sombart argues that the spirit of capitalism was crucially nourished by Judaism's rationality, its legalism, the commercial genius of its religious leaders, the Deuteronomic injunction which permitted different commercial dealings and a different moral code in relations between Jews and non-Jews (especially regarding usury), and so on. Sombart argues further that the Jews after their expulsion from the Iberian peninsula in the late fifteenth century, were vital to the growth of capitalism in Northwest Europe by virtue of their use of securities and instruments of credit that standardized (i.e., made impersonal) the money and credit system in Holland, their money lending and service to heads of states, their overseas trade and financing of colonial ventures, their expertise in luxury trading, and perhaps most significantly, their importation of the rational and calculating spirit of capitalism with all of its attendant techniques into England via Antwerp and Holland. In these and other vital matters, the Jews acted as the catalyst that shifted the center of European economic life to the northwest. They quickened the tempo of international trade and created the foundations of the modern nation state—without which capitalism could never have been established in the West. It is Sombart's contention that Jewish contributions to the emergence of capitalism went beyond influencing the forms of important institutions like the Stock Exchange and industrial organization and commercial procedures; he sees decisive Jewish influence in the formation of "the principles underlying economic life—that which may be termed the modern economic spirit. . . ."

Before we examine the thesis of *The Jews and Modern Capitalism* further, we should briefly resolve part of Sombart's disagreement with Weber. Basically, Sombart had to reconcile two contradictory notions: (a) that Puritanism, contrary to Weber, was hostile to capitalism, and (b) that Puritanism—at least with reference to capitalism—was indistinguishable from the Judaic religion

whose ethos was vital to the growth of capitalism. This reconcilia-
tion Sombart accomplished in two ways, both involving rather
ambiguous definitions of the early and modern stages of capitalism.
First, he defined modern capitalism much more loosely than Weber
did, so that its realization did not depend on the existence of characteristics like the bourgeois organization of labor in nondomestic
settings. Second, he gave chronological priority to Judaism in the
genesis of capitalism: it had already formed the spirit of capitalism
as far back as the sixteenth century. In effect, Puritanism was not
the moral force behind capitalism; capitalism was the shaping force
behind Puritanism. Thus Sombart argued that "true" Puritanism
"was absolutely inimical to capitalism" but was unable to ignore
it.[12] "With heavy hearts, no doubt, they (the Puritans) had to
reckon with it, and they sought as best they could to bring it into
accord with their religious views." This Puritan compromise was
reached because "economic conditions forced from Puritanism the
admission that the bourgeois mode of life was not opposed to the
state of Grace." "It was too late" for them to attempt to organize
their economic life consistently with the true nature of their other-
worldly beliefs. And Judaism in Sombart's analysis provided the
moral justification and rationale for this enforced Puritan trans-
valuation. For example, Sombart asserts that the Puritan's use of
religious figures of speech applied to commerce was derived from
Jewish literature and practice, and he claims "that capitalism was
already firmly rooted in their day, seeing that Jewish theological
thought was most suited to capitalist conditions." Sombart thus
never asserted that Puritanism was irrelevant to capitalism's development. Even in the chapter that analyzes the hostility of Puritanism to (early?) capitalism Sombart concedes that "Puritanism did
not altogether suppress the capitalist spirit. Indeed, certain of its
aspects unconsciously facilitated its growth."[13] The crux of the
issue seems to be his implied claim for Jewish priority in capitalism's genesis.

Sombart and Weber were one in their insistence on discovering the special role of religion in forming the spirit of Western
capitalism. Both were interested in countering the economic and
materialistic determinism of the Marxist interpretation of history;
for both the quest for an alternative explanation led to an emphasis
on discovering attitudinal factors, the ethos, the *spirit* that infused

the newly heightened commercialism of Western Europe. Thus, they were led—with their friend, the distinguished religious historian Ernst Troeltsch—to establish the new discipline of the sociology of religion.[14] In this and other respects Weber and Sombart were the two leading scholars of their generation; their interpretations of the origins of economic and social modernity helped to shift the historian's traditional focus from the industrial and technological sources of capitalism to the cultural, intellectual, psychological, and socio-religious origins of capitalism.[15]

But beyond these basic similarities they frequently diverged in ways that are instructive to an understanding of *Luxury and Capitalism*. Weber, for example, was critical of Sombart's work on the Jews. Though he did acknowledge their role in the growth of capitalism, he felt it was ancillary, not crucial. He did not see the Jews as essential contributors to that form of rationalizing and ascetic industrially based capitalism which became dominant in the West. Nor, he argued, had the Jews invented the bills of exchange, the legal forms of capitalist companies, or other characteristic forms of rational bourgeois commerce. Weber contended further that Sombart was mistaken in insisting that in the Jewish ethic one demonstrated one's divine election by means of the successful economic practice of this-worldly asceticism. So, for example, in the revised 1920 edition of *The Protestant Ethic and the Spirit of Capitalism*, Weber distinguished between Jewish and Puritan capitalism:

> To the English Puritans, the Jews of their time were representatives of that type of capitalism which was involved in war, Government contracts, State monopolies, speculative promotions, and the construction and financial projects of princes, which they themselves condemned. In fact, the difference may, in general, with the necessary qualifications, be formulated: that Jewish capitalism was speculative pariah-capitalism, while the Puritan was bourgeois organization of labour.

Numbers of significant elements are present in this disagreement between Weber and Sombart (see Weber's *General Economic History*): there are differences in defining capitalism's essence;[16] differences in dating various phases in the growth of cap-

italism; differences in theorizing about the origin of capital formation at critical periods in the emergence of capitalism. Finally, there
are differences of method, particularly evident in Weber's more
rigorously sustained control over the process of explanation. For
Weber the spirit of capitalism was quintessentially embodied in
Calvinist and Puritan activity, which gave commercial dealings
"the character of an ethically coloured maxim for the conduct of
life." The earlier capitalism of other civilizations or of the Middle
Ages lacked precisely this ethos which distinguished modern Western European capitalism. This ethos created the "new and distinctive forms of modern civilization, the rational organization of labor,
especially production in an industrial enterprise of the factory
type."[17]

In part what is at issue is a difference we may characterize as
historical explanation impelled by a search for causes (Weber) as
opposed to explanation in the form of genetic patterns or temporal
simultaneity (Sombart). Weber's "spirit" was a generic term intended to serve as a synoptic shorthand for the unique features of
modern capitalism. For him certain realities had to predominate in
order for modern life to be infused with the spirit of capitalism.
Among the most important were the respect for science and the
dependence on technology in production, rational organization
and control of industry manned by a free labor force, a rational
system of exchange which involved separating productive commercial activities from a domestic setting, and rational bookkeep-
ing. These matters Weber traced to their origins in the rationalizing ethics of ascetic Protestantism. But this was for him

> only one side of the causal chain. The later studies on the Eco-
> nomic Ethics of the World Religions attempt in the form of a
> survey of the relations of the most important religions to eco-
> nomic life and to the social stratification of their environment,
> to follow out both causal relationships, so far as it is necessary
> *in order to find points of comparison* with the Occidental de-
> velopment. For only in this way is it possible to attempt a
> causal evaluation of those elements of the economic ethics of
> the Western religions which differentiate them from others,
> with a hope of attaining even a tolerable degree of approxi-
> mation.[18]

Thus, Weber's insistence on comparative analysis provided a form of control in his search for a causal explanation of the capitalist spirit. His remarkable studies of other religions were, in effect, attempts to test hypotheses by recourse to comparative inquiries that provided non-Western cases against which to assess the efficacy of his findings. Numbers of commentators have pointed out that in his comparative studies Weber was actually asking: Why is it that industrial capitalism did *not* appear in China and India even though many conditions—such as the presence of great wealth—seemed to favor its appearance? His conclusions in these inquiries reinforced his belief that Protestantism was the indispensable factor in the formation of modern capitalism. His studies also revealed the inhibiting consequences of Asian religions with reference to the emergence of a capitalist ethos. Finally, Weber attempted to demonstrate that the rationality of capitalism's economic order was both cause and effect of a deeper process of extensive "rationalization" in the West. Just as capitalism's rationality has its reinforcing counterpart in the social, economic, moral, and religious activities of Protestantism, so capitalism's rationality also had its counterpart in the rational presuppositions and reinforcing principles of Western architecture, mathematics, experimental science, music, and so on. His comparative studies of these cultural variables revealed the absence of such an interrelated "rationalizing" causal nexus in Asia and led him to emphasize Protestantism's special role in the formation of the spirit of capitalism.

In many of these matters (e.g., the emphasis on rationality in the spirit of capitalism) the substance of Sombart's thought was remarkably similar to Weber's. But, ultimately, Sombart's definitions of capitalism lacked the range and sophistication characteristic of Weber's comparative methodology. Sombart's search for the genesis of capitalism produced a brilliantly uneven analysis. It often depended on phenomena that could be found throughout history and that therefore did not explain the emergence of the special properties of Western industrial capitalism. It drew on events that "coincided" with the emergence of capitalism—sometimes by virtue of Sombart's shifting timetable. In works such as *The Jews and Modern Capitalism, War and Capitalism,* or *Luxury and Capitalism* the analysis represented a rich mixture of conspicuous high scholarship and less visible partisan polemics.[19] While

Sombart's work revealed many factors related to the genesis of capitalism, their causal connections within and between cultures were not elaborated as they were in Weber. Raymond Aron has synthesized some of the elements of this contrast between Weber and Sombart in a discussion of the emergence of capitalism in the West:

> The fundamental reason for their disagreement is that they employ different definitions of capitalism. In Sombart's work capitalism is apparently contrasted with an economic system which is primarily concerned with the satisfaction of needs *(Bedarfswirtschaft)*. Capitalism is a system which is motivated by the desire for unlimited gain, and whose development has no bounds, a system characterized by exchange and money, by the concentration and circulation of wealth and by rational calculation. These features are delineated by an intuitive grasp of the system as a whole, rather than by comparison with other civilizations.[20]

In the space available here we have been concerned only with singling out some of the central themes of Sombart's work up to approximately the midpoint of his career—that period just before World War I which saw the publication of a group of specialized studies including *The Jews and Modern Capitalism*, *War and Capitalism*, and the present work *Luxury and Capitalism* (1913).

The general thesis of *Luxury and Capitalism* is that the thirteenth and fourteenth centuries witnessed the first significant step in the appearance of a new society: the emergence of great fortunes in Italy that were no longer based on the feudal economy. This capital accumulation came from trade with and exploitation of Asia, discovery of new sources of silver and other metals, and private moneylending at usurious interest rates. Germany followed this pattern of capital accumulation in the fifteenth and sixteenth centuries; Holland, France, and England followed it in the seventeenth. Meanwhile, the fifteenth century in Italy saw the growth of princely states characterized by an urbanized nobility, revitalization of arts and science, development of the absolute secular state, further concentration of great wealth, and the studied refinement of social graces. During the first half of the sixteenth century France in her turn provided Europe with the supreme model for this kind of state: the court of Francis I. In this splendid court women had unparalleled prominence. They contributed to court life a heretofore unheard of measure of intrigue and artifice, insistence on social graces, and a passion for luxury goods.

By the seventeenth century, another major phase in the emergence of a new society had begun. Toward the end of the reign of Louis XIV, middle-class fortunes had burgeoned in France and in England as well. From 1600 to 1800, Sombart argues, these *nouveaux riches* further altered the spirit of the times by forming new alliances with the impecunious nobility. In this early period of early capitalism, wealthy men aspired to be admitted to socially superior classes not merely by virtue of the accumulation of money but also by the possession of the expensive appurtenances of social standing. In the eyes of the aristocrat, however, it was still not respectable to earn money by commerce—a judgment that continued to prevail in upper-class circles during the seventeenth and eighteenth centuries.

Along with these developments came the phenomenal growth of the city. The great cities of Europe with populations numbered in six figures were, according to Sombart, "consumer cities," i.e., they owed their existence to large concentrations of consumers brought together because of the presence of a royal court with its lavish expenditures and sophisticated amusements. Those industries and businesses that thrived did so by supplying the wealthy with a massive flow of consumers' goods. Especially in the seventeenth century, the cities (or more exactly the capitals) were also enlarged by the presence of creditors of the state and financiers, men whose energies created banking businesses capable of rapidly mobilizing very large sums to cover state debts and the like.

Perhaps the most original aspect of Sombart's treatment of this phase of early capitalism is his analysis of the contribution of altered sexual values to the emergence of a new ethos. In Chapter III, "The Secularization of Love," Sombart attempts to demonstrate that from the eleventh century on, love became increasingly secularized in the West, i.e., it was less and less subordinated to religious goals, rules, or institutions. He examines attitudes toward sexuality in the art and literature of medieval Europe and in the Italian Renaissance in an attempt to show that the work of Fragonard, Boucher, and Greuze was the culmination of an era inaugurated by Boccaccio and Pietro Perugino. He perceives the "hedonistic aesthetic conception of woman" that gradually emerged after the thirteenth century as being in "irreconcilable opposition to the religious or institutional restraints to which love had been subjected in former times." Thus, Sombart is led to the conclusion that the values of Titian and Giorgione and of Ariosto and Rabelais were the expression of altered beliefs that made love its own justification—something which might exist "outside and beyond all institutions." Love, in a word, became more free, and with its "liberation" a new class of women appeared designated by various names: *courtisane, maîtresse, grande cocotte, cortegiana*, etc. They were present in the great and small courts and imparted to them and to society at large a desire for wealth, glitter, conspicuous consumption, grand entertainment, and the like. It was not only the courtier who kept a mistress but also the financier; the court dignitaries and the men of commerce spent enormous sums supporting women of easy virtue. And bourgeois wives, following the tastes and style of the court, carried into society at large the appetite for extravagance and expenditure for luxuries.

We have only begun to scratch the surface of Sombart's psychological theories of the dynamics of luxury in the genesis of capitalism. In numerous passages he reveals a knowledge of the mechanism and varieties of sensual gratification as well as of compensatory sexual sublimation that immediately brings Freud[21] to mind:

> All personal luxury springs from purely sensuous pleasure. Anything that charms the eye, the ear, the nose, the palate, or the touch, tends to find an ever more perfect expression in objects of daily use. And it is precisely the outlay for such objects that constitutes luxury. In the last analysis, it is our sexual life that lies at the root of the desire to refine and multiply the means of stimulating our senses, for sensuous pleasure and erotic pleasure are essentially the same. Indubitably, the primary cause of the development of any kind of luxury is most often to be sought in consciously or unconsciously operative sex impulses.

> For this reason we find luxury in the ascendant wherever wealth begins to accumulate and the sexuality of a nation is

freely expressed. On the other hand, wherever sex is denied expression, wealth begins to be hoarded instead of being spent; thus goods are accumulated, especially in such abstract forms as precious metals and, in more recent periods, money.

Or again, while discussing the enormous increase in consumption of luxuries in the home—from about the beginning of the seventeenth century—Sombart turns to an analysis of the economic consequences of refinements in the culinary arts and concludes that

> without the pervasive refinement and sensualization of our tastes which are due to the influence of women, this high development of the culinary art would never have taken place.

Especially does he see a vital connection between the rise of feminism (which he elsewhere describes as the triumph of the erotic Rococo over the Baroque) and the consumption of sugar:

> Because of the predominant role of women, during early capitalism, sugar rapidly became a favorite food; and only because of the widespread use of sugar were such stimulants as cocoa, coffee, and tea adopted so readily all over Europe. Trade in these four commodities, and the production of cocoa, coffee, and sugar in the overseas colonies, as well as the processing of cocoa and the refining of raw sugar in Europe, are outstanding factors in the development of capitalism.

He also argues for a crucial feminine influence on the growth of capitalism through influence on the style and content of residences, furniture, the opera house and theater, fashionable restaurants and shops, and luxury hotels.

Sombart provides a highly particularized analysis of the importance for the growth of capitalism of luxury consumption in wholesale and retail trade and overseas trade with the colonies—the latter inextricably tied to the international traffic in slaves. By the end of the seventeenth century the increased wealth prevalent in Europe gave rise to tremendously intensified demands for luxury goods which, Sombart contends, jolted traders from a handicrafts view of commerce to one focused on industrial capitalism. Agriculture, too, responded to the demand for luxuries, especially in the colonies. There, the demands of Europe brought into being a new rational capitalist agriculture, manned by slaves, and given over to the large-scale production of sugar, cocoa, cotton, etc. In the examination of industry especially, Sombart discovers the vital role of luxury consumption. Large-scale industrialism, he believes, was first developed in luxury industries, especially those producing silk and other cloth: "Indeed it is quite possible that the first concrete example of a factory founded on a capitalistic basis during the Middle Ages was in the field of silk manufacturing." And, by the eighteenth century, all true luxury industries were transformed into capitalistic enterprises usually characterized by large-scale production. Sombart's final sentence provides the study with its synoptic climax: "Luxury, then, itself a legitimate child of illicit love —as we have seen—gave birth to capitalism."

What is the critical reader to make of such an intriguing and bold book—a book which Sombart himself in his mid-1920's revisions of his magnum opus, *Der moderne Kapitalismus*, felt to represent a somewhat extreme statement of his point of view? It is a work that reflects Sombart's strengths and weaknesses. His powers of synthesis, the command and authority of many of his formulations hold the reader from the outset. Witness the first sentence of this work: "The history of the Court is the history of the State." Or the last sentence of the book quoted in the preceding paragraph. His marshaling of evidence in the defense of unexpected theses (e.g., the relationship of sexual values to patterns of consumption and the emergence of economic systems) sometimes reveals dimensions of philosophic and scholarly possibilities approaching those of thinkers like Nietzsche or Freud. For example, Sombart writes of the human attempts to "emancipate the flesh" that begin timidly and then move on to naive sensuality, followed by refinement, debauchery, and finally perversion: "This necessary cycle seems to encompass the deepest tragedy of human destiny; that all culture being an estrangement from nature, carries in itself the germs of dissolution, destruction, and death." It is surely a modest enough claim to suggest that there is much to be learned here not only about economic history but also about the subtleties of the human condition.

But there are also many problems. *Luxury and Capitalism* is not well coordinated with Sombart's other major theses about the origin and nature of capitalism, some of which we have touched on. For example, there is virtually no treatment of the relationship between luxury and the religious ethos that presumably helped to infuse the spirit of capitalism with its identity. What manner of compromises were reached to subordinate the values of a rational this-worldly asceticism to the demands of luxury production and consumption—demands that were themselves, presumably, an active agent in the dialectic of capitalism's growth. How were luxury consumption and production related to the religious need to be always ready with an ultimate accounting to God? Such questions remind us that capitalism is very ambiguously defined throughout the book: the ambiguous chronology of its development is again especially troublesome. Too often Sombart's generalizations about capitalism are general and free-floating: to what period do they refer; to what part of Europe are they relevant? In the same sense his generalizations about luxury consumption and production are often not well defined. As Weber had suggested, when the special properties of Western capitalism are obscured—and this holds for the allegedly special role of luxury in the genesis of capitalism as well—it may become a mere promiscuous slogan or a concept so omnipresent throughout history as to be useless as an explanatory term. In this work Sombart is especially vulnerable on the grounds of his rather cavalier management of relevant dependent variables and his careless control of empirical evidence. Too often he has recourse to mere postulation of the relationship between luxury and capitalism rather than demonstration. The reader is often perplexed about the direction of the arrows of causality: did capitalism create luxury or did luxury create capitalism? Did the city create luxury and personal and sexual freedom, or did personal and sexual freedom create the city? Part of the problem may be that virtually all recourse to such bold and (inevitably) reductivistic formulations are doomed by the complexity and diversity of reality. Indeed, relatively few successful formulations of this kind appear to have survived the scrutiny of succeeding sceptical generations.

One longs throughout *Luxury and Capitalism* for the kind of perspective and test that comparative evidence can provide in such macrocosmic forms of analysis where the controls characteristic of scientific inquiry—though always difficult to approximate—are nonetheless necessary. Sombart never quite proves that there was a necessary causal relationship between the growth of capitalism and luxury consumption and production in the West. An intervening variable or set of variables is missing from his equation. What was it that accounted for the fact that luxury production in the West helped to create capitalism? Were the demimondaine and mistress with their extravagant tastes unique to the West? Were not other cultures such as India and China highly advanced in their production of luxury goods? Is it a question of the order of magnitude of such preoccupations that accounts for the emergence of capitalism of one sort or of the complete absence of capitalism of any kind? What were the relative orders of magnitude involved in different cultures? Too often Sombart provides historical reconstruction of the sort that obscures causal explanation in favor of the loosely implied "influence" of luxury on capitalism's growth. Our earlier discussion of Sombart and Weber will serve as a reminder of Sombart's methodological limitations on this score.

And yet *Luxury and Capitalism* is a work of considerable merit, perhaps even a minor classic. Extravagant and loose as its assertions often are, it should be seen as one of a relatively small number of explorations of the terra incognita of modern capitalism. The problematical place of luxury (what psychological tensions, one wonders, were engendered by its repeated seduction of Puritan asceticism in capitalism's revolution of rising expectations?) has been probed by writers from Mandeville through Adam Smith, Marx, Thorstein Veblen, and John Kenneth Galbraith. Galbraith's book, *The Affluent Society*, would seem to suggest that we are still, in W. H. Auden's words, "Lives possessed by powers we pretend to understand." Surely, if there is anything to be learned from Freud it is that understanding can come through mastery of the past. Sombart guides us to subterranean parts of our social system's past. As we explore those depths with him, we can profit by his mistakes as readily as the scientist profits by the necessary study of the negative findings of his peers: the dead ends, the fallacy of false explanation, the vividly present and still unexplored past waiting to be aroused by the proper question. Sombart's work can also serve as a source of hypotheses that may be tested in comparative historical inquiries or in the realities of the contemporary underdeveloped world.[22] What, for example, would be the effect on Sombart's theories about the relationship of luxury to the development of capitalism if he had pursued a Weberian course and examined luxury consumption in Tokugawa Japan during the generation or two before the Meiji Restoration formally inaugurated Japan's economic development? What hypotheses can be generated from similar historical inquiries into the history of America's economic development that are relevant to those new nations aspiring to achieve modified forms of capitalism? Such queries could easily be multiplied. Their abundance tells us, among other things, that our inquiries into the classical writings of men like Weber and Sombart need never be limited merely to the revival of old controversies as ends in themselves. At their best such inquiries may help us to adjudicate those old quarrels that we continue to have with ourselves.

NOTES TO THE INTRODUCTION

1. Their rejoinder—then as in later years—was often equally doctrinaire: economics was made virtually indistinguishable from history, and criticisms of capitalism took the peculiarly German form of nationalist and romantic appeals to embrace socialism. Talcott Parsons has noted some of the modern consequences of this continuing emphasis in German social thought, especially as it relates to the appeals of Marxian socialism and National Socialism. He cites two "pre-Nazi" expressions of these leitmotifs, one "on a very high level," Ernst Troeltsch's *Deutscher Geist und Westeuropa* (1925) and a "much more vulgar version," Sombart's *Händler und Helden* (1915). See Parsons, "The Problem of Controlled Institutional Change," in *Essays in Sociological Theory* (rev. ed.; New York: The Free Press, 1964), esp. pp. 266–69. The force of such observations is particularly revealing when we remember that Sombart embraced the Nazi philosophy of folk nationalism in the early 1930's.
2. Benjamin Nelson, "Dialogs Across the Centuries," in *The Origins of Modern Consciousness,* John Weiss, ed. (Detroit: Wayne State University Press, 1965).
3. Professor extraordinary is the second stage of academic rank in Germany coming after Privatdozent and before ordinary professor.
4. The following remarks draw upon the observations of Talcott Parsons in his early dual essays: " 'Capitalism' in Recent German Literature: Sombart and Weber, Part I," *The Journal of Political Economy,* vol. 36, No. 6 (Dec. 1929) and Part II, vol. 37, No. 1 (Feb. 1929).

5. From *Socialism and the Social Movement* (1909 ed.), p. 1, tr. from the 6th German ed., 1908. The earliest edition, taken from a series of lectures delivered in 1896, was published in that year as *Sozialismus und soziale im 19ten Jahrhundert (Socialism and the Social Movement in the Nineteenth Century)*. Subsequent editions were revised and translated into seventeen languages. The fifth edition published in 1905 was virtually a new book and the sixth edition was expanded still further.

6. I owe this observation, in part, to Talcott Parsons' and Neil Smelser's *Economy and Society* (New York: The Free Press, 1956), p. 39, though they are dealing here with a somewhat different set of issues. In the course of demonstrating the central thesis of their study—that "economic theory is a special case of the general theory of social science"—they note that a version of the idea of the economy as a social system is "found in the Marx, Sombart, Weber line of continental European students of 'capitalism.'" They also note that only Weber carried out this conception with any success.

7. Weber is here alluding to *Der Bourgeois* (1913), a work of 440 pages that seems in one sense to deal with Weber by studied neglect. It contains one prominent though inaccurately cited general reference to Weber's Protestant Ethic essays in the *Archiv* (in the introduction to the section on Notes and References) and two brief references to Weber among its 442 footnotes. The text does deal rather elaborately and critically with numerous theses put forward by Weber, but the identity of their creator remains unspecified.

8. Max Weber, *The Protestant Ethic and the Spirit of Capitalism*, tr. Talcott Parsons (New York: Charles Scribner's Sons, 1958), p. 198.

9. All quotations in this paragraph are drawn from Sombart's *The Quintessence of Capitalism*, tr. and ed. M. Epstein (New York: E. P. Dutton & Company, 1915), ch. XIX.

10. The following quotation is drawn from the most recent edition of *The Jews and Modern Capitalism* (New York: Collier Books, 1962), p. 235, reprinted from the 1951 edition published by The Free Press. The latter is reproduced from the 1913 English translation prepared by M. Epstein. The two most recent editions contain an excellent introductory essay by Professor Bert F. Hoselitz on which I have drawn, together with an extended Bibliographic Note prepared by Hoselitz in association with Benjamin Nelson.

11. *Ibid.*, pp. 235–36.

12. The following quotations are from *The Quintessence of Capitalism*, chapter XXI.

13. *Ibid.*, p. 256.

14. Troeltsch supported Weber in the controversy over the special role of Protestantism in the formation of capitalism. With reference to *The Jews and Modern Capitalism,* he felt that "Here Weber's method is instructively applied to Judaism." Together with Weber, he was critical of the main thrust of Sombart's analysis: "I believe . . . that the actual importance of Judaism is here greatly overestimated, that the special character of Jewish capitalism as directed mainly to trade and money-lending, in contrast with the civic, industrial capitalism, is not sufficiently emphasized, and that the relations between Jewish religion and economic ethics are not grasped with sufficient thoroughness. What is certainly wrong is the simple identification of Puritan and Jewish religion and their economic ethics. Here the causes and effects are different in the two cases. . . ." See *Protestantism and Progress: A Historical Study of the Relation of Protestantism to the Modern World,* tr. W. Montgomery (Boston: Beacon Press), pp. 141–42. (The first English tr. of this was published in 1912.)

15. One difficulty in considering Sombart's views is here brought into focus: his interpretations of the history of capitalism varied throughout his career. The first edition of his major work, *Der moderne Kapitalismus,* was published in 1902; numerous editions followed including major revisions and expansions published in 1916–17 and 1926–27. By the mid-1920's Sombart had altered and refined his interpretation of the chronology of capitalism. While still emphasizing the emergence of its unique spirit as the controlling factor in its development, he shifted to more traditional views about the decisive contributions of technological innovations. Thus, in 1902, he traced capitalism's beginnings to 1204, a year marked by the fall of Constantinople to the Crusaders and the introduction of "Arabic notations" into European mathematics—an innovation with far-reaching economic and "rationalizing" consequences. In later revisions, capitalism was divided into "Early and High Capitalism," from 1500 to 1760 and from 1760 to 1914 respectively. "High Capitalism" was initiated with the introduction of the coke process in iron smelting in 1760. Some of Sombart's disciples exaggeratedly regarded these shifts in emphasis to be sufficiently large as to make the mid-1920's revisions a totally new work. Whatever the case, it is clear that this dating problem can have serious consequences: obviously Protestants and Jews will make different contributions to capitalism depending on the chronology of its development. Some of these changes apparently were traceable to criticisms of Sombart's work. They were complicated by the fact that Sombart

characteristically yielded little to the assaults of his critics. Thus, in shifting his point of view, he tended often to retain parts of previous theories along with later and more plausible revisions. Such unyielding intellectual retentiveness led to much controversy over his exact intentions. Some of these observations are derived from an excellent treatment of Sombart's work in Frank H. Knight, "Historical and Theoretical Issues in the Problem of Modern Capitalism," *Journal of Economic and Business History*, Vol. 1, No. 1 (Nov. 1928). A significant part of Knight's essay is a paradigmatic treatment of Sombart's pretensions and limitations as an economic theorist who was not content with being (in Sombart's own words) "a mere historian."

16. Raymond Aron makes this point about Weber and Sombart in discussing the critical function of concepts in historical inquiry. See *German Sociology*, tr. Mary and Thomas Bottomore (New York: The Free Press of Glencoe, 1964), pp. 95–96.

17. Max Weber, *The Sociology of Religion*, tr. Ephraim Fischoff (Boston: Beacon Press, 1964), p. 250. This was first published posthumously in 1922 as "Religionssoziologie," a self-contained book-length part of the unfinished *Wirtschaft und Gesellschaft (Economics and Society)*. The Fischoff translation is based on the extensively revised fourth edition prepared by Johannes Winckelmann (1956).

18. *The Protestant Ethic and the Spirit of Capitalism*, p. 27. This quotation is from the "Introduction" written in 1920 for the entire series on the Sociology of Religion. The series was never finished because of Weber's death. The first volume contained, among other things, a study entitled "Die protestantischen Sekten und der Geist des Kapitalismus," and studies of Confucianism and Taoism. Other posthumously published volumes contained studies of ancient Judaism, Hinduism, and Buddhism. Additional studies dealing with Islam and special aspects of Judaism and Christianity were initiated but never finished.

19. Weber specifically criticized Sombart on these grounds. For example: "In the writings of Werner Sombart, above all in the second edition of his most important work, *Der moderne Kapitalismus*, the *differentia specifica* of Occidental capitalism—at least from the view-point of my problem—the rational organization of labour, is strongly overshadowed by genetic factors, which have been operative everywhere in the world." *The Protestant Ethic and the Spirit of Capitalism*, p. 185.

20. Aron, *German Sociology*, p. 96.

21. As far as I have been able to tell, there is no evidence of Sombart's having studied or made conscious use of Freud's work during this period, but the likelihood of contact ought not to be completely eliminated. Weber, who moved in circles similar to Sombart's, seems to have been introduced to Freud's theories about 1907 and apparently read his work with great interest in the years after that date, though there are no direct references to Freud in his writings.

22. A recent work relevant to this point is by Robert Holt and John E. Turner, *The Political Basis of Economic Development* (Princeton: D. Van Nostrand Company, Inc., 1966). In a sense it is an excellent contrast to Sombart, given its concern for a carefully articulated theoretical framework: methodologically it is perhaps to contemporary social science what Sombart might have been to scientific inquiry in his own day. As Sombart customarily searched intuitively for the ethos of a social form, Holt and Turner search for empirical variables within a theoretical framework where facts can be brought together in controlled relationships for purposes of comparison and generalization. Their study tries to discover hypotheses to account for the influence of certain political forms on the historical economic development of four nations: Tokugawa Japan, Manchu China, France from 1600–1789, and England from 1558–1780.

CONTENTS

CHAPTER I

The New Society

The history of the court[1] is the history of the state. Yet, as far as I know, there have been no outstanding studies on this subject. I shall make special mention only of Heinrich Laube's *Französische Lustschlösser* (Mannheim, 1840), 3 vols. This comparatively unknown book is considered to be one of the most vivid historical accounts. We can learn more from it about conditions at the French courts than from most of the ponderous tomes on history (not excepting Ranke). By centering the narrative in a representative castle of each reign, Laube tries to recreate the entire period and thus does for France (on a smaller scale) what G. Freytag did for Germany in his *Bilder aus der deutschen Vergangenheit*. "Historians" will duly consider Laube trifling.

My *Moderner Kapitalismus* is the first attempt to describe the emergence of middle-class wealth.[2]

The history of the changes in the upper strata during the early capitalistic era[3] has an external and an internal aspect: the external aspect shows us only the genealogical events. A specialized literature rich in works on family histories, particularly abundant in England, serves this purpose. The most comprehensive descriptions are the following recently published by George Edward Cokayne, *Complete Baronetage, 1611–1800* (Exeter, 1900–1909), 6 vols.; and *Complete Peerage* (London, 1910–), 12 vols.

Among old works, which are very important in this connection, I mention the following: Arthur Collins, *The Peerage of England* (London, 1735), 3 vols., (London, 1812), 9 vols.; *The Baronetage of England* (London, 1720), 2 vols.; and *The English Baronage* (London, 1727); Francis Townsend, *A Catalogue of Knights from 1660 to 1760* (London, 1833); Charles Catton, R. A., *The English Peerage* (London, 1790), 3 vols.; Thomas Walkley, *New Catalogue* (London, 1652), 8 vols.

On rank, we have C. R. Dodd, *Manual of Dignities*, etc. (London, 1842). On constitutional problems, we have R. Gneist, *Adel und Ritterschaft in England* (Berlin, 1853), and the works mentioned in it.

French genealogical history is far less fertile. The most important of the works of a general nature is the *Dictionnaire de la noblesse* by D'Hozier. To make up for this deficiency there is a wealth of French sociohistorical monographs. Works like those of Normand, Thirion, Bonnaffé, which I shall often mention, are possessed by no other country.

In these works the other side of the question, the sociopsychological side, is also touched upon. I am, however, unacquainted with any comprehensive exposition of the internal changes in the upper classes during the last centuries. In this investigation we must draw our material from all departments of literature. Therefore, a separate bibliography will not be necessary. The reader will find a number of books mentioned in the quotations which will afford further information.

i. *The Court*

THE RISE of the great courts in the sense in which we understand the term today is an important consequence as well as a cause of the fundamental changes in the political and military structures of the European countries at the close of the Middle Ages.

In this, as in so many other spheres, the princes of the Church were the precursors and prototypes of later developments. Avignon was perhaps the first "modern court." Here, for the first time in history, two specific types of persons are found together who established the tone which in the subsequent centuries went into the making of what was called "court society": noblemen with no vocation other than that of serving the court's interest, and beautiful women "often distinguished in deportment and spirit," who (as we shall have occasion to see later) gave life at the court its distinctive character. The significance of the Avignon episode lay above all in the fact that it was here that the ecclesiastical princes of almost all Europe gathered about the head of the Church and displayed that splendor which we find colorfully described in the decree *Etsi deceat* of Pope John XXII.

We know that during the fifteenth and early sixteenth centuries the court of the Roman popes and the papal nepotes was the most splendid in all history and was considered a model of magnificence and courtliness, as well as of freedom of manners, causing even a man like Erasmus to go into ecstasy. The Roman courtier closely resembled the ideal portrait of the contemporary courtier drawn by Castiglione. We shall see later how worldly splendor reached its apogee in Rome during the reign of the great Renaissance popes.

The other princely courts in Italy competed with that of the pope. One of the first secular courts bearing a modern stamp was the court of Alfonso of Naples, of whom it was said that he loved "splendor, magnificence, and the fair sex" above all things. By the fifteenth century, the courts at Milan, Ferrara, and the other small residential towns also developed a thoroughly modern mode of life. It is natural that we find the beginnings of this type of life first in Italy because it was there that, earlier than elsewhere, the necessary conditions were developed: the decline of knighthood, the urbanization of the nobility, the creation of the absolute state, the revival of the fine arts and sciences, the cultivation of social graces, the accumulation of great fortunes, etc.

However, the decisive factor in the history of court life was the emergence of a modern court in far greater and more powerful France, which from the close of the sixteenth century on through the two following centuries became the unrivaled model in all things pertaining to court life.

The founder of the French court is Francis I. To be sure, Louis XI had already wrought a great change by giving his *officiers de la maison* the title *officiers de France*, thus identifying France with the royal house. It was by this act that the way for the creation of the court was paved. Prior to this, the court was considered only an enlarged circle of the king's family. The true creator of the court, however, was Francis I, since it was through his influence that women came into power. He is said to have remarked that a court without women is like a year without spring or spring without roses. That is why he gathered about him the ladies of noble birth who before then had pined away behind the gray walls of their ancient castles. Francis, aided by his personal charm and the cleverest despotism, created the court in which all activity and high life were to be centered around the king: "His mother managed these great gatherings and selected the beautiful girls, his sister Margaret added her own ingredient of spice and her play of fancy and wit, and Francis spread over it all splendor of ceremony in setting and entertainment, his whimsical desires providing rhythm and animation."[4] In this way the women were responsible for intrigue and gallantry and luxury. The courts of the great Louis were but copies, although on a gigantic scale, of the original created by Francis I. A glance at the court reveals that this special world rested on the great power exerted by women, an impression corroborated by the descriptions of contemporaries.

I cite the accounts of two men—one at the beginning and the other at the close of this woman-ridden court epoch—Sully and Mercier. Although differing in other respects, these two men are undoubtedly authorities on these matters.

> We need only take a view of that great number of mongrel gentry with which the court and city is filled, and we shall find them wholly destitute of the plain and manly virtue of their ancestors—with no depth of thought, no solidity of judgment, but rash, inconsiderate, passionately fond of play, naturally inclined to dissoluteness, solicitous about dress, with a vitiated taste in every kind of luxury, so that one would imagine they thought to exceed even the women in the effeminacy of their manners. . . .[5]

> The court has overwhelmed them (the nobles) with its pomp; entertainments have been arranged to cater to their desires. Women who used to live in solitude among their domestic duties are flattered by receiving public notice. Their coquetry and feminine ambitions have found their fulfillment. Glittering and charming, they hover about the throne, and their slaves perforce do not leave the seat of their power. They have become the queens of society and the arbiters of taste and pleasures; they have given trivial matters an air of supreme importance, the style of ornaments—all the puerile conventions. . . .[6]

The other courts of Europe had either no significance in the cultural life of their countries, or they were mere slavish copies of the French court. This is particularly true with regard to the English court, which was not founded until the time of the Stuarts. Even back in the days of Henry VIII, a contemporary writes: "Every gentleman flyeth into the country. Few that inhabit cities or towns; few that have any regard for them."[7] Even the court of Elizabeth was not what we mean by a modern court, as exemplified by the classical form of the French court, for it lacked the most important characteristic: the rule of women. With a woman on the throne this may sound paradoxical. But it will be understood if we bear in mind that feminine rule was based mainly on the rule of the mistress.

ii. *Middle-Class Wealth*

Elsewhere, I have described in detail how during the Middle Ages and the subsequent centuries new wealth poured forth from a thousand sources. This new wealth may be designated middle-class, as opposed to feudal, wealth. The insight gained there may assist us here in studying the vital modifications in the social structure of the old society as a result of this newly created wealth which led to a shift in the composition of that upper stratum as between the princes and the *misera contribuens plebs*. For this purpose we need only arrange the previously systematized facts in chronological order and consider the abstract possibilities of the growth of fortunes (which we know) in their actual social context. We then perceive approximately the following picture of this change in the upper social stratum.

The fortunes of the early Middle Ages were composed almost exclusively of landed property, and it was the big landowners (the Church being excluded) who formed the nobility. At that time rich burghers were practically nonexistent. Like that Poinlane of whom we hear again and again, they were rare exceptions.

This situation changes in the thirteenth and fourteenth centuries. During that period we observe the rapid multiplication of great fortunes which did not originate in the fuedal nexus, so that we may now speak of capital fortunes. This process was most conspicuous in Italy. It was the time when Europe began to despoil the Orient, when, probably, rich mines of precious metals were discovered in Africa and when the profits from money-lending at usurious interest rates to big landowners and, particularly, to rich princes reached large figures.

What is true of Italy in the thirteenth and fourteenth centuries applies also to Germany in the fifteenth and sixteenth centuries. In that period great wealth began to accumulate in the South German cities in consequence of the opening of the Bohemian and Hungarian gold and silver mines and, later, of the arrival of the American silver treasures, which stimulated the great finance operations of that era, the "Era of the Fuggers."

Holland followed in the seventeenth century, participating in the plunder of Spain and Portugal and developing new sources of wealth in the Far East, where she exacted tribute from the peoples by means of forced trade, robbery, and slavery.

In the seventeenth century the growth of wealth sets in also in France and England. However, middle-class wealth in both countries apparently remained within relatively narrow limits until the end of the seventeenth century. Financial enterprises, which almost exclusively form the foundation of the great capital fortunes, were not extensively engaged in until the end of the reign of Louis XIV and after the Glorious Revolution.

This situation is clearly illustrated by the only estimate of incomes that has come down to us from those days. The well-known calculation of Gregory King[8] for the year 1688 estimates the average income of a "big merchant and overseas trader" at not more than £400, that of a "big merchant and inland trader" at only £200. King places the number of the former at 2000, of the latter at 8000. Opposed to this middle-class element stand the following representatives of landed property:

		Average Income in Pounds
160	secular lords	2800
26	ecclesiastical lords	1300
800	baronets	880
600	knights	650
3000	esquires	450
12000	gentlemen	280

Among those listed above there must have been some representatives of new wealth. But I am certain that, had Gregory King made his tabulation thirty years later, he would have also mentioned the rapidly acquired wealth of the stock-exchange speculators and the promoters of the South Sea Bubble, who, during the second decade of the new century, had created an entirely new type of wealth. When the fortunes of the South Sea Company were confiscated, two were over £200,000 (£243,000 each), five from £100,000 to £200,000, five between £50,000 and £100,000, and ten between £25,000 and £50,000.[9]

The figures for income and fortunes which we find in Defoe

begin to show an entirely different aspect. Guy Miege[10] places the average income of a gentleman at £500.

The causes of this great change are obvious: Brazilian gold and the wars of Louis XIV with their large-scale financing operations and army contracts, all of which stimulated speculation. These are the three most important sources of great fortunes in more recent times. (What enormous wealth must have been acquired through the issuance of shares by such companies as the Hudson Bay Company or the African Company—whose shares soared within a short time from one hundred to four hundred, to drop later to two—not to speak of the profits made in the South Sea Bubble!)

It was then that middle-class fortunes (i.e., mobile fortunes), which would not suffer by comparison with fortunes of our own days, sprang up in great numbers. With the advent of Brazilian gold, the silver era of modern capitalism ended, and the era of gold began.

As in England, so we observe in France, at the turn of the seventeenth century, the sudden development of great fortunes. Because of the existence of accurate records in France we are able to trace the change even more definitely than in England. I offer a series of data, taken at random, on the wealth of French financiers (i.e., possessors of new fortunes), which I have completed by the addition of some relevant figures.

A country squire has drawn up a list of the amounts which were the subject of marriage contracts in his family[11]:

	Florins
1433	300
1477	1,000
1534	1,200
	Écus d'or
1582	1,200
	Livres
1613	7,500
1644	16,000
1677	15,000
1707	44,000
1734	360,000
1765	150,000

The following figures give us an idea of the dowries which the rich Turcarets[12] of the eighteenth century used to give their daughters:

> La Live de Bellegarde: for each daughter 300,000 livres in cash and 10,000 livres in diamonds.
> La Masson: 1,700,000 livres.
> Antoine Crozat: 1,500,000 livres (plus a "gratuity" of 50,000 livres for the mother-in-law, the duchess of Bouillon).
> Sam. Bernard: 800,000 livres.
> Olivier, comte de Senozan (He himself had dealt in rabbit skins): 1,100,000 livres in cash and 100,000 livres in furniture.
> Haudry: 400,000 livres.
> La Reynière: 600,000 livres in cash and 200,000 livres in installments to fall due in quick succession.

Such figures do not surprise use when we learn the extent of the profits and wealth of these nouveaux riches.

	Livres
Vincent Le Blanc (profits)	17,000,000
M de Saint-Fargeau	28,000,000
Marquis de la Faye	20,000,000
Mme de Chaumont	127,000,000
S. Bernard	over 100,000,000
Crozat	over 100,000,000
Fillon de Villemur (died in 1753) left an estate of	40,000,000
Peirenc de Moras left an estate of	12-15,000,000
Dangé left an estate of	13,000,000
Tournehem (the foster-father of Mme de Pompadour) left an estate of	20,000,000

The financier Paris profited by 63,000,000 livres from the floating of a single issue. (I have drawn these data from the above-mentioned book of Thirion.)[13]

Most of the amounts are probably exaggerated (as, for instance, are also most of the statements concerning the wealth of modern American billionaires). However, they leave no doubt that huge fortunes had begun to accumulate. This inference is borne out by many other indications of which we shall speak later. Moreover, we find a corroboration of our assumption in the accounts of the best-informed contemporaries:

> We speak nowadays of a million as people used to speak about a thousand louis d'or a hundred years ago. We count by millions, hear only of millions in every enterprise, and millions dance before our eyes whether it be a question of a ship, a voyage(!), or a court pageant. . . .[14]

III. *The New Nobility*

We are now interested in seeing by what means these important upstarts (and especially their wives, daughters, and sons!) effected their advance in the social scale after their rise in the commercial world. We are also interested in the attitude taken toward them by the nobility which, until then, had exclusive claim to the upper social stratum, and how, if at all, these nouveaux riches became a part of the "ruling class."

The correct answer to these questions is the following. In the course of the two centuries between 1600 and 1800 an entirely new stratum of society had been formed from the amalgamation of the old nobility and the new wealth. Inwardly, this new stratum represented the new fortunes, although outwardly it still exemplified the feudal manner of living. This means, in other words, that a great part of the nouveaux riches was elevated to noble status. Elevations could be accomplished in several ways: (1) through the conferment of a title, either on the grounds of distinguished service or in consideration of a suitable sum of money; (2) through the conferment of orders or offices to which hereditary nobility was attached; (3) through the acquisition of an estate to which hereditary nobility was attached.

On the other hand, members of the old nobility sank to the level of Turcarets, and through marriage, drew from the lower planes of society the necessary millions to regild their faded coats of arms. This is basically the same procedure which is common in our day.

The amalgamation of noble ancestry and bourgeois money has

taken place at the same rate in all capitalistic countries, in Italy and
Germany as well as in England and France, the two countries
which are representative of all the phenomena of the early capitalistic epoch. Despite a disparity in their social stratifications,
nevertheless, on this decisive point these two countries passed
through the same evolutionary stages.

In England the nobility had to be entirely re-created after the
accession of the Tudors or, more precisely, by Henry VIII. After
the Wars of the Roses the families of the old nobility had dwin-
dled to twenty-nine; even those remaining were in part outlawed
or they were weakened and impoverished. Henry VIII restored
these old families to power and wealth, thus making them dependent on the crown, whose domination went uncontested from
then on. The means for the endowment of these families consisted
in confiscated Church lands. These properties, as H. Hallam
correctly points out, were, in this manner, made available again
for secular use, which is of prime significance in our study. From
the time of Henry VII and Henry VIII, however, the number of
noble families was steadily increased by new conferments. The
new peers, who were in every respect on an equal footing with
the old landed nobility, were selected by the king from among all
the notables, and especially from among the rich bourgeoisie.
James I actually sold peerages. The following is a list of peers
created or elevated by the English kings from Henry VII to
James II:

Monarchs	Peers Created
Henry VII	20
Henry VIII	66
Edward VI	22
Mary	9
Elizabeth	29
James I	62
Charles I	59
Charles II	64
James II	8

After ninety-nine peerages had become extinct under the
Stuarts, the following titles were reconferred or created between

1700 and 1800: 34 dukes, 29 marquesses, 109 earls, 85 viscounts.

Naturally, all these elevations were not shortcuts for members of the Third Estate, as in the case of the Russells and Cavendishes whom Henry VIII lifted "from obscurity through the grant of church lands" (Green). Often, in fact almost always, the new peers had to pass through various preliminary stages—those of esquire, knight, and baronet. Yet, we know of numerous cases in which the pedigree can be traced back to a rich *novus homo* of the city. As proofs I offer merely the following examples: The dukes of Leeds are descendants of Edward Osborne who came to London as a poor merchant's apprentice; the dukes of Northumberland take us back to a Hugh Smithson who was a clerk in an apothecary shop and was chosen by Lady Elizabeth Seymour as her husband. The following titleholders likewise had middle-class antecedents: the Russells, the marquesses of Salisbury, the marquesses of Bath, the earls of Brownlow, Warwick, Carrington, Dudley, Spencer, Tilney (the first earl of Tilney is none other than the son of Josiah Child!), the earls of Essex, Coventry, Dartmouth, Uxbridge, Tankerville, Harborough, Pontefract, Fitzwater, the viscounts Devereux, Weymouth, the earls of Clifton, Leigh, Haversham, Masham, Bathurst, Romney, Dormer, the dukes of Dorset and the dukes of Bedford. Some of these titles have long since disappeared but they all, unless created at a more recent date, flourished in the first half of the eighteenth century. (The examples are taken from the aforementioned sources.)

It is the gentry, more than any other class, which gives English society its characteristic stamp, especially during the period with which we are here concerned. The gentry is composed of a body of persons who do not belong to the nobility proper; yet, they are nobles, lower nobles, but not in the eyes of the law. The uppermost stratum of the gentry is formed by the knights, among whom the baronets hold the highest rank; both titles confer the prefix of sir to the Christian name. The title of knight was originally reserved to the feudal landholders; later, since Edward III and Henry IV, the members of certain orders, such as the Garter and the Bath, and certain officeholders were also made knights. Eventually, it was possible to buy the title of knight. The venality of knighthood titles (the price was £1095) was introduced by James I in 1611. These knights, by the grace of the pocketbook, were called baronets; they were assigned precedence over the old baronets and ranked second only to the nobility. The new baronetage was increased by hundreds during the seventeenth and eighteenth centuries; by the middle of the nineteenth century, the number of new baronets had reached seven hundred. This, then, was the manner in which a large part of the newly rich common-ers rose to nobility (to which the knights, from a social standpoint, undoubtedly belonged). The peculiar fact, in regard to the En-glish gentry, is that it is utterly impossible to define its lines of demarcation, especially in relation to the stratum below. "No historian or jurist knows how to define them. This vagueness of class distinction is not a fortuitous circumstance but the result of the entire historical and legislative development of England."[15]

Esquire and gentleman were general terms and designated the independent man who lived on his rents, or followed some "re-spectable" occupation. Naturally, such a distinction is virtually obliterated today and is on the point of disappearing altogether, even in England. However, it was always recognized, even up to the middle of the nineteenth century, that a man had to command a certain income to be counted among the gentry. But the amount of such an income and the definition of a "respectable" occupation has at all times been left to "public opinion."

These peculiar conceptions implied that in England noble rank was determined almost automatically by an advance in the economic status. The rising financiers were always admitted to the nobility in direct relation to their growing significance in society. At first only a manorial lord of noble blood or, at most, a member of a liberal profession, such as a lawyer, could become a "gentle-man." This concept was still prevalent at the time of Elizabeth, a period vividly depicted by Thomas Smith. Perhaps it was also possible to become a member of the gentry through the acquisition of a noble estate, if we care to interpret the following quotation from Harrison to that effect: "Citizens and burgesses have next place to gentlemen"; yet, "they often change estate with gentle-men as gentlemen do with them, by a mutual conversion of one into the other."[16] This conception underwent essential modifica-tions toward the end of the seventeenth and at the beginning of the eighteenth century so that it was no longer impossible for the children of a business man to become gentlemen, after one or two generations, on the strength of their father's money. Defoe, for instance, must have had this condition in mind when he wrote the following:

> Trade is so far here from being inconsistent with a Gentleman that, in short, trade in England makes Gentlemen, and has peopled this nation with Gentlemen; for, after a generation or two, the tradesmen's children, or at least their grandchildren, come to be as good Gentlemen as those of the highest birth and the most ancient families.[17]

But this was, at first, true only of the sons or grandsons of tradesmen who had risen to wealth. (In Defoe, tradesman denotes both wholesale and retail dealers.) Mere wealth, however, did not as yet make the gentleman. Defoe sharply distinguishes the tradesman, however rich and well situated, from the gentleman, who might live in penury.

The tradesman, as long as he was in business, lived among his "fellows." When he retired from business he could, under certain circumstances, cultivate relations with gentlemen, even "commencing a Gentleman."[18]

Defoe also mentions that many members of the gentry were by no means disposed to accept the sons or grandsons of the newly rich commoners, to say nothing of the enriched first generation itself.[19] Obviously, the power of money was beginning to assert itself; during the eighteenth century the conquest was completed.

Postlethwayt, Miege-Bolton,[20] and others who wrote about the middle of the eighteenth century, reveal a somewhat more liberal conception. To be sure, the man in trade, as well as the wholesale merchant, who did not stand at a counter, could not become a gentleman until he had retired from business. "As to Merchants (i.e., persons engaged in foreign commerce) . . . , they deserve indeed to be ranked among Gentlemen," whereas Gregory King, in his survey of the national income of England, above referred to, distinguishes the merchant from the gentleman. Thus, the writers, who at the beginning of the nineteenth century gave their views on "current opinions," consider the following of a trade or the keeping of an open store incompatible with the position of a gentleman; this does not apply, however, to merchants generally or to factory owners.[21]

During the whole early capitalistic era the notion persists that eventual acceptance into a socially superior class, the gentry or the nobility, must be the ultimate aim of the wealthy man; it is important to stress this point. The aristocratic character of this noble class was preserved, however, in that admission to it was not granted for wealth alone, but required the possession of qualities of an entirely nonbourgeois character. A certain distance from actual business life, as well as the cultivation of a family tradition, etc., which found expression in the invariable custom of the gentleman to bear a coat of arms, were prerequisites to admission. In this connection it is Defoe again who is our informant, telling us about the newly rich storekeepers who besieged the Heralds' College and retraced their lineage in order to discover, if possible, a "noble ancestor": "We see the tradesmen of England, as they grew wealthy, coming every day to the herald's office, to search for the coats of arms of their ancestors, in order to paint them upon their coaches, and ingrave them upon their plate, embroider them upon their furniture, or carve them upon the pediments of their new houses. . . . In this search we find them often qualified to raise new families, if they do not descend from old; as was said of a certain tradesman of London, that if he could not find the ancient race of gentlemen, from which he came, he would begin a new race, who should be as good gentlemen as any that went before him."[22] (Manifestly a virtue was made of necessity.)

The relation between nobility and wealth grew still closer when the sons and daughters of both groups intermarried and had children. This linking of nobles and parvenus has been a commonplace in England, at least since the Stuarts. If Sir William Temple actually made the statement that, as far as he recalled, it was about fifty years since the noble families had begun to marry into the city and "for downright money," the great authority of this very excellent observer permits us rather definitely to establish the beginning of these mixed marriages in the reign of James I. At any rate, one hundred years later, when Defoe wrote, mixed marriages between the nobility and the bourgeoisie were apparently frequent, for Defoe refers to them as everyday occurrences. Usually, of course, noblemen married rich heiresses of the tradesman class in order to regild their coats of arms. Defoe lists seventy-eight marriages between noblemen and shopkeepers' daughters, with names,[23] but we need not repeat them here. After all, it makes hardly any difference whether Lord Griffin married Mary Weldon, a merchant's daughter from Well in Lincolnshire, or whether Lord Cobham took as his wife Annie Halsey, a brewer's daughter from Southwark; these marriages interest us solely as mass phenomena, which, considering the number of nobles, they had certainly become in the England of the eighteenth century.

However, the concept of the mutual exclusiveness of respectability and business prevailed in France even more strongly than in England. "If there is contempt in this world, it is directed against the merchant," epitomizes the attitude of the upper classes, transmitted to us by a competent observer of the time of Henry IV.[24] A member of the nobility might participate in a profitable undertaking even though he belonged to the oldest, most illustrious family; he might marry the daughter of a newly rich shopkeeper; he might not disdain to give up the position of privy councilor in order to accept the more profitable one of a fiscal official (today we would say bank director); yet the plebeian was looked down upon with contempt. High finance gained a little in respectability during the eighteenth century; but in the seventeenth century we find newly rich financier Turcarets of the rank of the Cotteblanches or of the Du Plessis Rambouillets interspersed among aristocratic society. Great wealth reconciled the nobility with the commoner, an attitude which La Bruyère very nicely expressed in this manner: "If the financier fails, the courtiers say: 'He is bourgeois, a nobody, a boor.' If he is successful, they ask for his daughter's hand." Wherever we look we meet with the notion, intrinsic to the whole precapitalistic and early capitalistic culture, that it is entirely compatible with respectability to spend money, but not to earn it. Montesquieu uttered the ever-memorable words: "All is lost if the lucrative occupation of a financier promises to become respectable too. Then all the other classes will be filled with disgust, honor will lose its significance, the slow and normal means of distinguishing oneself will fall into disrepute, and the state will be rocked to its very foundations."

This view was maintained not only by the members of the feudal society, but it pervaded also those strata of the population which had arrived at a level above the *misera contribuens plebs*. Thus, the better—the richer tradesmen and the capitalistic entrepreneurs—"bourgeois" felt prompted to establish barriers between themselves and the lower ranks of tradesmen and artisans. (We shall have occasion to observe these tendencies in other connections also.) But above all, the newly rich bourgeois cherished a longing for noble titles. In France this desire was possibly even stronger than in other countries because the nobility was politically in a privileged position and to belong to it meant, therefore, not only social but also considerable material advantage.

At all times we observe an influx of newly rich merchants into the nobility. This movement, as I should like to point out, is a very common occurrence which may be observed in all countries since the earliest epochs of the Middle Ages. I am tempted to say that this tendency is more marked during the earlier than during later periods. It is well-established that the noble families in the German cities continually received additions from below, that is to say, they accepted the fortunate individuals of the Third Estate who had risen above trade and handicraft.[25] The noble families of the Italian cities, which from the early Middle Ages onward were largely composed of wealthy merchants, present the same picture.[26] Similarly in England, the nobility had at all times received an influx from the low planes of the *artes sordidae*. In this connection I wish to refer to a neglected but, what seems to me, significant excerpt from Anglo-Saxon legal sources, containing a decision by King Athelstane of England: "And if a merchant thrived so that he fared thrice over the wide sea by his own means (craft) then was he thence forth of thane-right worthy."[27] Furthermore, it is evident that the development of the French nobility proceeded in a like manner.[28]

Yet, I believe that we should not lose sight of the fact that it actually makes a difference whether a wealthy merchant or banker was elevated to noble dignity in the thirteenth century or in the seventeenth century. As long as the rule of the feudal system was unchallenged, the nobility consisted almost exclusively of landed proprietors of noble descent; the commoner who was admitted to the nobility did not alter the mode of living of the feudal class. Within a very short time he adjusted himself inwardly and outwardly to his new environment which, as it were, absorbed him as a sponge would a drop of moisture. This process of complete absorption was due to the relative social power between the old, established families and the newcomers, a comparatively small group. A century later, these new elements added to the old feudal nobility appear to have fused with the latter into one homogeneous entity. The "old families," which were still in existence about 1550 in Genoa, Florence, England, or France, were families whose genealogy went back two hundred years or more. With the best will in the world, one could no longer distinguish among those whose ancestors had once been freemen, feudal landowners, officials, or porters. They all belonged to the "feudal nobility" and stood in contrast to the newly founded families, which were created later and in great number, especially since the seventeenth century. The newcomers descended in most cases from the Third Estate and, because of the temper of the period, were destined to have a determining influence on the whole structure of the nobility.

In tracing the changes in the society of our civilization, which are due to the amalgamation of the nobility with the wealthy families of a lower estate, it would hardly be appropriate to mention the rare elevations of rich burghers to nobility during the Middle Ages in the same breath with the influx of commoners into the nobility which has taken place since the beginning of modern times. It is the power of discernment, the flair for the peculiarities of different historical periods that make the good historian.

In France the turning point of this development came toward the end of the sixteenth century and the beginning of the seventeeth century. During that period several sources which gave rise to a numerous new nobility suddenly sprang up.

1. Since the reign of Henry IV, the ennoblement of manufacturers, by means of privileges for newly founded industries, grew more frequent.[29]

2. By the Edict of Paulet, in 1684, venal offices became hereditary. This meant a change of system, for afterward the *Grande Robe* which, for the most part, had been connected with the nobility, recruited itself more especially from among wealthy men of the world of finance.[30]

3. The year 1614 is marked by legalization of the transference of feudal land holdings into the hands of commoners. Such conveyances had always taken place, but without that sanction.[31] This mode of acquiring a noble title was of particularly great significance for France. The eighteenth century was teeming with brand new seigneurs who had risen to their position by the simple expedient of purchasing a seigneurial estate. The rich adorned themselves with seigneuries as people do nowadays with exotic orders. Jean Paris de Montmartel, the son of a small innkeeper of Moirans, signed at a christening as comte de Sampigny, baron de Dagouville, seigneur de Brunoy, seigneur de Villers, seigneur de Foucy, seigneur de Fontaine, seigneur de Chateauneuf, etc.

In addition to these three sources from which a new nobility sprang, a new one is opened toward the end of the seventeenth century.

4. Outright purchase. The number of titles sold was five hundred in 1696, two hundred in 1702, and one hundred in 1711.

It is no matter for wonder, then, that eventually the French nobility consisted almost entirely of ennobled Turcarets. It is no exaggeration when Cherrin says that what was called "noblesse" in France during the seventeenth and eighteenth centuries, was essentially a "wealthy, elevated, decorated and propertied Third Estate," or when the marquis d'Argenson writes, about the middle of the eighteenth century, that, judging by the ease with which a title of nobility can be acquired for money, there was no wealthy person who would not soon become ennobled.

The fairly accurate statistics which we possess of the composition of the nobility at the end of the French Revolution confirm the correctness of these opinions. At that time the number of noble families reached 26,000. Only 1300 to 1400 belonged to *la noblesse immémoriale ou de race* (the nobility of blood or race), and only about 4000 of them were of the *noblesse de robe ou d'office* (nobles of the bench, etc.). The part played by high finance in the composition of the French nobility is even greater than these figures would indicate, for we must keep in mind the numerous marriages of nobles with wealthy heiresses from the Third Estate.

This process of amalgamation is in full operation by the beginning of the seventeenth century, if we are to believe that old blusterer, the duc de Sully, who bitterly complained of this condition: "At this day . . . the notions of mankind are changed, and . . . everything is rated by the money which it brings. . . . And, indeed, how should it be otherwise when we see the nobility of the same mind with regard to this point as the meanest of the people and making no scruple to mingle the most illustrious blood in a shameful alliance with a dirty pedlar, who knows nothing but barter, his shop, his counter, or knavery? . . . This subversion of all order is indeed to be lamented. . . ."[32] A century and a half later, entirely different views were entertained even by the nobility. The editor of Sully's Mémoires, M de l'Ecluse (1752), cannot refrain in a commentary from adding words of apology to Sully's reproaches.

When, at about the same time, the duc de Picquigny married the sister of the financier La Masson Montmartre and received a comfortable dowry of 1,700,000 livres, the duchesse de Chaulnes said to her son: "My son, this is a good marriage. It is only fitting that you take some dung to enrich your land."

The descriptions of existing conditions by the ever-clear-sighted Mercier, undoubtedly correspond to actual conditions: "The world of finance is nowadays related by marriage to the nobility, and there lies its real strength. The dowries of the wives of almost all our noblemen come straight from the strongboxes of our bankers. It gives me satisfaction to see a count or a viscount, with nothing but a fine name, seeking the hand of a wealthy financier's daughter, or a financier, wallowing in wealth, asking the hand of a girl of high rank, without a sou to her name, but of noble family. . . ."[33]

Again, I shall refrain from giving names and enumerating these mixed marriages in detail, although it would be easy to draw up long lists of them. I shall call attention to only a few characteristic examples which will throw a revealing light on the singular social conditions of the eighteenth century (which in this respect resembles the nineteenth and twentieth centuries).

One son of Samuel Bernard, who was known generally as "le juif Bernard," is comte de Coubert; he married Mme Frottier de la Coste Messelière, the daughter of the marquis de la Coste. The other son bought the office of president at the parliament of Paris, styling himself comte de Rieur, and married Mme de Boulainvilliers. Through this marriage the Jew, Bernard, became the grandfather of the comtesses d'Entraygues, de Saint-Simon, Courtorner, and D'Apchon, later the marquise de Mirepoix.

Antoine Crozat, whose grandfather was a servant, married off his daughter to comte d'Evreux, of the princely house of Bouillon.

His second son, baron de Thiers, married Mlle de Laval-Mont-morency. Their daughters married the marquis de Bethune and the marshal de Broglie.

Pierre, the brother of Antoine Crozat, gave his daughter to the marquis de Montsampère, Seigneur de Glèves. A relative of the duc de la Vrillière married the parvenu Panier. The marquis d'Oise married the two-year-old daughter of the Mississippi specu-lator André (in consideration of an annuity of 20,000 livres until their actual marriage, and a dowry of 4,000,000 livres).

The daughter of the Berthélot de Pleneuf married the marquis de Prie; she was the notorious mistress of the regent. Mlle des Pondre became Mme de la Rochefoucauld. Le Bas de Montargis became the father-in-law of the marquis d'Arpajon, grandfather of the comte de Noailles and the duc de Duras. Olivier Senozan, whose father still dealt in old clothes, gave his daughter to the count de Lucé, later prince de Tingry. Villemorien gave his daughter to the marquis de Béranger.

The comtes d'Evreux and d'Ivry, the ducs de Brissac and de Picquiny—one and all found their way to the money bags of the Turcarets.

Does it not seem as if we were dealing here with the marital chronicles of the daughters of American meatpackers during the last twenty years?

CHAPTER 2

The City

I am unacquainted with any literature on the history of the city, which could be used in connection with our study. A great many writings dealing with the history of individual cities are at best mere histories of municipal law or of monuments. The economic and cultural points of view are almost never taken into consideration. It would hardly be of use, then, to cite these books here.

The material presented in the following pages on the origin and the organization of the early capitalistic city, has been compiled almost entirely from original sources. Travel books and descriptions of other kinds take first place among the sources used. Needless to say that Mercier's *Tableau de Paris* (1781), 12 vols., has no counterpart for any city. Still, we find reasonably accurate information about London in the seventeenth and eighteenth centuries in the descriptions by Defoe-Richardson, Miege-Bolton, Archenholtz, etc.

The sources for Naples in the sixteenth century are to be found in E. Gothein, *Culturentwicklung Süd-Italiens* (Breslau, 1886); Naples in the eighteenth century is described in *Essai sur la société et les moeurs des Italiens* (1782), Letter LV, *et seq.*

With regard to Madrid in the seventeenth century, some travel journals and the memoirs of Mme d'Aulnoy[1] are adequate for our purposes. (Cf also, Karl Justi, *Diego Velasquez und sein Jahrhundert* [Bonn, 1888]; English tr., *David Velasquez and His Time* [London, 1889].)

1. The Cities in the Sixteenth, Seventeenth, and Eighteenth Centuries

ONE OF the most significant events in the whole history of our civilization (which is essentially a result of the processes described in the preceding chapter) is the rapid increase in population of a number of towns at the beginning of the sixteenth century. The product of this development is the city with a population running to six figures. Toward the end of the eighteenth century this type of city, exemplified by London and Paris, comes close to the modern metropolis.

During the sixteenth century the number of cities with 100,000 inhabitants and over, increased to thirteen or fourteen.[2]

The first group to be considered are the Italian cities: Venice (1563: 168,627; 1575–77: 195,863), Naples (240,000), Milan (about 200,000), Palermo (1600: about 100,000), and Rome (1600: about 100,000). On the other hand, Florence, in 1530, had a population of only 60,000.

The next are the Spanish-Portuguese cities: Lisbon (1629: 110,800) and Seville (at the end of the sixteenth century had 18,000 households representing a population of about 100,000), and the cities of the Netherlands: Antwerp (1560: 104,972) and Amsterdam (1622: 104,961).

Let us finally consider Paris and London. Paris, against whose expansion royal edicts had already been issued by the middle of the sixteenth century (I shall revert to them presently) obviously decreased in population because of the religious wars; in 1594 the population of Paris was about 180,000. London grew rapidly and by the end of the sixteenth century exhibited all the signs of an overpopulated city, as we may gather from a decree by Queen Elizabeth in 1602.[3] We must place its population for that period at about 250,000.

During the seventeenth century a few of the formerly large cities decreased in population. Lisbon and Antwerp fell below the 100,000 mark, and the population of Milan and Venice likewise shrank considerably. On the other hand, Vienna (1720: 130,000) and Madrid grew into big cities.

Rome, Amsterdam, Paris, and London continued to expand. Rome had a population of 140,000 at the end of the seventeenth century; Amsterdam, one of 200,000. At the same time, Paris reached half a million, while London, in 1700, exceeded this mark with 674,350.

While London grew only gradually during that century, Paris developed more rapidly, particularly in the reign of the first two Bourbons. Now we frequently meet with those odd edicts, to which I have referred above, forbidding the erection of new houses with a view to checking the growth of the city. They usually begin with phrases like "Whereas the increase in size of our good city of Paris is highly prejudicial," or "Whereas it has been the intention of His Majesty that the city of Paris be of a fixed and limited size. . . ." (These prohibitory edicts express a spirit kindred to that of the guilds of the Middle Ages: opposition to an unrestrained growth of an organic structure, opposition to the tendency to unrestrained expansion and quantification inherent in the capitalistic system, opposition of the old frugality, and conservatism to the boundless urge to expand inherent in the commercial spirit.)

As might have been expected, these prohibitions proved useless. In spite of their reiteration (1627, 1637), Paris kept on growing mightily during these very decades. Baudrillart, a judicious historian, holds that there is a greater difference between the Paris of Louis XIII and that of the League than between the Paris of the League and that of the Third Republic. The awareness of contemporaries of this change is expressed by Corneille in his comedy, *Le Menteur*, written in 1642 (II:5):

> *Tout un ville entière, avec pompe bâtie*
> *Semble d'un vieux fossé par miracle sortie*
> *Et nous fait présumer, à ses superbes toits,*
> *Que tous ses habitants sort des dieux ou des rois.*

The eighteenth century brought the following changes: The 200,000 mark in population was passed by Moscow, St. Petersburg, Vienna, *Palermo (1795: 200,162), with Dublin not far behind (1798: 182,370, as against 8,159 in 1644 and 128,870 in 1753).

The 100,000 mark was reached by Hamburg, Copenhagen, Warsaw; Berlin and *Lyon grew to 141,283 (1783) and 135,207 (1787), respectively.

*Naples approached the half-million mark (1796: 435,930), London the million mark (864,845 according to the census of 1801), while *Paris had a population of between 640,000 and 670,000 at the outbreak of the Revolution.

II. *Origin and Inner Structure of the Cities*

When we inquire into the reasons for the gigantic growth of these cities we discover the same kind of city-building factors at

---

*An asterisk before the name of a city in the text indicates that the relevant figures are taken from the article by Inama-Sternegg in *Handwörterbuch der Staatswissenschaften.*

work which we have found in the growth of the towns in the Middle Ages. Moreover, this is worth noting—the large cities of the early capitalistic epoch are basically consumer cities. The most important consumers are familiar to us; the princes, prelates, and nobles, who are now joined by a new group, "haute finance" (which may be regarded as a class of consumers without disparaging its "productive" function in the politico-economic organization). The largest cities have attained that degree of expansion because they were the residence of the largest number of great consumers. Hence, the expansion of the cities is essentially due to a concentration of consumption in the urban centers of a given country.

The correctness of this view can be proved negatively by pointing out that the "producers," commerce and industry, were unable to develop the cities in which they were situated beyond mere middle size.

Purely commercial cities as, for example, Bristol, which a traveler, about the middle of the eighteenth century, called the "largest, most populous and flourishing place in the island, and one of the principal cities in Europe,"[4] or the other flourishing commercial cities of England at that period, Exeter, Lynn, Norwich, Yarmouth, etc., numbered no more than 30,000 to 40,000 inhabitants when London had long passed the half-million mark. In general, industry had no inherent ability to develop large cities. The industrial centers of the eighteenth century, the mining cities or the centers of the household industries, like Newcastle, Glasgow, Leeds, Manchester, and Birmingham in England; Iserlohn, Paderborn, Jauer, and Hirschberg in Germany, are middle-sized or smaller cities. Neither Great Britain nor Germany, with the exception of their capitals, could boast of a city with a larger population than 100,000, before the end of the eighteenth century.

When we closely examine the so-called commercial cities, for instance, Amsterdam or Hamburg, it is not long before we discover that they owe their rise to city status to forces other than trade. Hence, we can name but one commercial town which, prior to the nineteenth century, had risen to the rank of a city: Lyon, the site of the greatest luxury industry of the early capitalistic epoch. And even in the case of Lyon, banking activities probably have played an important part in the growth of the city.

It will now be easy to show conclusively that it was the concentration of consumption which brought about the early development of the cities. Such a development occurred everywhere under the pressure of a germinating capitalistic system, irrespective of the peculiar character of the country.

Using the most important cities of the seventeenth and eighteenth centuries as illustrations, I shall proceed now to test my assertion.

1. Berlin is the model of the purely residential city, in which only the court, the government official, and the military appear as urbanizing factors. The first signs of an accelerated rate of growth appeared in the latter half of the eighteenth century; it was not until the beginning of the 1760's that its population passed the 100,000 mark. But even at the end of the eighteenth century, Berlin was almost exclusively a city of soldiers and officials and, consequently, of necessity a poor city. In 1783 the garrison, including the families of officers and soldiers, numbered no less than 33,088 people, or 23 percent of the total population of 141,283. (In 1895 this same group comprised 29,448 persons, or 1.8 percent of the entire population.) The state and municipal officials totaled 3433 or, with their dependents, about 13,000. In addition to these two groups there was an extraordinarily large number of servants (10,074). These three sections of the population, and the section depending directly on the court, formed a group totaling 56,000 persons, or two-fifths of the entire population of the capital.[5] How poor these salaried employees of the king of Prussia were is evidenced by the fact that they, in turn, could give employment and homes to a group no more numerous than their own. During that period, 50,000 salaried employees in London or Paris would have fed a population from 200,000 to 300,000 at least.

2. Amsterdam, too, began as the residence of a prince. We gather this from the fact that the departure of the court toward the end of the seventeenth century resulted in great losses in every direction.[6] The gap was soon bridged, however. Amsterdam became the home of the creditors of all European states, a city which consumed the surplus of the wealthiest colonial empire of the world.

3. Venice is similar in character to Amsterdam. The extensive possessions acquired in the early colonial days of the Republic produced in due course a smug, over-wealthy class with incomes from abroad, which swelled the substantial group of land owners. A writer of the fifteenth century informs us with respect to the colonial families of Crete: "A number had accumulated large fortunes and lived in Venice on their income."[7] Nor should it be overlooked that Venice, prior to the loss of her colonies, was the capital of the third largest state in Europe. The great wealth spent in Venice was conducive to a rich, lavish life of pleasure which attracted many foreign visitors. Next to Rome, Venice was the most celebrated city in the sixteenth century: *sede principalissima del piacere* (principal pleasure resort), as it is described in a letter of the year 1565; *paradisus delitiarum* (paradise of delights), as it is called in Hentzner's *Itinerarium* (1617).[8] The greatest attractions of Venice were amusements and women.

4. Rome, in the opinion of Gregorovius, "the only metropolis" because of its physical extent, combined a multitude of important consumers of various kinds:

I. The pope, with the numerous court attendants, who relied on Peter's pence and, in most cases, on a very considerable private income.

II. The pilgrims. Two hundred thousand are said to have been in Rome in 1500.

III. The cardinals and the prelates. Cartesius de Cardinalatu estimates[9] that as early as the fifteenth century a cardinal had to have an income of 12,000 gold florins and a staff of about 140 persons. Some of the cardinals had incomes of 30,000 ducats, and more.[10]

IV. The relatives of the popes on whom riches were lavished. Pietro Riario, the son of Sixtus IV, drew an annuity of 60,000 gold florins.

V. The great noble families, the Orsini, Colonna, etc., who had huge estates and a correspondingly great income from ground rents.

In the period when the popes resided in Avignon, Rome threatened to decay. Cardinal Napoleone Orsini assured the French king after the death of Clement V that, through the departure of the popes, Rome was brought to the verge of ruin. In 1347, Cola di Rienzi held that Rome resembled a robbers' den rather than a habitation fit for respectable people.[11]

5. Madrid. What Rome and Venice meant to the fifteenth and sixteenth centuries, Madrid became in the seventeenth century —*the* Metropolis. The mightiest king on earth held court in Madrid; it was the center of the greatest empire in the world, and to it flowed all the silver treasures of America. No wonder, then, that Madrid attracted all who represented power and riches in Spain. Nothing was more keenly coveted than the honor of being received in the king's household. The court offices bestowed by the king were the especial goal of the younger sons of the nobility. It is fairly easy to trace the growing importance of Madrid to the congregation of the great of the country in that city, particularly since the accession of Phillip III. "The rural districts," so we learn from a contemporary, "are being abandoned by the rich notables."[12] It also seems that Madrid, next to Rome, was the first modern city to have an appreciable influx of pleasure-bent foreign visitors. For this reason Madrid was called " the noble inn of foreigners."[13]

6. Naples. If Madrid, in the seventeenth century, was the third, or perhaps the second, largest city in Europe (it is estimated to have had 400,000 inhabitants at the height of its glory), Naples now grew so rapidly that during the following century it ranked immediately behind London and Paris.

Naples is a textbook example of the vindication of the thesis advanced in this work, namely, that the early development of the cities is based on the concentration of consumption in them. Naples was never anything but the residence of a prince. It owes its status as a city to this circumstance and to the fact that it was the capital of Italy's first unified state, possessing a centralized administration and judiciary.

The greatness and wealth of Naples flowed from two sources: the royal court and the church. These facts were well recognized in their time. "*Regis servitum nostra mercatura est*" (Serving the king is our business), says Caracciolo, in whose writings we see mirrored the social structure of Naples. Indeed, the number of offices in Naples was infinitely large, for centralization led to hypertrophy of offices. The payment of fees was worked out as a system, which was likewise recognized by contemporaries as an essential source of income. An observer moving in the higher strata of Naples' society must have gained the impression that there was hardly anything besides the "unlimited number of jurists, lawers and clerks." (Folieta). With the definite establishment of Spanish rule, Caracciolo at once notes the wane of that influence which had been exerted by the court. The king is now far away, he says, and the city is declining. The barons have given up their large retinues, and, in consequence, public life has lost rhythm and brilliance. No longer does anyone here display princely splendor. The city loses its population, rents are falling, and all merely because Naples has ceased to be the residence of the king.

Later, everything changes again. Naples had another period of prosperity under Spanish rule. When the nobility resumed its lavish mode of life, Naples witnessed a greater pomp than ever before and the population again increased rapidly.[14]

7. Paris. When Lavoisier, the founder of modern chemistry, dedicated his not inconsiderable faculties to the "public good" and fought in the National Assembly for the fiscal reform of France, he made an extremely interesting calculation in order to ascertain the quantity and value of the goods brought into Paris for local consumption. His very accurate computations disclose that every year the people of Paris bought necessities worth 260,000,000 livres for themselves, and feed worth 10,000,000 livres for their horses. Of course, all this had to be paid for. The answer which Lavoisier gives to the question as to the sources from which the 250,000,000 livres were paid, interests us because it contains a remarkable estimate of the composition of the population of Paris at the outbreak of the Revolution. The answer, after eliminating certain obviously erroneous statements which crept into Lavoisier's computations, presents the following picture.[15]

Export industries and trade brought in about 20,000,000 livres; 140,000,000 livres constituted the share of Paris in the interest paid on the public debt *(revenu des intérêts et dépenses payé par le trésor public)*; 100,000,000 livres represented ground rents and profits from industries outside of Paris spent in the city *(revenu des propriétaires de terre, de biens ruraux et de manufactures)*. Brilliant indeed! What depth of insight and comprehension! Paris, with a negligible exception, is revealed as purely a consumers' city which drew its livelihood from the court, the officials, the public creditors, and the receivers of ground rents.

The same idea is advanced by all well-informed contemporaries. And in the absence of statistical material we must, to our regret, depend on their statement for the correctness of our opinion.

Mirabeau the Elder, the author of *L'Ami des hommes*, estimated that the population of Paris would be reduced by about 200,000 if, in conformity with his proposal, the following persons were to be ordered back to the provinces: (1) the court officers who are drawing large salaries; (2) all the large landowners who have come to Paris to carry on their litigations before the courts. They should be made to understand that the cases could best be handled in their own rural districts, where they would enjoy greater consideration and more ease; (3) mischievous litigants.[16]

In his opinion, and that of all physiocrats, there is "a false distribution of population and wealth," for, "all the gentlemen, all the rich people, all those who have independent incomes or pensions which enable them to live comfortably, install themselves in Paris or some other large city where they spend almost the entire interest from the bonds of the state. This spending of money attracts a host of merchants, artisans, servants and laborers."[17] These wealthy rentiers, with whom the "financiers who maintain a direct connection with the royal treasury..."[18] and others were associated, stimulate the growth of a highly developed and, in the opinion of the physiocrats, an overrefined luxury industry. "The landowner, a rustic when on his estate, becomes in Paris an *arbiter elegantiarum* and gives new ideas to the artisan who, thus lifted above routine work, becomes eminent in his line...."[19]

To what extent all industries and businesses thrived only on the expenditures of the wealthy, who thus become the founders of the city in the sense which we have given to this term, is again told by Mercier, in his usual incisive manner:

> How are we to help this mass of needy who have no other guarantee of livelihood than the depraved luxury of the great...
>
> We see in this capital men spending their whole life making toys for children; varnishing, gilding, and tufting occupies a whole army of workers; a hundred thousand are busy day

and night mixing sweetmeats or making ornamental pastries. Fifty thousand other men, comb in hand, wait for the moment of awakening of those idlers who vegetate under the impression that they are alive and who make their toilet twice a day to overcome the boredom which weighs them down.[20]

In most cases the physiocrats forget to stress in their discourses the fact that a not inconsiderable portion of the population of Paris lived on the income of the Church and her servants. It is Mercier again who serves as the most valuable source on this point also:

> Paris is filled with abbés, tonsured clerics, serving neither Church nor State, who live in continuous idleness, whiling away their time with futilities and inanities. ... In many a house we find an abbé who is called "friend of the family" but is only a simple valet in charge of servants. ... Then come the tutors who are also abbés. ...[21]

The bishops violate without much concern the residence laws and leave the posts assigned to them by the holy canons. Boredom drives them from their dioceses which they look upon as places of exile. Most of them come to Paris to enjoy their wealth.[22]

We are indebted to the same authority for the only reliable account of the various strata which made up the population of Paris at the end of the early capitalistic period. In conclusion, I shall present the survey furnished by Mercier. In order to bring out the picture in sharper relief, and also for the sake of greater clarity, I shall reproduce the survey in schematic form.

> Paris has eight distinct classes of inhabitants:
> 1. Princes and nobles
> 2. Gentlemen of the robe
>   a. bar
>   b. church
>   c. medical profession
> 3. Financiers, from the farmer-general to those who lent money on estates; the stockbrokers, those new vultures, occupying the center of this predatory brotherhood, dispicable and despised

4. Business men or merchants, living exclusively on the great, who, being gentlemen, never buy anything for cash, and are obliged to humiliate themselves daily before them or their servants

5. Artists

Painters ⎫
Architects ⎬ inferior rank
Sculptors ⎭

Music composers, ranking high

Men of letters, ranking highest, the *nobilitas literata*

6. Artisans, wealthy artisans deriving their comfort exclusively from the work performed for the wealthy (as I have shown elsewhere)

7. Laborers

8. Servants

9. Populace

(There are nine classes after all?!)

Above all there are also a great number of unproductive people, such as the monks performing religious services in private chapels; and so many nobles, court clerks, bailiffs, constables, attorneys' clerks, armed guards, beadles, rentiers, coachmen, postilions, grooms, and, moreover, the foreigners who come to Paris in droves.[23]

8. London. A great royal court, surrounded since the end of the sixteenth century by a circle of feudal lords spending their income there, is still the core of London when we enter the seventeenth century. We sense the power of attraction of the capital for the nobility and gentry in the seventeenth century from the numerous decrees issued—strangely enough, by the first two Stuarts—against the tendency of country gentlemen to reside in London. One of these decrees, from the year 1632, runs as follows:

The King's Most Excellent Majesty hath observed, That of late yeares a great number of the Nobility and Gentry, and abler sort of his People with their Families have resorted to the Citties of London and Westminster, and places adjoyning, and there made their Residence more then in former tymes

... by their Residence in the said Citties and Parts adjoyning, they have not imployment but live without doing any Service to his Majesty or his People, a great part of their Money and Substance is drawn from the severall Countries whence it ariseth, and is spent in the Citty in excess of Apparell provided from forraigne parts ... and of the great Numbers of loose and idle People, that follow them and live in and about the said Citties, the disorder there groweth so great. . . .[24]

However, these residence prohibitions suffered the fate of all decrees that purport to drive the river upstream; they were simply disregarded. During that century the migration of landowners to London must have taken place with increasing frequency. This movement was the chief factor in the growth of London in the seventeenth century, for at the turn of the following century, London was described as "the mighty Rendez-vous of Nobility, Gentry, Courtiers, Divines, Lawyers, Physicians, Merchants, Seamen and all kind of excellent Artificers of the most refined Wits and the most excellent Beauties."[25]

Since the end of the seventeenth century and the beginning of the eighteenth century, a new element appeared as a city builder, the creditors of the state and the big financiers. As early as the seventeenth century, London had a well-established banking business. What great amounts of cash could be mobilized on short notice is demonstrated, for instance, by the fact that the subscription of the capital stock of the Bank of England (£1,200,900) was completed between June 21 and July 2, 1694. D. Hume recognizes, with profound acumen, the power of the state debts to promote the growth of the city: ". . . [Our] national debts cause a mighty confluence of the people and riches to the capital, by the great sums levied in the provinces to pay the interest [on these debts]."[26]

In the middle of the seventeenth century we find society still living in the city, as evidenced by the complaints of city ladies with sensitive olfactory nerves about the nuisance of coal smoke (coal was then beginning to be widely used): "O Husband wee shall never bee well, wee nor our children while wee live in the smell of this Cities Seacoale smoke."[27]

This period inaugurates the transfer of the mansions of the

nobility to the suburbs. Bolton, who continued the work of Guy Miege, has left us a vivid picture of this process of transformation which the city of London underwent in the middle of the eighteenth century. "The Nobility and chief among the Gentry are at this time much better accommodated in fine Squares and Streets where they breath a good Air and have Houses built after the modern way." He lists a great number of these new houses. We also conclude from his descriptions that the character of elegant London was, in his time, still determined by the establishments of the gentry.[28] The nobility was living at that time in the immediate vicinity of London. Defoe counts seventeen localities in the outskirts of London, "all crowded and surrounded with fine houses or rather palaces of the nobility and gentry of England."[29]

In attempting statistically to ascertain the part played by the several urbanizing elements of the population in the development of London in the eighteenth century, I have sought to do for that city what Lavoisier has similarly done for Paris, although by quite a different method. The conclusions arrived at by me naturally make no claim to absolute accuracy. Undoubtedly, however, they gain considerably in credibility by the fact that the components calculated closely approximate those given for Paris by Lavoisier. The apparent disparity exists only insofar as the turnover of trade in London exceeded that of Paris.

We can readily understand why descriptions of London, as the one by Chamberlayne, for instance, place such great emphasis on the importance of trade as a city-forming element. Trade impressed all observers as the most prominent feature of English life. Statistics, however, plainly show that trade could have supported only a small part of the population of London. In 1700, the imports and exports of England amounted to about RM 214,000,000, (about £10,500,000), a figure reached by the trade of the city of Bremen around the middle of the nineteenth century. The tonnage of incoming and outgoing vessels in all harbors of England in 1688 totaled 285,000 tons, equaling Hamburg's traffic about the year 1800, or one-fiftieth of its present volume.[30] With all due respect to the commercial greatness of London in that day, we should not uncritically accept the extravagant statements of contemporary writers who speak of the "infinite number of ships, which by their masts resemble a Forest, as they lie along this

Stream" (Themas), or of the "infinite number of great wellfur-
nished Shops." (Chamberlayne). In order to appreciate the true
part that trade shared in the development of London, we should
present the following calculation.

In 1700, the imports and exports of all England amounted to
not quite £11,000,000. Assuming a net profit of ten percent,
which is high enough even for that period, this will give us a
profit of £1,100,000. Assuming London's share to be two-thirds
of the total English trade, which is certainly ample, we arrive at
the round sum of £750,000 as the yearly profit of the London
merchants. Considering, as King does, that in 1688 the average
income of an artisan's family was £40, and that of a laborer's
family £15 a year, the foregoing sum could have furnished an income for only about 7000 artisans' families and 24,000 workers'
families, or 12,000 families in each category. King holds that the
average number of persons in these families was three and a half
or four. Hence, it is unlikely that trade could have supported
much more than a population of 100,000 souls, i.e., from one-
seventh to one-sixth of the total population of London at that
period.

Moreover, we must not lose sight of the fact that trade trans-
acted in London could be a factor in the promotion of the growth
of the city only insofar as it was not engaged in merely supplying
the needs of the population of London itself. When we deduct
that portion from the total trade, the part which was operative in
the growth of the city is considerably reduced.

The civil lists of the English kings of that period may serve
as a basis of comparison. In 1696 Parliament granted William III
a civil list of £700,000. Queen Anne received the same sum.
Under George I the civil list was increased to £800,000 and under
George II to £900,000, (£100,000 for the separate household of
the queen). In addition to this, the prince of Wales had a private
income of £100,000. Thus, the king, the queen-mother, and the
heir apparent disposed of a combined income of approximately
the same amount as that of all the merchants of the realm together
and consequently, constituted a source of income for as large a
population as that supported by the merchant class. The figures
here are taken from the above-mentioned work by Miege-
Bolton.[31] This work offers in an appendix ("A regular collection

of series of lists containing all the offices and the whole establishment civil, military and ecclesiastical in Great Britain and Ireland"), a nearly complete roll of the salaries of the military and civil officers of the kingdom, which reveals salaries of almost incredible size, especially in the upper brackets. Not infrequently these salaries rise to £1000, £1500, and even £2000. Continuing our calculation, we find that if £2000 had to be earned as profit, such a profit, even assuming a rate of 20 percent and two complete capital turnovers a year, would have necessitated an investment of £200,000 or one-fortieth of the yearly turnover of all goods in London. If we assign the various portions, by their source of income, to the several city-forming strata, we may effect the following distribution: two-sixths of the population derive their livelihood from the king and his court, one-sixth from the officials, two-sixths from the landed rentiers and the indirect rentiers of the state (high finance), and one-sixth from trade and industrial activities.

III. *Theories of the City in the Eighteenth Century*

The sketch of the social structure of the city in the early capitalistic epoch, which I have attempted to draw in the preceding pages, finds unequivocal corroboration in the numerous "city theories" of the eighteenth century, from which we may infer the character of the city at that time. For, although most authors believed they were describing the origin and the conditions promoting the development of the city or the metropolis, their theories are in reality only generalizations regarding the actual municipal structures accessible to their observation. For this reason I shall now, in conclusion, quite some of the most widely read and respected contemporary authorities on the theory of city growth.

Cantillon, as far as I can see, is the pioneer in this field as in so many other fields of political economy in the eighteenth century. He assigns the origin of the city to the following causes:

> If a Prince or Nobleman . . . fixes his residence in some pleasant spot, and several other Noblemen come to live there to be within reach of seeing each other frequently and enjoying agreeable society, this place will become a City. Great houses will be built there for the Noblemen in question, and an infinity

of others for the Merchants, Artisans, and people of all sorts
of professions whom the residence of these Noblemen will
attract thither. For the service of these Noblemen, Bakers,
Butchers, Brewers, Wine Merchants, Manufacturers of all
kinds, will be needed. These will build houses in the locality
or will rent houses built by others ... all the little houses in
a City such as we have described depend upon and subsist at
the expense of the great houses. .... The City in question will
increase still further if the King or the Government establish
in it Law Courts. .... A Capital City is formed in the same
way as a Provincial City. .... Thus, all the Lands in the State
contribute more or less to maintain those who dwell in the
Capital.[32]

A similar train of reasoning is found with minor modifications
in almost all contemporary treatises on the formation of the city.
This concept was developed with particular emphasis by the
physiocrats, who made it the foundation of their theory, but it
was also taken up by many nonorthodox physiocratic writers.

The politico-economic literature of the eighteenth century is
devoted to the discussion of the most desirable way of spending
incomes from ground rent. This subject is the theme of a host of
pamphlets and treatises dealing with luxury, which are as characteristic of the politico-economic literature of the eighteenth century as the treatises on the subject of population.

Since this economically important portion of the national
income is expended in towns and, especially, in the large cities,
the problems posited by luxury and the cities soon coalesced. In
almost every instance the discussions of luxury are extended to an
examination of what caused the cities to become populous, to the
very composition of this population, to the specific items and the
distribution of the expenditures of the rich, with the resulting
economic effects.

In order to ascertain the connection between theories of
luxury and the city, one need only refer to Quesnay's "Questions
intéressantes sur la population, l'agriculture et le commerce,"[33]
which deals, in the twenty questions set forth in the section
"Ville," with the nexus between city formation and economic
circulation. Question XV,[34] for instance, propounds: "Are the
great fortunes forming in the city not prejudicial to agriculture

... does their existence not prove that they accumulate in the cities and do not return to the country?" Then in Question XVIII: "Does the restoration of the income from landed property permit the proprietors and all other people, who are able to spend lavishly, to live in the country?"[35] etc. Or, in the section "Richesse," article VI: "Ever since the great and rich have gone to the capital, have their expenses not augmented enormously, and would one not judge therefrom that luxury has increased? Has luxury not always been a measure of the wealth of a nation?"[36] etc. Quesnay, too, bases his argumentation on Cantillon, whose brilliant treatise, in its first part, is concerned with many of the same problems. See, for example, chapter XIV,[37] the title of which constitutes a whole program.

For comparison with the theory of Cantillon, I quote the following passage from Helvétius: "The wealth of the city has attracted pleasure seekers. The rich landowners who want to enjoy themselves leave their estates and spend several months in the city where they have mansions built for themselves. The city will grow with every day. . . . Eventually it will become a capital."[38] We have already seen a similar view expressed by Quesnay. Wholly kindred in spirit are the arguments of Count Mirabeau.[39]

Of Italian writers, Beccaria and Filangieri should be mentioned. "The big landowners, with their greater needs and a life more refined than the lowly and simple customs of the common people, became victims of ennui—the plague of the rich. In order to distinguish themselves from others and to assert their superiority over the working classes, which are just as good as they are, they eventually had to congregate and live near one another at the sources of the law, near the highest courts of the land where, while extending the sphere of their pleasures, they extended their powers as well. This is the origin of the large cities and, in consequence, of the capitals."[40] Filangieri, likewise, attributes the formation of the city to the rich landowner: "In that place (the city), in order to display his luxury he (the landowner) prostitutes the canvas of the painter, the chisel of the sculptor, the talent of the architect, the imagination of the poet, and all sorts of artisans. In the city he also maintains a band of idlers, more for the sake of display than for his own convenience. In the city, he eats up finally his own income as well as that of future generations."[41]

The English theory of Stuart is but a restatement of Cantillon's ideas with only this modification. Stuart recognizes as free, city-forming elements not only the landlords ("to whom this surplus [of food] directly belongs") but also the new class of financiers, i.e., people with a vested claim to the nation's income ("with a revenue in money already acquired") around whom are grouped tradesmen and artisans ("those who purchase it [their food] with their daily labour or personal service").[42]

CHAPTER 3

The Secularization of Love

SOURCES AND LITERATURE

A.

I. The Renaissance

The works of Capellanus, Petrarca, Boccaccio, L. Valla, Bembo, Castiglione, Beccadelli, Firenzuola, Aretino, Montaigne, and Rabelais.

II. The Seventeenth Century

The collection: *Cabinet satyrique ou recueil parfait des vers piquants et gaillards de ce temps,* printed in many editions, one of them in Paris in 1632; the books by Auvray and by P. de Brantôme (*Vie des dames illustres, Vie des dames galantes,* were recently published in German by Insel Verlag, 1905 and 1907), etc.

III. The Eighteenth Century

The works of Restif de la Bretonne, especially *Le Palais royal* (1790), 3 vols. New edition in the collection: *Les Moeurs légères au XVIIIe siècle,* introduction and notes by Henri d'Alméras; above all, the extensive literature of memoirs.

B.

I. The Middle Ages

A. Schultz, *Das höfische Leben zur Zeit der Minnesänger* (2d ed.; 1889).

II. The Renaissance

Of prime importance are the well-known historical works of general character by Burckhardt, Gregorovius, Grimm, and others, also Chledowski's fine work, *Die Menschen der Renaissance* (Rome, 1912), tr. from Polish; the recent literature on the life of the great courtesans of the Renaissance is particularly extensive: C. Biagi, *Un Etera romana, Tullia d'Aragona* (1897); P. L. Bruzzone, *Imperia e i suoi ammiratori, Nuova antologia* (1906), fasc. 828; even the letters of these ladies have found editors: L. A. Ferrari, *Lettere di cortegiane del secolo XVI* (1884); Lothar Schmidt, *Renaissancebriefe* (n.d.), vol. IX of "Kultur."

III. The Seventeenth and Eighteenth Centuries

Besides the universal works on cultural history: Imbert de Saint-Amand, *Femmes de Versailles: Les femmes de la cour de Louis XV* (1876), 2 vols., and *Les femmes de la cour de Louis XVI* (1876), 2 vols.; Arsène Houssaye, *Galerie du XVIIIe siècle*, 6th ed., second series: *Princesses de comédies et déesses d'opéra*, fourth series: *Hommes et femmes de cour*, (1858), very witty and clever.

IV. Le Régime des Dames

Theodor Griesinger: *Das Damenregiment an den verschiedenen Höfen Europas in den zwei letztvergangenen Jahrhunderten*, first series: *Die grossen französischen Vorbilder* (1866–67), 2 vols.; second series: *Versailles in Deutschland* (Dresden and Hanover, 1869–70), 2 vols., extensive material, but compiled in the form of anecdotes, and containing no sources. Albert Savine, *La Cour galante de Charles II* (1908), good, authoritative.

A good introduction into the world of the theatre star is *Souvenirs de Mlle Duthé de l'opéra* (1748–1830), apocryphal; new edition by Paul Ginisty with an instructive preface.

V. The Goncourts

The superb and instructive works of the brothers Goncourt place them in a class by themselves. *Portraits intimes du XVIIIe siècle*, new ed. (1873), 2 vols. *Les Maîtresses de Louis XV* (1860). *La Femme au XVIIIe siècle*, 1862. *L'amour au XVIIIe siècle* (1875), and particularly the two works, *La Pompadour* and *La Du Barry*.

VI. Famous Mistresses

Each of the famous mistresses, particularly those of the kings, has become the subject of an extensive literature. The most important works are on *La Pompadour* by Capefigue, Compardon, Goncourt, and others. The *Montespan* by Arsène Houssays, Clément, Bonnassieux (*La Château de Clagny et Mme de Montespan*, 1881), and others.

VII. Various Courts

The literature on the history of the various rulers is also to be mentioned, but cannot be cited here, just as we cannot cite the literature on the various courts. Vehse's work of ill-fame, *Geschichte der deutschen Höfe seit der Reformation* (1851–58), 48 vols., on account of its size, takes first place among the latter.

VIII. French Kings

For France should be noted: Saval, *Les Galanteries des rois français sous plusieurs races*.

ix. French Financiers

H. Thirion's *La Vie privée des financiers au XVIIIe siècle* portrays the régime of the mistresses of the high financiers in detail.

x. Influence of Women

The (not very informative) works on the history of women should also be mentioned. Comte de Ségur: *Les Femmes* (1803), 3 vols. G. Klemm: *Die Frauen. Kulturgeschichtliche Schilderungen des Zustandes und Einflusses der Frauen in den verschiedenen Zonen und Zeitaltern* (1859), 6 vols. The title is the best part of the book. Only the second volume is of interest. In it the author has compiled some articles on the "cocu" (p. 355). H. Scheube, *Die Frauen des achtzehnten Jahrhunderts* (1876), 2 vols., and the well-known works by Scherr, Henne am Ryhn, and others.

xi. Manners and Customs

The books on the history of manners and customs are generally instructive: R. Günther, *Kulturgeschichte der Liebe* (1899); Eduard Fuchs, *Illustrierte Sittengeschichte vom Mittelalter bis zur Gegenwart; Renaissance* (1909); *Die galante Zeit* (1910), with supplementary volumes containing the obscenities, valuable on account of their illustrations; E. Dühren, *Sittengeschichte, Englands* (2d. ed.; 1912), 2 vols.

xii. Art

Naturally the literature on the history of art belongs here but I cannot enumerate the various books. I will only mention one book because it does not belong to any special class and for that reason is most enlightening: Virgile Josz, *Fragonard: Moeurs du XVIIIe siècle* (1901).

xiii. Love and Marriage

The recent books on love, on sex problems, and on marriage offer us very little information because they do not deal with historical data. A good introduction into this literature is: Max Rosenthal, *Die Liebe, ihr Wesen und ihr Wert* (1912).

xiv. Prostitution

Of the books on the history of prostitution, the best known is by the Frenchman Dufour, translated into German by Adolf Stille and Bruno Schweiger and brought up to date by Franz Helbing (5th ed.; 1910), 6 vols. Because of the author's moral conceptions, according to which all love relations without benefit of clergy or the marriage register are termed "prostitution," Lucrezia Borgia and Madame d'Etoiles, for instance, are classified as prostitutes. The book treats the subject expansively; unfortunately, it is carelessly written and lacks references.

xv. Bibliography on Erotic and Obscene Literature

Hugo Hayn, *Bibliotheca Germanorum erotica. Verzeichnis der gesamten deutschen erotischen Literatur,* ... (2d ed., 1885); and (more important) *Bibliotheca erotica et curiosa Monacensis, Verzeichnis französischer, italienischer, spanischer, englischer, holländischer, und neulateinischer Erotica und Curiosa* (1887). *Bibliographie des ouvrages relatifs à l'amour, aux femmes, au mariage et des livres facétieux, pantsgruéliques, scatalogiques, satyriques* ..., par M. le Cte D'I***; par J. Lemonnyer, 4th ed. (Paris 1894–1900) the chief work, 4595 columns of encyclopedia size!

1. *The Triumph of Illicit Love*

I KNOW of no event of greater importance for the formation of medieval and modern society than the transformation in the relations between the sexes which occurred during the Middle Ages and through the eighteenth century. In particular, comprehension of the genesis of modern capitalism is closely bound up with a correct appreciation of the basic changes in this most important domain of human activity.

The change in the conceptions of love and love relations was in the beginning, of course, an internal process. We have two sources of information which help us to appreciate that process fully: observations of representative men (in this instance, of women as well) and characteristic acts of contemporaries. These observations appear in a great variety of forms; they may be made *ex professo* in treatises on love, "*ne'quali si ragiona d'amore,*" as they say in the dialogues of Asolani; we may find them also in the poetry and other works of art that reflect the "spirit of the times." Moreover, it goes without saying that the "spirit of the times" is but the "spirit" of a certain social class, in this case, the society of the courts and the nobility and their sycophants. The love life of the burgher develops in a fundamentally opposite direction to that of the courtiers; and these social contrasts give birth eventually to the capitalistic entrepreneur.

The changing modes of life follow one another like waves of the sea. The wave carrying us at the moment has nothing in common with the one whose rise and fall we wish to study. Social and moral attitudes emanate from the guildhalls and from the sermons of Calvin and John Knox to whom we owe all concepts of middle-class respectability. Development never takes an absolutely linear course, not even within one and the same cultural circle, for now and then the direction is diverted by countertendencies. Only in a general way is it possible to speak of a fundamentally uniform and linear development which has influenced the conception of love and its manifestations in our era.

Europe, during the Middle Ages, subordinated the cosmic phenomenon of sexual love, like every other human activity, to the service of a higher order: God—either worldly love received its religious consecration and was diverted to heavenly goals (as in Mariolatry) or love became institutionalized and this institution (marriage) was recognized as willed and blessed by God—a sacrament. All unsanctioned and uninstitutionalized love was branded with the stigma of "sin."

A fundamentally different conception of the nature of love first becomes palpably evident in the period of the minnesinger. This would set the date in the eleventh century, which marked, in every respect, the beginning of the secularization of love. The year of terror, 1000, had passed, new silver mines had been opened, and the trade connections with the Orient had been extended and consolidated. Provence, which during the eleventh and twelfth centuries was likened to a "peaceful, gaily blossoming island in a stormy sea" was the first to hear the airs of a free, worldly love in the songs of the troubadours who appeared about the year 1090, flourished, and reached their highest peak between the middle of the twelfth and the middle of the thirteenth century. They are followed by the German minnesinger but, above all, in Italy by a large number of lyrical poets, singing of nothing but love. In a collection from the century preceding that of Dante, which I have at hand, I count no less than 126 names of these love minstrels.[1]

Today the whole lyric of the troubadours (the feelings expressed in these lyrics) impresses us as false, affected, and stilted. But it is exactly in this that they are the worthy precursors of modern love. They are a distinct example of adolescent eroticism, which exhausts itself in the glorification of the beloved one, in languishing, sighing, yearning, and adoring. It is not until the beginning of the thirteenth century that we reach the firm ground of natural sensuality. We even cannot state definitely whether the

era of the minnesingers finds its direct continuation in the socie-
ties forming the papal court at Avignon or assembled about Boccaccio's Fiametta. If we are to believe an authority like Ulrich von
Lichtenstein, the amorous period of minnesong was an episode
which ended during the thirteenth century. In his *wrouwenbuch*
(1257), he complains that women were no longer free in the
society of men, did not don pretty costumes any more, covered
their faces with heavy veils, and piously wore rosaries around their
necks. Ulrich von Lichtenstein feels that women have been es-
tranged from the joyous spirit of living which gave so much zest
to former years. The men found pleasure only in hunting; they
set out with their dogs at the break of dawn, and when they returned weary at nightfall, they spent their time throwing dice and
drinking with their boon companions instead of devoting themselves to the ladies.[2]

Perhaps this condition concerned Germany only. Germany,
with few exceptions, is lost to the history of love until the birth
of another era, Goethe's Weimar. It is much more in keeping with
the spirit of the countries of Southern Europe to have perpetuated
a mode of life which had been ushered in by the troubadours. In
any event, a spirit like that which pervades the *Decameron* appears to us as the direct continuation of the rapturous lyrics of the
preceding centuries. It is the reaction of a healthy sensuality
against an overstrained idealism, still expressing itself at the outset
in childish forms: the allure of sexual pleasures is rediscovered, as
it were, and the lifting of veils and garments causes undreamed-of
delights. The keynote to which everything is attuned can be
found in the words of the pious and lascivious nun of Boccaccio:
"I have heard from several women, who came to see us, that all
delights in the world are quite worthless in comparison with those
given by woman to man." Woman, in the imagination of man, appears still fully clothed; let us remember that the *Decameron* is a
product of Giotto's times.

Realistic representations of nude figures in the guise of religious myths, predominantly Adam and Eve, appear as harbingers
of a new conception in art.[3] The paintings and illustrations of the
first half of the fifteenth century already give clear evidence of
the fact that the eye has begun to perceive flesh and blood again.
The Adam and Eve by Jan and Hubert van Eyck on the panels

of the altar in St. Bavon's in Ghent (now in the Museum of Brussels), in Jacopo della Quercia's reliefs on the doorjambs of S. Petronio in Bologna (c. 1425), Massaccio's frescoes in the Brancacci Chapel of Santa Maria del Carmine in Florence, but above all Ghiberti's (1378–1458) reliefs on the bronze gates of the baptistery in Florence are like the dawn of a new era.

But only the late quattrocento sees women in complete nakedness and discovers the intimate beauties of the female body and drinks in to the full the charms of sensual love. One fights for love and for woman: the painters have a partiality for the subject of "The combat of love against chastity" (Pietro Perugino, Sandro Botticelli), but the issue never is doubtful; in the frescoes which Francesco Cossa paints in the Palazzo Schifanoia, in Botticelli's "Primavera" and "Birth of Venus" the love of woman and her beauty triumphs.

What Lorenzo Valla came near to expressing theoretically, in his treatise *De Voluptate* (1431), new emerges palpably from the works of painters and poets as the spirit of concrete life: "What is sweeter, what is more delightful, what is more worthy of love than a beautiful face. The gates of Heaven cannot be a greater pleasure to man's eyes."[4] Valla is indignant that women do not bare to the world the most beautiful portions of their bodies. The manner in which he describes the female body reminds us of the beautiful stanzas in the *Hohe Lied* by Heinrich Heine. (A hundred years later Valla would have found many of his demands fulfilled.) Firenzuola, in the cinquecento, almost canonized the ideal of beauty of the new era.[5] To love means to enjoy these pleasures. "Love is nothing but pleasure. I love women as I love wine, games, and the sciences. The ultimate meaning of life is pleasure. We do not enjoy pleasure for the sake of an ulterior end. Pleasure itself is its own end. . . ."[6] Love becomes the essence of life. The poets Boiardo, Poliziano, Ariosto devote their works to love and women. The words of the poet: "I sing of women, lovers, our clean swords, love, gracious manners, and adventure" might be inscribed on the gates to this era, which, as Ariosto sings, ". . . was submerged up to the eyes in a sea of delights and beautiful things." Love impels men through life as depicted symbolically by a woodcut in the *Poliphilo*.[7]

One of the most glamorous illustrations of the amorous character of those days is transmitted to us by Thomas Garzoni in the ninety-seventh discourse of his *Piazza Universale* (1587), dedicated to Alfonso II of Este:

> These fools do not know what calamities disguise themselves under the name of women friends and ladies. I would not say that they revere them, nay, they worship them as their goddesses who are responsible for so many whims, illusions, and vanities, and with this weak foundation the mansion of love crumbles into an ocean of misery and sorrow. These women are also the idols and godheads, deities of the third heaven and the Graces of the tenth heaven, the beautiful lithe nymphs and the virginal followers of Diana to whom men offer their arduous tears as an incense, their afflicted hearts as censers, their cringing souls as host and sacrifice, their protestations of love as incantations, as their hymns, amorous sonnets and madrigals and the sight of weak, confused countenances as rituals. As oblation they bring the submission of a dog who fears neither cold nor heat, neither night nor daylight, undismayed by pain or by sorrow, who returns when repulsed, does not remain to be protected, never counts the wrongs and insults, never thinks of harm done him, does not think of revenge because like the dead he is blind and mute as to his own interest. They run after these savage beasts, willing to become the prey of these she-bears, ready to submit to these she-panthers and to love these tigresses.

In this manner he continues for pages and pages which glitter and sparkle like a rapid stream so that one feels tempted to copy the entire chapter. In general, one can see how the good Garzoni must have singed his wings if he has gathered so much wisdom in the fires of love.

The century of Titian dawns—a century in which soul and senses unite in a hitherto unknown harmony, in which to love woman means to love beauty and to love beauty means to love life. To what height of refinement love is developed is not so much revealed by the works of poets, painters, and sculptors as by the "theoretical treatise" on love which that period has produced. I mean the writings of the Asolanian Pietro Bembo: "Love is the first cause of everything" we hear; "love is the sweetest of all sweet things."[8] And what is love but a longing for beauty? All wise men agree on this. Beauty, then, is nothing else but gracefulness, born of propriety, symmetry, and harmony in all things. The same idea holds true for body and soul. "As the body with well-proportioned limbs is a thing of beauty, so is the soul with harmonizing virtues." "Love spreads its wings toward beauty—and two windows are opened to love in its flight; the ear, through which it reaches the soul; the eye, through which it is carried to the body."[9]

At that time Italy was probably the only country where the cults of love and beauty found a home; France was still in a chrysalid stage. Montaigne bitterly bewails the awkardness of the French in the conventions of their love life; the younger France was still too impetuous to enjoy fully the pleasures of love as Montaigne would have liked to see them enjoyed. Next to the Italians, he considers the Spaniards to be masters of the pleasures of love: "They are more given to preamble and, thus, make love linger; a twinkling of the eye, a nod, a word, or a slight gesture becomes a favor or a reward."

But this situation was to be radically changed. With the Valois dynasty, Italian art came to France and with it the woman cult. Brantôme extols the amatory art of the French. Needless to say, in the seventeenth and eighteenth centuries France became the recognized school of love which she has remained up to the present day; it was in France that love life attained the ultimate refinement which approaches perversion. The true essence of the eighteenth century was life for love's sake, which found its highest consummation in Paris.

In the works of Fragonard, Boucher, and Greuze, we see the culmination of an era which began with Boccaccio and Pietro Perugino; or better yet, the glamorous finale, because Tintoretto, Rabelais, Ariosto, and Rubens really mark the zenith of that period. The theorists of love, first the minnesingers, Cappellanus, then Lorenzo Valla, and finally Bembo, now become Brantôme and Restif de la Bretonne and also perhaps the marquis de Sade.

These stages seem to mark the normal development which has been repeated in numerous civilizations. "The emancipation of the flesh" begins with timid attempts; this is followed by an epoch of strong natural sensuality in which a free, naive love life reaches its full climax. Then follows a certain refinement, then debauchery, finally perversion. This necessary cycle seems to encompass the deepest tragedy of human destiny; that all culture, being an estrangement from nature, carries in itself the germs of dissolution, destruction, and death.

Ein wenig besser würd' er leben,
Hätt'st du ihm nicht den Schein des Himmelslichts gegeben;
Er nennt's Vernunft und braucht's allein,
Um tierischer als jedes Tier zu sein.[10]

Evidently, this purely hedonistic aesthetic conception of woman and of the love of her, as it gradually emerged after the fifteenth century, stood in an irreconcilable opposition to the religious or institutional restraints to which love had been subjected in former times. Possibly religious ecstasy may yet be reconciled with a detached view of love, e.g., the marvelous poem ascribed to Saint Francis of Assisi, beginning with the words:

In foco l'Amor mi mise:
in foco l'Amor mi mise:
in foco d'amor mi mise
Il mio Sposo novello. . . .[11]

Such lines could have been written by every worldly lover. The ecstasies of the Mary cult certainly were not far removed from the "free love" of that time. What free love, however, could never become reconciled to was the institutionalization of love by marriage. The cosmic love instinct as well as the refined pleasures of love recognize no legal barriers. By its very nature "free love" is illicit or, better, nonlicit. And the ability of a woman to be womanly, beautiful, and lovable can neither gain nor lose an iota of its penetrating power by any man-made social institution such as marriage.

Men, pondering at that time on love problems, could not help but realize that, in marriage, two quite heterogeneous elements were combined—love and order: thus we find this problem thoroughly treated by all "theorists" of love. Probably one of the first to accept the inevitable conclusions arising from his natural conception of love and to declare the relations of the sexes to be nonlicit, was Lorenzo Valla. He says, without circumlocution, that it does not concern anyone if two people choose to love each other: *"Si mulier mihi et ego mulieri placeo, quod tu tanquam medius non dirimere conaberis?"*[12] Therefore, says Valla, it is of no consequence whether a woman has intercourse with her husband or her lover. This conception then finds its free expression in the belles-lettres of the period, particularly those of lighter genre. Boccaccio still had a semblance of respect for marriage, but now derision of marriage and mockery of the duped husband is not only admissible but almost good form; even in the less lascivious novels, which were introduced with Piccolomini's *Euryalus* as well as in the less obscene comedies, adultery is always the "predominant theme."[13]

Montaigne carries this thought one step further. If love is pleasure and marriage a social or ecclesiastical institution with any very noble aims (Montaigne always speaks of marriage with the greatest respect, and precisely because of his opinion of marriage, he arrives at his radical views regarding the interrelation of love and marriage), then the achievement of the goal of love is not only independent of previous matrimonial alliance, but the two, love and marriage, are mutually exclusive. He bases his conception on the following reasoning: Love loathes anything which deals with other matters and shuns every relation contracted for other reasons, such as marriage, where connections and wealth are at least as important as charm and beauty. We do not marry for marriage's sake alone but principally for reasons of offspring and family connections. So it would be short of incest to give free rein to the extravagance of amorous passions in this honorable and holy institution of marriage. A good marriage rejects the association with love and seeks the pleasures of friendship. To love and to bind oneself are two fundamentally different matters which contradict each other.[14]

What Titian and Giorgione expressed in their paintings, what Ariosto and Rabelais declaimed in their writings was formulated in these views. Love finds in itself its highest and only justification and must necessarily dwell outside and beyond all institutions created by man for social and moral purposes, even though sanctified by the Church.

It is, however, more important and decisive for the development of culture that society had lived for centuries in accordance with these ideas; that for centuries, in certain classes, marriage and love had been regarded, almost as a matter of course, as distinct entities which existed side by side, possessing equal rights. In the latter instance we see actually only the resumption of the mode of life of Greek (and late Roman) antiquity. This continuity will be traced more exactly in the following section, especially insofar as it introduced the hetaera into European society.

ii. *The Courtesan*

When free love becomes established in society beside institution-alized love, the women serving this new cult are either seduced daughters of respectable families, adulteresses, or prostitutes. What significance purely erotic love has attained among the upper strata of European nations since the period of the minnesingers may be gathered from the fact that seduction, adultery, and prostitution have shown a great increase.

Figures for the first two forms of free love are not available. But we may infer from the opinions of contemporaries and from many other indications that, for centuries, free love played indeed an important role. Petrarch believes that the festering sore of adultery came to a head in his time. It became good form for a young man to seduce a married woman; he must do it lest he be laughed at by his friends, hence, the feverish craving of young men for gallant adventures, which springs less from sensual needs than from an erotic ambition. Too often the success does not repay the efforts.[15]

It is the same period in which princes ceased to be embar-rassed about their natural offspring and, on the contrary, began to boast about them, as Jacob Burckhardt and Luigi Cibrario prove by numerous examples.

From that time until the end of the epoch, premarital or extramarital sexual relations steadily supplemented marital rela-tions in all circles desirous of being in "style." It is unnecessary to adduce evidence from contemporary biographies; every general "history of morals" is replete with the subject. I will, however, point out one significant symptom which makes adultery appear almost as a social institution; the public recognition of the cuc-kold, as it appeared in Italy during the fourteenth century and in France in the reign of Francis I.

It is also known that prostitution greatly increased in extent and importance after the close of the Middle Ages. Naturally, prostitution finds its best markets in the large cities. Starting in Avignon, this institution reaches its height in London and Paris. Petrarch, in his magnificent Latin, complains that Avignon is invaded by a veritable flood of harlots. Rome was long famous for the abundance of public women within its walls; a reasonably reliable census of the year 1490 lists 6800 meretrices. Considering that the population of Rome at that period had not yet reached the 100,000 mark, this proportion is considerably higher than that for London and Paris, at the end of the eighteenth century, with a count of 50,000 and 30,000, respectively.

Still more important, especially for the development of our external culture, is the circumstance that with the spread of illegitimate love, love for its own sake, a new class of women appeared and took a position between the "respectable woman" and the *putain*. In the Romance languages these women are designated by a multitude of names: *cortegiana, courtisane,* concubine, *maîtresse, grande amoureuse, grande cocotte,* and *femme entretenue,* etc. (The German language and perhaps the English have no single expression for them, although the rather indefinite German word *buhlerin* might be acceptable. This is, perhaps, proof that the entire question was confined to countries of the Romance tongue or was introduced by them.)

Through these women, love—having become a free art—emerges again from the dilettantism of the preceding centuries, and its cult is now placed in the hands of its "vestals." While talent and long practice are necessary to the execution of every art, they are particularly needed in the art of love. Thus, the art of loving could reach its climax only after eminently gifted women, through a natural process of selection, had been elevated from the great mass and given the opportunity to become masters of that art by devoting their whole life to its practice.

Courtisane, cortegiana, meant in the beginning merely "court lady." There were also ladies at the court with purely legitimate love relations. In the third epistle of his book on the courtier, which Castiglione devoted to the court lady, Magnifico goes so far as to say that the love relations between gentlemen and ladies of the court should only be of a licit character. Certainly, most members of the inner circle smilingly contradicted him. They must have known why, for Magnifico's demands were far removed from reality. There seems little doubt that the illicit relations of illustrious ladies were identified at an early date with the social life at the courts. I presume that life at the papal courts had a considerable influence in the formation of this idea. In Avignon (where probably the modern courtesan originated), we find a set of clever, witty, and beautiful women at the courts of the pope and the princes of the church. Such a situation led many to designate the courts *académies de femmes aimables*. We have but to recall such names as Mabille de Villeneuve, Briande d'Agoult, Huguette de Forcalquier, Beatrix de Sault, Laure de Noves, Blanche de Flassans, Isnarde de Roquefeuille, Doucette de Moustiers, Antoinette de Cadenet, Magdeleine de Salon, Blanchefleur de Pertais, Stephanette de Gantelme, the beautiful Adelise of Avignon, the cousin of Laura, to realize the justification of this phrase.

It is natural that a woman in the entourage of the princes of the church could only be a mistress if her relations to the high dignitaries went beyond the merely intellectual, and this, indeed, was probably not unusual. The *cortegiana*, for purely extrinsic reasons, had to become a courtesan.

What Avignon began, Rome continued. For here, too, the lady at the court was "illegitimate" by her very nature. This outward compulsion towards illegitimacy did not exist at the secular courts; the inner urge, however, amply replaced it. The selection of concubines by princes was not an innovation of the Renaissance; the princes had done it at all times. But the daughters of commoners, whom Louis XI of France invited to his royal chambers were not "courtesans" by any means; they became so only when they were received at court and given official recognition as favorites of the ruler. The first tyrants who elevated their mistresses to princely rank are believed to have been Bernabò and Gian Galeazzo Visconti. But the reign of the *cortegiana* does not actually begin until the time when we see Cossa painting the frescoes in the Palazzo Schifanoia; when the court, as we understand that term today, was formed by women and with women. After this period, gallantry became the soul and the ornament of court life. "No court, however great, can sparkle or be gay without women, nor can a courtier be, or achieve, anything of importance without being filled with or urged on by love of women." Thus, Castiglione in his book *Il Cortegiano*.

Taking into account the temper of that period, it is self-evident that our author did not have in mind connubial love; thus, one *cortegiana* after another became the mistress of a *cortegiano* until the term *cortegiana* became identical with courtesan (in its modern connotation).

At this stage we enter the era of the unrestricted sway of the *maîtresse* which, in view of what we have found to be the prevailing relations between the sexes, was the inevitable concomitant of monarchic rule. In the measure that small courts grow, the system takes on larger proportions. We know that from the beginning of the Reformation, France took the lead in this most important matter also; the lady-loves of Francis I are the first royal mistresses who appear as such in history, for it was this king who, as we have seen, conceived the essence of court life to be gallantry and "the most significant act of gallantry was that he made his mistresses the most important personages at the court."[16]

The entire guild of the professional priestesses of Venus was ennobled, as it were, in the persons of the king's *maîtresses attitrées* who now began to govern the world. Thus, also, was the outward stigma removed from these illicit relations, at least from those at court.

In that epoch the influence of the court on any one wishing to belong to society was so great that the legalized illicit behavior gradually resulted in freer love relations outside of the court circles also. Women, in the growing cities, began to live like ladies of the court. This condition produced the courtesans who had nothing to do with the court. They were *femmes entretenues*, if they bestowed their favors on one man, or cocottes, if they were more promiscuous. In the upper crust of the demimonde the term "venal love" becomes slightly blurred.

The courtesan, who was not a courtesan at all, emerged at about the same time as her sister at court (from whom she received her name) and in the same localities, above all in the large Italian cities, especially Rome and Venice. Conditions here were particularly propitious to the creation of a new type of woman; wealth, delight in the revival of antiquity, and the idea that its hetaera could be brought back to life. The spirit of the large city, together with the general liberality of that period, was conducive to surrounding a few selected prostitutes, a small upper stratum, with a halo of distinction. (This liberality always refers to the upper social strata, for there were in those times also respectable tradespeople and merchants who, no doubt, shunned the glittering courtesan just as a Sunday school teacher or purity crusader would avoid her modern sister today.) These were the "honest harlots," the *honeste cortigiane* or *cortesane famose* as they are called in a fragmentary register of Roman prostitutes of the year 1500. The two hundred listed in that register were contrasted with the prostitutes of the lower class, *cortesane puttane* or *cortesane de la minor sorte*.[17]

This document indicates conclusively that the process of differentiation to which I have referred had been completed already.

Much has been written lately regarding the *cortesane famose* of the Renaissance. Many new sources have been made available. We now know by name all the famous cocottes who lived in Rome, Florence, or Venice during the period of the reign of Sixtus IV, Alexander VI, and Leo X. There are even learned discussions regarding the degree of their "education," which they displayed ostentatiously, and the quality of their poetry, which they wrote more or less with the assistance of "ghosts." As if this were so important! Certainly it was only a very superficial education, and their verses were poor. Be that as it may, the significance of this new species of humanity does not lie in these items, but in facts such as, for instance, that a Tullia d'Aragona could, for years, make a fool of Filippo Strozzi and that an Imperia could make the richest man in Italy, Agostino Chigi, keep her during many years of her life. Such achievements are certainly not due to their proficiency in poetry; rather, they require, as Maupassant says, other *qualités rares*, which they amply possessed. And through these qualities they became a power which has had considerable influence on the development of culture. The significance of this class of women is not embodied in the fact that an Imperia could inspire one of her distant admirers to compose the following glorifying epitaph: "Imperia, Roman Courtesan, how worthy are you of this name. Seldom has nature created a being of such beauty"; nor does this significance lie in other manifestations of gallantry bestowed on the *grandes amoureuses* in the Italy of that period. The evidence of their sway is found in facts such as the privilege of interment in the chapel of Santa Gregoria granted to the same Imperia and the solemnization by the pope and fourteen cardinals of the baptism of Agostino Chigi's first son by his new Venetian mistress, Francesca Andreosia.

Like the courtesan and favorite, the woman of the town first attained her full development in France. It is there that she became that definite type with which all European countries are now familiar.

It is of particular significance for the formation of the type of the modern courtesan that, at the turn of the sixteenth century, women appeared on the stage of Paris theaters. In England this custom was introduced in the reign of Charles II. Now, at last, this era had a substitute for the glamour which had surrounded the Renaissance cocotte, herself emulating the hetaera of antiquity; the theater provided the nimbus, which seems to be so essential for free love relations on a higher level. The actress, the prima donna, and the dancer at the Grand Opera took the place of the versifying and painting courtesans of the fifteenth century.

The number of "women of the town" steadily increased during the seventeenth and eighteenth centuries, particularly in cultured centers such as London and Paris, where it became "the thing" to keep an elegant mistress instead of, or besides, a lawful spouse. If we are told that at least fifteen out of every twenty court dignitaries did not live with their wives, but with their mistresses,[18] we may rest assured that this estimate approximated pretty nearly the actual situation. But it is not only the courtier who keeps a mistress; the Turcarets also believe they owe it to themselves to be in the good graces of ladies of easy virtue, the *demoiselles de moyenne vertu*, as they were called. The expenses incurred through these liaisons (I shall discuss this later) constituted the largest items in the budgets of the financiers, as we are reliably informed by Thirion who has made a thorough study of these "affairs." The annals of gallantry in the eighteenth century reveal the close relations between illicit love and the tax farming system.[19] London is not different from Paris. We are told that a bachelor with an income of £2000 spends scarcely £200 for his immediate needs; the rest go for pleasure, which means girls, first and last. (Archenholz.)

In view of such judgments we cannot but accept the figures

given us by reliable observers regarding the number of the "women of the town" in Paris and London. Mercier, for instance, estimates that in his time 10,000 women were "kept" in Paris. In one single parish of London (Marylebone), 1700 courtesans lived in their own town houses at that period.

The prominent place held by venal love in eighteenth century society is best revealed by the custom of publishing, every year, directories of the better class of cocottes, giving names, addresses, and various other information regarding facial pulchritude, deportment, and talents. In London, one printing (8000 copies) of Harry's List of Covent-Garden Ladies was sold as fast as it came off the press. In Paris, a "similar guide" was published with the following title: *Almanac des adresses des demoiselles de Paris de tout genre et de toutes les classes. Calendrier du Plaisir. A Paphos.*

One outgrowth of the new prominence of the elegant courtesan in social life was that bourgeois wives followed her example in style and taste. Not directly though. First, it is the court society which shapes the habits and manners of all good society: "Paris apes the court," says La Bruyère. Court society in turn is molded by the acknowledged favorite of the prince, who thus puts her stamp on all strata of society. The court favorite is above all the model which is copied by the ambitious woman of the town, the *grande cocotte*. At the outset, the latter almost becomes a competitor of her sister at court.

Ninon de l'Enclos follows in the footsteps of Madame de Maintenon: she carries on the old traditions of gay life when her predecessor grows old and pious; the rue de Tournelles challenges St. Cyr.

On the other hand, the respectable lady had to adjust herself to competition with the mistress; the alternative was complete elimination from social life. From this more or less open struggle resulted certain minimum standards of culture to which every lady, whatever her superior social position, had of necessity to conform.

It does not seem improbable that it was the cocotte who indirectly compelled the respectable lady to wash. Marieu de Romieu, who lived in the sixteenth century, advises, in her "Instruction to Young Girls," "all women to keep their bodies clean, be it only for their own good or that of the husband." The "salon," an institution through which, in the seventeenth and eighteenth centuries, the woman of the world exercises her greatest influence, is probably only the successor of the meetings of great minds at the houses of the great Italian courtesans in the fifteenth century.

But the most important result of this development is that the style of life of the demimonde determined that of the women of the world, i.e., society. Hardly anything has changed in this respect since then. Even in the respectable middle-class world of today, the woman of secure position (I am not referring to the eccentric people in "rational" dresses, vegetating in three-room apartments) studies the costumes worn by the *grandes cocottes* at the Spring races in Paris. All the follies of fashion, luxury, splendor, and extravagance are first tried out by the mistresses before they are finally accepted, somewhat toned down, by the reputable matrons. In those bygone days which we discuss here, when the burgher lived in a sphere of his own, far removed from what was then "society," the courtesan in her restricted circle naturally exercised an influence which was more thoroughly and directly felt than is possible today.

In the following chapters we shall endeavor to show in greater detail the effects of this influence on the external mode of life of the new society.

CHAPTER 4

The Development of Luxury

It is hardly possible to speak of any specific sources for the history of luxury, as it may be necessary to consult almost every historical source. First of all, we shall examine the tangible heritage—such as buildings, garments, utensils, account books and invoices for construction costs, travel reports, and contemporary descriptions of conditions of which a very important group (to be used with caution!) is represented by moralistic writings. The extensive literature of memoirs of the sixteenth, seventeenth, and eighteenth centuries furnishes much material. I shall refer to the most important sources at the proper place.

The standard work on the history of luxury is H. Baudrillart's *Histoire de luxe privé et public*, (2d ed.; 1881), 4 vols. One may say of this work, as may be said of many such historical books, that although it is an admirable piece of work, we learn almost nothing from it. The studies of Wilhelm Roscher, "Über den Luxus" in the *Ansichten der Volkswirtschaft*, and those of Emanuel Herrmann, "Die Launen der Pracht" in the *Miniaturbilder des Wirtschaftslebens* (1872), are, for lack of better material, important. Compare also Theo. Sommerlad's article "Luxus" in *Handwörterbuch der Staatswissenschaften*, 3d ed., and the bibliography mentioned therein.

Thorstein Veblen's *Theory of the Leisure Class* (1899 and later editions) is a brilliant attempt to explain luxury and its changes from the psychological as well as the sociological viewpoint.

Besides these works of a general nature dealing with luxury and its history, the specialty literature on the separate phases in the evolution of luxury should be consulted.

Concerning the art of luxurious eating, it is best to read the numerous gastronomic almanacs (originating naturally in France), the first of which was published in 1530. The second which we know was written by Abbé Claude Cherrier and was published under the title *Almanach de la table à Paris*. The *Almanach du comestible*, published first in

1778, had the largest sale (*see* the *Almanach des gourmands* of 1904).

With regard to the history of luxurious residences, we must consult all works dealing with the history of styles in architecture and furniture. Moreover, travel books and descriptions of palaces, etc., should be looked into; a compilation of such descriptions may be found in the *Dictionnaires des amateurs* by P. Bonaffé (1884).

Concerning the luxury of dress, the most useful books are those dealing with the history of costumes and fashions, the manufacture of materials such as silks, laces, jewelry, etc., and the craftsmanship displayed in fashioning them. The economic aspect is clearly pictured in such writings as E. Langlade's *La Marchande de modes de Marie Antoinette: Rose Bertin.*

Much interesting material may be found in the works of Humbert de Gallier: *Les Moeurs et la vie privée d'autrefois* (1911) and *Usages et moeurs d'autrefois* (1912).

1. *Definition and Nature of Luxury*

LUXURY IS any expenditure in excess of the necessary. Obviously, this is a relative definition which becomes intelligible only when we know what constitutes "the necessary." This again may be determined in either of two ways. We may view "the necessary" subjectively, with reference to some judgment of value (e.g., ethical or aesthetic), or we may attempt to establish an objective standard to serve as the measure of "the necessary." Such a yardstick is found either in man's physiological needs or in what may be called his cultural wants. The former vary according to climate; the latter, according to the historical period. As regards cultural wants, or cultural needs, the line may be drawn at will; however, this arbitrary act should not be confused with the above-mentioned subjective evaluation of "the necessary." In this case, luxury has two aspects: quantitative and qualitative.

Quantitative luxury is synonymous with prodigality; such as the keeping of a hundred servants when one would do, or the simultaneous striking of three matches to light one cigar, etc. Qualitative luxury is the use of goods of superior quality. These two types can be, and in most cases are, combined.

From the concept of qualitative luxury we derive the concept of "luxury goods," which may be characterized as "refined goods." "Refinement" is any treatment of a product, over and above that which is needed to make it ordinarily useful. As a rule, refinement is applied either to the material or to the outward form.

Just as we have been able to distinguish between an absolute and a relative concept of luxury or luxurious living, in the same way we must use discrimination in treating the basis of qualitative luxury, i.e., refined goods.

If refinement were to be understood in an absolute sense, most of our articles of use would have to be assigned to the category of refined goods, for almost all of them gratify needs over and above our animal needs. Consequently, we must speak relatively of a demand for luxuries and use the term "refinement" merely for that degree of elegance which surpasses the prevailing standards of luxury in goods. This narrowly circumscribed demand for refined goods may then be called the demand for luxuries, and the goods which serve its gratification, luxury goods proper.

In this restricted sense of luxury demand and its gratification, luxury serves widely divergent purposes and may, therefore, have been brought into being by as wide a range of causes. Whether one dedicates to God a golden altar or buys a silk shirt for one's self, one is indulging in luxury. There is, however, a world of difference between the two; by distinguishing between purpose and motive, we may term the dedication of the altar, idealistic or unselfish luxury and the purchase of the silk shirt, materialistic or selfish luxury. In considering the development of luxury expenditures, we discuss only the latter type of luxury, which, being of selfish origin, serves to fill the individual's life with "idle vanities." It is just this kind of luxury which expanded greatly during the Renaissance, to be more specific, in the period between Giotto and Tiepolo. In any case, I shall treat here only of the origin and growth of personal luxury.

All personal luxury springs from purely sensuous pleasure. Anything that charms the eye, the ear, the nose, the palate, or the touch, tends to find an ever more perfect expression in objects of daily use. And it is precisely the outlay for such objects that constitutes luxury. In the last analysis, it is our sexual life that lies at the root of the desire to refine and multiply the means of stimulating our senses, for sensuous pleasure and erotic pleasure are essentially the same. Indubitably the primary cause of the development of any kind of luxury is most often to be sought in consciously or unconsciously operative sex impulses.

For this reason we find luxury in the ascendant wherever wealth begins to accumulate and the sexuality of a nation is freely expressed. On the other hand, wherever sex is denied expression, wealth begins to be hoarded instead of being spent; thus, goods are accumulated, especially in such abstract forms as precious metals and, in more recent periods, money.[1]

But once luxury has been established, we find that a number of other motives further its growth. Ambition, love of display, ostentation, and lust for power may be weighty motives; they are really the desire to outdo the next man. Veblen, in his brilliant book on the "leisure class," attributes all valuation of luxury and property to this urge to distinguish one's self. Even if we grant that this instinct, like hunger and love, is one of the basic instincts of man, we must admit that its manifestation in the form of luxury depends somehow on the concurrence of certain conditions. Plainly, this presupposes that luxury already exists and that the display of similar or greater luxury furnishes the means of gratifying the impulse to outdo others. The most convenient means for gratifying the craving for superiority is the accumulation of things, quantitative luxury: number of slaves, size of property or fortune, order of rank, and the like. But if luxury is to become personal, materialistic luxury, it must be predicated on an awakened sensuousness and, above all, on a mode of life which has been influenced decisively by eroticism.

Turning to the period under discussion, we note that the stage had been set for the advent of great luxury. All the necessary elements were present: wealth, sexual freedom, the striving of certain groups of the population to get ahead, and a preference for living in large cities which, as we have seen in the previous chapters, were exclusively centers of pleasure before the nineteenth century.

Such a conclusion, however, might seem a little anemic and appear to many not sufficiently convincing. For this reason I propose, in the following analysis, to reverse the procedure. I shall begin with the fact that in the centuries following the close of the

Middle Ages there existed considerable luxury, which by the end of the eighteenth century attained staggering proportions; later, I shall explain these phenomena. It is first necessary to demonstrate the existence of an intense development of great luxury.

For this purpose let us recall the frequently recurring statements of contemporaries which are concerned with the unbearable burden of luxury. "The whole world is insane: Luxury has been carried to extremes; and we have been told that half the people of Paris have been ruined, and that the other half live by swindling," writes a provincial visitor to his wife from Paris in 1787. "One of the downright obsessions of our day," observes Mme d'Oberkirk, the old gossip, "is to ruin one's self in every possible manner." We owe the most graphic description of the hopeless situation of society of that day to Mercier.[2] He calls luxury the executioner of the rich *(luxe, bourreau des riches),* and tells us in incisive language how the rich, going to extremes in all pleasures, have lost their capacity for enjoying them. "The senses are no longer satisfied; they are jaded. Instead of meeting with stimulating variations, we come face to face with bizarre and nauseating extravagance; this is why everything keeps changing, continually and for no good reason: fashions, dress, customs, manners, and speech. The rich soon become insensible to new pleasures. The furnishings of their houses have the character of changeable stage settings; to dress up becomes a real task; their meals are pageants. In my opinion luxury is to them as much an affliction as poverty is to the poor. Oh, it has indeed been worth while to sacrifice everything for luxury! The great scourge of the rich in Paris is their frenzy of spending; they alawys spend more than they intended to. Luxury has taken on such dreadfully expensive forms that there is no longer any private fortune which is not undermined by it. Never has there been a more profligate age than ours! People squander their income, devour their substance; and everyone seeks to outshine his neighbor by a display of shocking extravagance."

The same picture everywhere, and almost the same words to describe them: Never has there been an age more extravagant, is the opinion of Defoe in the *Complete English Tradesman.* "It is next to incredible what a share the luxury of the age has . . .

'vanity, gaiety and luxury' are our masters, 'excesses' have the upper hand."[3]

Living in Warsaw, where luxury reached its apogee, Kochanowski wrote: "Luxury swallows up everything as though it were a bottomless sea; if the Almighty would send down upon us a rain in which every drop were a ducat, covering Poland ankle deep, all this gold would not stay with us for long. Like water falling from hill and mountain to stream and field, it would flow swiftly to Breslau, Leipsig, Frankfort, Berlin, Danzig, Riga, and Königsberg, to pay for silver plate, carriages, furniture, and so forth."[4]

We do not content ourselves with such second-hand evidence, but will endeavor to present the facts themselves, that is to say, to give concrete examples of the luxury of the period under discussion. I may as well assume that the reader is familiar with such facts; and indeed, to a certain extent, such knowledge will be assumed throughout. I do not believe it superfluous to cite definite figures regarding not only the general development of luxury, but also such figures as deal with individual instances of luxury, and, a fortiori, to cite the figures behind a whole mass of such instances adequately to illustrate the important role of the demand for luxuries in the growth of the market. It is this relation, above all, which we seek to understand.

Having thus established beyond any doubt that excessive luxury was characteristic of the period we are concerned with here, we shall proceed to determine how the demand for luxuries is related to the social factors considered in the preceding chapters. More particularly—and this is the fundamental thesis of the present inquiry—we must ascertain the extent to which women, especially women as objects of illicit love, have influenced the life pattern of our age.

ii. *The Courts*

Good living and pleasure, like every other manifestation of life at that time, had its origin in the courts which were, in a very real sense, the source of all socially vital forces.

In surveying the past in order to find the period in history where sumptuous worldliness first made its appearance, our attention is inevitably attracted to Avignon:

> *Covetous Babylon of Heaven so hated,*
> *Has by her sins now drained the brimming flagon*
> *Her knees now bend to Baal and hideous Dagon.*
> *Pallas and Jove are fouled and Bacchus fêted.*
>
> . . . .
>
> *Rome erstwhile, now the Babylon whore of hire!*
>
> . . . .
>
> *Founded in want and honour unpolluted,*
> *Against thy founders pointest thou thy horn,*
> *Impudent Jezebel? Is thy faith rooted*
> *In thine adulteries and gold ill-born?*
>
> . . . .

To be sure, Petrarch,[5] who has bequeathed us this as well as other descriptions of the papal court of Avignon, was not an entirely impartial and unprejudiced judge, but that he draws an essentially true picture of the situation is corroborated by the testimony of reliable witnesses. Nicolas de Clamenges exclaims: "Perverse morals have invaded our Gaul."[6] A pointed reference to the papacy indeed! Yet, these statements alone do not give us a complete picture.

It is preferable to depend on more objective sources of information, such as, for instance, a contemporary account[7] of banquets given in honour of Pope Clement V, which closes with this glowing description: "The eyes of our Holy Father surveyed all these things (the bacchanal climax of the sumptuous banquets, with all the guests dancing through the gardans), taking delight in the variety of refined pleasures, and with the benignity and serenity befitting such holiness as is His."

Or again, I should like to refer to the inventories of the papal palace, brought to light by E. Müntz.[8] These lists establish, in a dispassionate manner, the justice of Petrarch's observations. But if we wish to have a correct impression of the atmosphere at Avignon, we must take into account also the numerous satellite courts of the prelates residing there. Probably the ecclesiastical courts taken together did produce that splendor and magnificence which we find reflected in the descriptions of eyewitnesses. The expenditures of the papal household, as recent research has shown, were not excessively extravagant. Thus, for instance, in the period from June 24, 1305, to April 24, 1307, a total of 175,317 gold florins were disbursed for officials and servants attached to the papal household. (It is true that these records date from the first years of the pope's residence at Avignon; schedules for later periods have, to my knowledge, never been published.) An average of 826 florins 8 dinars a week was spent for kitchen, bakery, wine cellar, and stables; the stables contained 135 horses.[9]

In our minds the resplendent Avignon period is followed immediately by the most brilliant period of papal history in Rome—the reign of the great popes of the Renaissance, from Paul II to Leo X. Each new incumbent of the throne of St. Peter sought to surpass his predecessor in sumptuous magnificence. "A pagan spirit pervaded the city, with the theatrical splendor of ancient imperial times. Secular pomp became a necessity of the papal government. The pampered populace called for festivals, and festivals were given in abundance."[10]

The bacchanalia began with Paul II (1464–71). His court was magnificent. He himself was entirely given to worldly pleasures; the carnival in Rome, to which he gave a secular, pagan character, he regarded as a symbol of his own life.

Sixtus IV emulated his predecessor. In his reign it was especially the nepotes who led a merry life in Rome. His son, Pietro Riario, with 60,000 florins a year to spend, dissipated his whole fortune within the short span of two years. When Leonora of Aragon, the natural daughter of the king of Naples, came to Rome in 1473, the "feasts given surpassed, in their insane extravagance, anything that had been seen before."[11] When the time for her departure had come, she could leave Rome with a conviction that there was nothing on earth that could even remotely compare with the opulence of a nepote's court in Rome.

The luxury of that period is especially evident in the lavishness displayed in the festivals, public spectacles, receptions, and state pageants. No less than 100,000 persons assembled on the Piazza Navona on St. Mark's Day, in 1476, when Girolamo Riario held a tournament. When the princess of Urbino was married to Giovanni Rovere, in 1478, contemporaries said that the nuptials were celebrated with Persian pomp, *persico apparatu*.[12] The diary of Johann Burchard, a papal secretary, gives us a minute description of the pomp displayed when Prince Federigo of Naples entered Rome.[13] Worldly splendor exhibited by the papacy reached, however, its zenith on April 11, 1513, in the memorable Lateran procession of Leo X. The pageant, for which hundreds of artists were hired to give their best, consumed 100,000 ducats.[14] We need not be surprised, for this was the age that saw Raphael Santi riding through the streets of Rome like a crowned sovereign, followed by a retinue of never less than half a hundred admirers, friends, and pupils.

The secular courts of Italy, particularly those of Milan and Naples, as we know, vied with each other in the display of material splendor. Regarding the luxury at these courts, we have as authority the diary known as *Le Vergier d'honneur*[15] kept by André de la Vigne, secretary of Anne of Brittany, who accompanied Charles VIII on his journey through Italy.

Of greatest significance in the history of court luxury, as well as in the general history of court life, is the fact that the kings of France became the cultural heirs of the Italian princes. Caterina de' Medici only completed what the house of Valois had begun. Charles VIII and Louis XII manifested strong leanings towards Italian culture, which were embodied in their policies. In consequence—and this is of decisive importance—the external possibilities for developing luxury increased in the degree that France became greater and richer than the Italian principalities. Already the last kings of the house of Valois had spent sums for their households which exceeded the combined public revenues of the richest Italian states. The revenues of these states at the close of the fifteenth century have been estimated at the following figures[16]:

States	Maximum Gold Florins
Venice	1,000,000
Naples	600,000
Milan	600,000
Florence	300,000
Papal State	200 to 260,000

In striking contrast with these figures are the 1,500,000 écus which Francis I and Henry II could afford to spend on their courts per year.

The Venetian ambassador, Marino Cavalli, to whom we owe this estimate, adds this remark: "If you could but see the court of the French king, you would not be surprised at such huge sums. He usually provides for the maintenance of from six to twelve thousand horses. His reckless extravagance knows no limits. The cost of traveling increases these expenditures by at least one-third, because the multitude of mules, coaches, litters (sedan chairs), horses, and servants needed for such undertakings are of a kind that costs twice as much as those used by others."[17] Another ambassador estimated the train that accompanied the king on his journeys at 8000 men and an equal number of horses.[18] According to the same authority the 1,500,000 scudi (écus) which in 1913 would have amounted to 10,000,000 francs, were spent for the following items:

	Écus
Buildings	100,000
Hunts	150,000
Banquets and entertainment	100,000
Wardrobe and gifts	100,000
Household of the king	200,000
Household of the queen	300,000

Since it is instructive to follow up the development of the several items of expenditure, I shall quote from the report of another ambassador, which, as far as I know, has gone unnoticed hitherto.[19] In 1542 the total spent by the king was 5,788,000 livres.[20] Of this amount the following items may be classified as luxury expenditures:

	Livres
The king's privy kitchen	85,000
The king's horses (including wages of stable attendants)	80,000
Gold and silver garments for gifts	50,000
Wages and board of court attendants	190,000
The queen's household	140,000
(The household of the dauphin)	280,000
Falconry	60,000
Château of Chambord (on which 400,000 livres had already been spent)	30,000

	Livres
Château of Fountainebleau	50,000
The king's privy purse	500,000
Gifts and grants	500,000
Purchases for the king, such as trinkets, etc.	160,000
Funds for undisclosed purposes	400,000
Menus plaisirs	750,000
	3,275,000

The *menus plaisirs*, adds our authority, include items of a nature which call for discretion, such as gifts to ladies for very personal services, etc.

Under Henry IV, luxury expenditures tend rather to decrease. In the last year of his reign expenditures of that sort are distributed in the following manner[21]:

	Livres
Royal stables	261,590
Household of the king	435,538
Silver plate	197,334
Miscellaneous minor items	162,180
Hunts	88,670
Household of the queen	541,439
Buildings	633,298
Traveling	107,185
Gratuities, gifts, etc.	85,798
Purchases	71,575
	2,584,607

Thereafter the court's expenditures increased each year, reaching their peak in the last years of the reign of Louis XIV. The budgets for the period between 1680 and 1715 do not differ greatly from one another. I shall quote a typical budget (year 1685)[22]:

	Livres
The king's household	606,999
The king's privy purse	1,618,042
Silverware, including articles for the royal toilet and other precious objects	2,274,253
Pocket money	400,850
Purchase of horses	12,000

	Livres
Keeping of the royal stables	1,045,958
Gifts	313,028
Stewards	61,050
Hunting small game, hunts with falcons and wolf hunts	388,931
Household of monsieur	1,230,000
Household of madame	252,000
Gratuities	160,437
Petty expenses of the king	2,186,748
For construction of royal buildings	15,340,901
Secret fund	2,365,134
Traveling	558,236
	28,814,567

That is to say, of a state budget of 100,640,257 livres about 29,000,000 are appropriated by the king for his personal uses, to wit, mostly luxury expenditures. Examining the single expense items, we see even more clearly what huge sums of money were diverted to luxury trades.

First and foremost is, of course, the enormous outlay for building purposes. In the minutely itemized accounts for the years 1664 to 1779, we possess the most detailed information regarding all the money spent on royal residences. The data contained in these records constitute sources of information on the economic history of the period the value of which cannot be overestimated. As far as I know, this source has not as yet been drawn upon, still less exhaustively treated, although an excellently edited collection of these documents was published a long time ago.[23] To be sure, Levasseur and other French economic historians knew, and quoted, this collection; but they scarcely seem to realize what rich harvests were here in store for the industrious scholar. In this connection I can naturally utilize only a small part of these abundant materials which certainly deserve thoroughgoing study. Despite the fact that the word "guild order" is not mentioned even once throughout the five quarto volumes of this work—or perhaps because of it—this source, skillfully treated, will yield the necessary raw material for a complete history of important crafts and of industrial capitalism in the seventeenth and eighteenth centuries.

In order to convey a comprehensive idea of this type of luxury expenditure, I shall first give the total of the disbursements for the construction of royal residences during the reign of Louis XIV (1664–1715): 198,957,759 l. 14 s. 11d.[24] (The livre had by then a value of $0.33 only; hence, this amount is equivalent to about $66,000,000.)

Far more than one-half of this amount was disbursed during the first twenty-seven years of his reign, to wit: 73,977,269 l. 14 s. 5 d. between 1664 and 1680, 57,657,478 l. 6 s. 2 d. between 1681 and 1687.

The lion's share of this money was, of course, absorbed by Versailles, which, with its gardens and water works, cost 65,651,257 l. 18 s. 3 d.[25] (the equivalent of $20,000,000). Previous estimates placing the cost variously from 600,000,000 to 700,000,000 francs ($120,000,000 to $140,000,000) are, thus, very wide of the mark.

The painstaking recapitulations, for which we are greatly indebted to the editor of the aforementioned work, present itemized lists of expenditures. The following items are illustrative[26]:

Purchases from manufacturers and merchants	1,730,206	l.	10	s.	2 d.
Purchases from the *Manufacture royale des Gobelins*	4,041,068	l.	2	s.	7 d.
Large silver plate	2,245,289	l.	14	s.	10 d.
Marble, lead, and tin	3,790,446	l.	16	s.	2 d.
	11,807,011	l.	3	s.	9 d.

Expenditures for actual construction work at Versailles, the Louvre, the Tuileries, St. Germain, Fontainebleau, Vincennes, Trianon, Clagny, and Marly are given in detailed enumeration[27]:

Work	*Expenditures*				
Masonry	17,300,995	l.	8	s.	1 d.
Carpentry	2,334,108	l.	11	s.	2 d.
Roofing	826,148	l.	10	s.	5 d.
Plumbing	2,268,087	l.	19	s.	7 d.
Lock and blacksmithing	1,878,242	l.	8	s.	4 d.
Panelling	2,087,541	l.	5	s.	10 d.
Painting	2,877,875	l.	16	s.	3 d.

Work	Expenditures
Statuary (plaster)	2,041,321 l. 11 s. 6 d.
Glazing	289,524 l. 11 s. 11 d.
Paving	729,738 l. 16 s. 10 d.
Gardening	2,306,003 l. 19 s. 1 d.
Landscaping	3,791,064 l. 18 s. 9 d.
Miscellaneous	350,104 l. 12 s. — d.
Extraordinary expenses	4,456,733 l. 6 s. 9 d.
Total expenses for 1664–80	43,537,491 l. 16 s. 6 d.

In 1689 and again in 1709, financial difficulties forced Louis XIV to have all the silver plate of the court melted down.[28] In 1689, the silver thus obtained weighed 82,322 marcs 5 ounces 9 grains,[29] representing a total value of 2,505,637 l. 4 s. 9 d. (approximately $750,000).

The lavishness of the furnishings of the royal palaces can be gleaned from the profusely illustrated inventories which have been published in recent years. One list, to take but one instance, enumerates 334 complete wall tapestry sets composed of 2600 smaller pieces and 140 individual pieces; the *Manufacture royale des Gobelins* had furnished 882 pieces constituting 101 sets.

A few of the orders placed with various merchants give an idea of the luxurious appointments of the royal residence[30]:

Paid to Messrs Duc & Marsolier, merchants,
    for 64 yards of gold and silver
    brocade   — 138 l. 10 s. per yd.
    44 yards of gold brocade, poppy-red
    and green   — 133 l. 5 s. per yd. 16,545 l. 5 s.
    for Lyon brocade   22,155 l.
    for 62 yards of gold and
    silver brocade on violet
    background — 66 l.   per yd.
    259 yards of crimson-red Tours
    damask   — 11 l. 10 s. per yd. 7070 l.
Paid to M Reynon for gold and silver
    brocade   70,716 l. 18 s. 11 d.
Paid to M Marcelin Charlier for velvets
    and brocatelle   5572 l. 5 s.

The costumes worn by court society were in keeping with the furnishings of the castles. To what heights of lavishness they rose may be read in *Le Mercure galant*, in which a writer of the seventeenth century dwells at great length on the costumes of the exalted personages admitted to the court.[31] On one occasion, Louis XIV wore a coat covered with diamonds worth 14,000,000 francs. On a visit to a lace factory in Paris he bought lace worth 22,000 livres.[32] Luxury in dress at the French court assumed ever more extravagant proportions during the eighteenth century, reaching its culmination a few years before the outbreak of the Revolution. The accounts of Marie Antoinette's wardrobe have been preserved. The figures quoted below are taken from a first-hand source.[33] In 1773 the dress allowance for the dauphine was 120,000 livres. This amount was exceeded by considerable sums in subsequent years. Thus, the expenditures for the wardrobe of Marie Antoinette, during four years as queen of France, were as follows:

Year	Expenditure
1780	194,118 l. 17 s.
1781	151,290 l. 3 s.
1782	199,509 l. 4 s.
1787	217,187 l. —

Thereafter this item of expenditure grew smaller.

And woman—the woman of leisure and pleasure—did she have any share in the sky-rocketing multiplication of luxury expenditures? And, if so, to what extent was she responsible?

When we consider the Italian princes and the French kings of the house of Valois, we need not pause for an answer: their lives, we have learned before, were an endless pursuit of the love of women. As regards Louis XIV, who unquestionably was the first to introduce luxury on a truly magnificent scale, was it not rather conceit and craving for display that completely dominated him and gave rise to his extravagance? No, indeed! In his case especially we have, in state records, documentary evidence, as it were, of the influence of his favorites on his style of living. Love for Louise de la Vallière impelled him to build the new palace at Versailles, for it had been there, in his father's hunting lodge, that he had kept his first trysts with her. "There, on the wooded hill, the beloved was to see her master's magic castle." His relations with this woman mark the beginning of the lavish festivities which characterized the French court. The outstanding entertainment of that epoch, a divertisement named *Les plaisirs de l'île enchantée*, lasted three days; it included the performance of Molière's *La Princesse Elide*, based on Ariosto's *Isola magica*, in which the king himself took the role of Roger. During the following six years he built the Château de Clagny, at a cost of 2,000,000 francs, in order to gratify the whim of his mistress. And the same thing repeated itself invariably. For Louis XIV every new love affair was the signal for a new outburst of riotous spending, eclipsing the previous one. The climax was reached with Mlle de Fontanges, through whose fingers money ran like water; she spent 100,000 écus a month and was surprised at people calling her extravagant. That the French court during the eighteenth century was completely dominated by the royal mistresses and that court life was governed by them in every detail is a fact too well known to require proof. Mme de Pompadour, who possessed very good taste, set the fashion in everything. "We live now only by Mme de Pompadour; coaches are à la Pompadour, the color of dresses is à la Pompadour; we eat meat stews à la Pompadour, and in our houses we have mantelpieces, mirrors, tables, sophas, chairs, fans, boxes, and even toothpicks à la Pompadour!" writes a contemporary.

Madame de Pompadour symbolizes the culture of the ancien régime; but above all, she embodies the tastes and style of living of her day. She brought her influence to bear on the economic life of France in order to mold it into conformity with her tastes. After sending her brother to Rome to study, she has him appointed director general of buildings, gardens, arts, and crafts; later she has him elevated to the rank of marquis de Marigny. She builds one château after another: the Petit-Château, the Château de Bellevue, to which she later added Le Taudis, a retreat later renamed Brimborion. She beautified Choisy. She herself designed the gallery of the Château de Bellevue, which was to be decorated by Vanloo, Boucher, and Brunetti, and for which Couston made a statue of Louis XV. There it was that Mme de Pompadour gave sumptuous gala feasts for which she prescribed the costumes to be worn by her guests. Telling her guests what to wear, she also had these costumes made at her own expense; some of these costumes cost as much as 14,000 livres. The guest linen in the Château de Choisy alone had cost 600,452 livres. Her annual expenditures reached sums no queen ever had at her disposal. According to extant records she spent 36,327,268 livres for her personal needs during the nineteen years in which she held sway over Louis XV.[34]

Madame Du Barry was no less reckless a spender. M. A. Leroy has painstakingly computed the sums spent by her during her dazzling career at the French court (1769–74) and has arrived at the impressive total of 12,481,803 l. 11 d. Of this amount, 6,427,803 livres were honored by the court banker Baujon. The Abbé Terray, as we know, had arranged that her drafts be treated like *bons du Roi*, the personal drafts of the king.

Marie Antoinette is the last *grande cocotte* to rule supreme over a French court. At any rate, until the early eighties she gave further impetus to the rising tide of luxury. The figures cited above plainly demonstrate that even a legitimate royal spouse could follow in the footsteps of the royal mistresses. But we must not forget that Marie Antoinette, in the happy years when she was only the wife of the dauphin, had to live up to the traditions of that court in order not to be effaced by such formidable rivals as Mme Du Barry and her clique.

The accounts of Mme Du Barry, which have been preserved in their entirety, are an inestimable source of information for a true understanding of the role that woman, especially the woman of leisure, pleasure, and sensual tastes, played in the development of luxury at the close of the era of early capitalism. It is fair to say that these records throw more light on the economic life of the eighteenth century than dozens of guild charters and government decrees which always repeat substantially the same thing. From the great wealth of figures I shall quote only a few, namely, bills for various purposes paid by drafts on the court banker:

Article I

From goldsmiths, jewelers, and dealers in trinkets:

Goldsmiths	313,328 l.	4 s.	— d.
Jewelers	1,808,635 l.	9 s.	— d.
Dealers in trinkets	158,800 l.	— s.	— d.
	2,280,763 l.	13 s.	— d.

Article II

From silk merchants,
lace dealers,
and millinery establishments:

Silk stuffs	369,810 l.	15 s.	— d.
Linen and laces	215,988 l.	6 s.	— d.
Fashionable articles of dress	116,818 l.	6 s.	— d.
Haberdashery	35,443 l.	14 s.	— d.
	738,061 l.	1 s.	3 d.

From different perfumers,
furriers, hatters:

Braziers	52,148 l.	9 s.	— d.

Article III

For furniture, pictures, vases
and other ornaments:

Furniture	24,398 l.	18 s.	— d.
Pictures, vases	91,519 l.	19 s.	— d.
	115,918 l.	17 s.	— d.

Article IV

From tailors and embroiderers:

Tailors	60,322 l.	10 s.	— d.
Embroiderers	471,178 l.	— s.	— d.
	531,500 l.	10 s.	— d.

Article V

For purchases of carriages and
horses and forage:

Carriages and keep	67,470 l.	1 s.	— d.
Horses	57,347 l.	— s.	— d.
Forage	6,810 l.	— s.	— d.
	131,627 l.	1 s.	— d.

Article VI

From painters, sculptors, etc.:

Gilders	78,026 l.	— s.	— d.
Sculptors	95,426 l.	— s.	— d.
Gilders	48,785 l.	12 s.	6 d.

Article VI (cont.)

Founders	98,000 l.	— s.	— d.
Marble cutters	17,540 l.	8 s.	10 d.
Joiners and locksmiths	32,240 l.	8 s.	— d.
	370,018 l.	9 s.	4 d.

Article VII

For the old and new works of
Luciennes:

Old works	111,475 l.	6 s.	9 d.
Gardens	3,739 l.	19 s.	— d.
New works	205,638 l.	16 s.	8 d.
Gardens	3,000 l.	— s.	— d.
	323,854 l.	2 s.	5 d.

The remaining expense items, clothes, gifts, etc., are of too personal a character to interest us here. The prices paid for them, however, speak for themselves:

	Livres
A full-dress costume of white velvet	12,000
Trimming of another	10,500
Other robes, costumes,	
toilettes at prices varying from	2400 to 9000

A set of twelve armchairs, 7200 livres; an ottoman to match, 2400 livres; the bed at the Château de Luciennes, 5945 livres (it is so elaborate that its description occupies a whole page, very much worth reading); a clock, 5400 livres; a snuffbox, 576 livres; fifteen coffee napkins of mousseline, 225 livres. The gilt frame of a portrait of *Madame la comtesse* (the one depicting her as one of the Muses), cost 2250 livres. A particularly expensive item in this inventory is the porcelain used in the household. A Sèvres service was billed at 21,438 livres; another, presented by Mme Du Barry to her brother-in-law, was valued at 4856 livres. One of her Gobelins cost 488 l. 5 s. a square yard. Two tapestries, representing Vanloo's "Neptune and Amimone" and Boucher's "Venus and Vulcan," respectively, were priced at 3534 l. 14 s. 5 d. each.[35]

For a short period, from the opening of the silver mines in Potosí and Guanaxuato to the reign of Philip IV, that is, from about the middle of the sixteenth century to the first third of the seventeenth century, the Spanish court surpassed in luxury anything that could later be seen at the French court. The influence of the Spanish court style then began to manifest itself everywhere, and its formal ceremonial has since become a part of most other courts. The revenues which made possible the pomp and circumstance of the Spanish court were still considerable in the time of Philip III. According to estimates of the Venetian ambassador, Tomaso Contarini, they totaled 16,000,000 ducats a year.[36] The accuracy of this estimate is confirmed by the results of a secret investigation undertaken by Henry IV who had a vital interest in discovering the resources of his rival. This inquiry revealed a yearly revenue of 15,658,000 ducats, which actually reached the treasury of the king of Spain. Another 5,000,000 ducats found their way into the coffers of viceroys, tax-gatherers, and so forth. A considerable part of the king's revenue, to be sure, was used to pay the interest on the state debt, but, as we shall see, this debt had to a large extent been incurred by luxury expenditures. Thus, according to figures compiled in 1610 by Count Francesco Gomez de Lerma, a Spanish statesman, only 4,487,350 ducats remained for the king's own expenses; of this sum, not quite one million was used for the maintenance of the royal household.[37]

In Western Europe, England's court life was not far behind that of France and of Spain. There the zenith of court pageantry had been attained in the reign of the Stuarts, who took the French kings for models. The splendor of the court under these sovereigns is mirrored in the paintings of Van Dyck, Peter Lely, and Huysmans; they show us foppish men and beautiful, proud ladies in magnificent brocade and satins after the great fashion of the day. The literary descriptions of contemporaries, such as Pepys' in his *Diary*, correspond faithfully to the picture of buoyant and exuberant life evoked in us by the paintings of these masters. We are reminded of Louis XIV when we read that Charles I had furnished twenty-four castles with such meticulousness that he was able to travel from one to the other without having to take along any baggage, or when we remember that James I spent £93,278 for the celebration of his daughter's wedding. The difference, however, between conditions in France and in England becomes apparent; in England, Charles II could be forced into meek submission and made to promise the House of Commons that he would be less extravagant in the future and stay within the limits of his civil list. At moments like this, the respectable burgher might have felt the approach of a new era when even kings would have to live within their income. The prince of Orange also loved a brilliant and gay court.[38] The House of Hanover, in the persons of its two first kings, followed in the footsteps of its predecessors.

The funds at the disposal of the English kings do not compare with those Louis XIV wrested from his country. Nevertheless, they were large enough for that period and are indicative of a very considerable demand for luxury articles.

In 1549, the expenditures of the royal household amounted to £100,000, which is five times the amount spent under Henry VII. Within the span of two generations, expenditures increased again five-fold. After the Restoration, the kings were granted a civil list; from this time on, we are able to follow expenditures in great detail.[39] But the £1,200,000 voted for that purpose was never paid in full, and Bonnie Prince Charlie, whose needs were so many, was, therefore, always short of funds. The amount allowed him for expenditures was £462,115 in 1675–76.

William III, in his reign from November 5, 1688, to March 25, 1702, spent a total of 8,880,506 l. 2 s. 9 d. for his own needs and those of his court. Queen Anne, during the twelve years following his death, used up £7,604,848, or an average of £586,900 a year. Her civil list was £700,000, the chief item of a total peacetime budget of £1,965,605. The civil lists of King George I and King George II ranged from £800,000 to £900,000; under George III it reached £923,196.

The intimate history of the English court shows that here too, luxury was fostered by illustrious mistresses and promoted for their sake. Ever since a royal court was established in England, there were royal favorites, and we are well aware of their propensity for lavishness and a life of ease and pleasure. Before our eyes appear Barbara Palmer, Louise Kéroual (who received the attentions of Louis XIV when she visited Paris, and of whom it has been justly remarked that the silken waistband of her dress had held together France and England for fifteen years), Catherine Sedley, Baroness Darlington, the countess of Dorchester, and many another *maîtresse en titre* of the Stuarts. We know also that the Elector George Lewis, when elected king of England, brought his mistresses along with him and subsequently created them countess of Arlington and duchess of Kendal, respectively. And his son, George II, was so attached to the land of his forefathers that he had his mistresses brought from Hanover. One of them, Frau von Wallmoden, was created countess of Yarmouth by him.

It is needless to describe similar conditions at the courts of the German princes, among which those of Saxony, Hanover, and Württemberg were the most lavish, or to recall the conditions at the courts of Eastern Europe, as these did not exert anything like the influence of the courts of Western Europe on economic development.

I shall mention, therefore, only one particularly noteworthy aspect of the demand for luxuries at these courts: the expenditures for porcelain. At the beginning of the eighteenth century, it had become possible to manufacture porcelain in Europe. This achievement laid the foundation of one of Europe's first large-scale industries, encouraged above all by the huge orders of the princes, whose fondness for this novel material by that time had assumed the proportions of a major craze. The following order placed by the court of Saxony on February 25, 1732, will serve as an illustration[40]:

Specifications of chinaware to be placed in the new front gallery in the upper story of the Royal Dutch Palace (today the Japanese Palace)

30	pieces—6 sets
266	separate vases of different forms
198	pieces, large and small animals
198	pieces—birds
48	tureens with covers
170	pieces—dishes
910	pieces

III. *The Cavaliers and the Parvenus as Imitators of the Court*

The luxury prevailing at the courts spread gradually to all the circles that were in any way connected with the court or saw fulfillment of their ambitions identified with court life. This description, we may safely state, applies to the entire moneyed class which was gripped with the same fondness for luxury as the court circles. That members of the court were actually compelled to take their part in luxurious living can be accurately traced and attributed to the kings, particularly to Louis XIV. The powerful influence exerted upon society by Louis the Great is thus described in the memoirs of a reliable eyewitness: "He loved splendor, magnificence, and profusion in all things, and encouraged similar tastes in his court; to spend money freely on equipages and buildings, on feasting, and at cards, was a sure way to gain his favor, perhaps to obtain the honor of a word from him. Motives of policy had something to do with this; by making expensive habits the general fashion, and, for people in certain positions, even a necessity, he compelled his courtiers to live beyond their income and gradually reduced them to depend on his bounty for the means of subsistence. This was a plague which, once introduced, became a scourge to the whole country, for it did not take long to spread to Paris and, thence, to the armies and the provinces, so that a man of any position is now estimated entirely according to his expenditure on his table and other luxuries. This folly, sustained by pride and ostentation, has already produced widespread confusion; it threatens to end in nothing short of ruin and a general overthrow."[41]

The king, especially in France, was looked up to as a god; Louis XIV became the arbiter of taste for Paris ("Paris—that has always sedulously aped the court," as La Bruyère remarks), for the provinces, and for the rest of Europe. Mansart, Le Nôtre, Lebrun, and Rigaud were the recognized court artists. Hence, everyone who could afford it wanted to have his house built in the style of Mansart, to lay out his garden after the fashion of Le Nôtre, to have his furniture in the Lebrun manner and his portrait painted in the style of Rigaud. This is all too well known.

But the longing for luxury would not have descended to

wider strata of Europe within so short a time, nor would luxury expenditures have assumed such gigantic proportions almost overnight, if it had not been for other contributing causes. The very great need for luxuries on the part of the nouveaux riches, whose rise we have followed in a previous chapter, initialed a craving for enjoyment and a striving for pleasure and vain ostentation which swept Europe like a plague. It is now our task to study the influence of this new class upon the changing mode of living and, above all, its contribution to the quantitative expansion of the demand for luxuries.

The tendency of people to spend their quickly acquired wealth mostly on luxuries is an ever recurring phenomenon in our civilization. The underlying facts are easily understood. What incites the demand of the upstart shopkeeper or flunky for luxury (unless he is a hoarder of wealth, in which role we shall observe him elsewhere) is, on the one hand, the inability of a natural and untutored man to get out of life anything but purely material pleasures such as an abundance of enjoyable goods may afford and, on the other hand, a consuming desire to attain a respectable position on the level of well-bred society. The two incentives to luxury, ambition and pleasure, work together in promoting parvenu luxury.

Hence, in history the growth of wealth is marked by as many stages of development as the growth of luxury; both begin with the emergence of the *homo novus*.

Diderot certainly must have been mistaken in stating that while in former times a man of the people who became rich made himself inconspicuous, it was only in his own time that wealthy commoners made a display of their riches. He is so sure of his ground that he goes as far as to say that a certain Bonnier was one of the first bourgeois to show off by an extravagant display of wealth.

Already in Dante's time we meet the type of the insanely extravagant parvenu; in this instance, Giacamo da Sant Andrea, who tossed silver and gold plate into the river or set fire to buildings in order to give his guests a thrill. There were many like him, who lived in similar fashion, forming a whole set of prodigal spenders: the *brigata godericcia, spendericcia,* or, as we would say today, the fast set. The lines from Dante's *Inferno*, cited by every Florentine "historian," read:

> *La gente nuova e i subiti guadagni*
> *Orgoglio o dismisura han generata*
> *Firenze in te, su che tu gia te piagni.*[42]

> (*The new inhabitants and the sudden gains*
> *Pride and extravagance have in thee engendered,*
> *Florence, so that thou weep'st thereat already!*)

Diderot was wrong in the case of France. Is there any reason for omitting from our list of parvenus Jacques Coeur who, in the fifteenth century, had grown rich as a money-lender and possessed palaces in Paris, Lyon, Tours, and seven other places; or Semblancay, or Thomas Bohier, the builder of Chenonceaux, in the sixteenth century; or should we forget the moneyed *canaillo* of the seventeenth century, which, in the words of Louis XIV, gave offense by their "brazen display"? The judgment ascribed to him is exceedingly revealing; he speaks of "financiers who, on the one hand, seek to cover their fraudulent practices by all kinds of deceptive maneuvers and, on the other, expose such acts by their insolent and challenging luxury, as though they were afraid that I would otherwise be unaware of their depredations."[43]

Last but not least in this line of worthies is Fouquet, the archswindler who squandered between 20,000,000 and 30,000,000 francs on his private luxury; of this amount, 18,000,000 francs were spent exclusively to defray the cost of the Château de Vaux. Colbert, who was himself averse to luxury in the grand manner, almost explodes with indignation as he puts down these figures in his requisition for Fouquet.

The intimate connection between the rise of the plebeian and the spread of luxury demands can be followed closely if we try to visualize the periods when people "*quos virtus aut fortuna e faece hominum extulit*"[44] appear in considerable numbers. These periods correspond to the stages in the development of modern luxury: the Italian era of the fourteenth and fifteenth centuries; the German era of the fifteenth and sixteenth centuries; the Spanish-Dutch era of the seventeenth century; and the French-English era of the eighteenth century.

Of greatest importance for our study is the tremendous progress toward "prosperity" and, above all, physical comfort, which the European nations made during the eighteenth century and thereafter. Considerable help in this study is gained from the numerous "Poor Richards" who already played a very considerable role during that period. The decisive transformation taking place at that time (around 1720) consisted in the spread of luxury demands over wider and wider areas. Many household accounts of that time have been preserved. About the middle of the eighteenth century, even in rich countries, one notices a contrast between the upper strata of that period and those of the seventeenth century. It is just as glaring as the one the Germans feel when they compare our times with, let us say, 1870. The universal complaint is: "It is very difficult to make ends meet with what is left to us."[45] (In a different connection I have mentioned similar complaints frequently expressed at that time.) We are not surprised at the views expressed in them if we consider that a large part of the huge fortunes amassed during that era was dissipated on luxury.[46] Between 1751 and 1755, d'Epinay spent 1,500,000 livres; Roussel squandered 12,000,000; Dupin de Chenonceaux, between 7,000,000 and 8,000,000; Savalette, 10,000,000; Bouret, 40,000,000 livres. The count of Artois, the neighbor of the rich Faventenès, remarked: "May a branch of the golden stream coming from that rock flow my way!" No one thought of accumulating wealth. Everyone spent everything on luxury—luxury in furniture, in houses, in clothes. The shelves in the shops of the Rue St. Honoré, which supplied France and foreign countries with the finest materials, were emptied within a few days. When, in 1720, a shower of gold poured down on Paris, Duhautchamp, who is our informant, states: "It is no longer possible to obtain velvets and gold brocades; yet all the looms are turning them out." In his book, he draws a picture of the streets of Paris, filled with people wearing gorgeous costumes of silk in all colors, and of silver and gold brocades covered with beautiful embroidery.

A point that appears to be of great significance for the economic development of modern society is the fact that the nouveaux riches, possessing nothing besides their money, have no other distinctive quality than their ability to spend the large means at their disposal on lavish living; that they communicate their materialistic and plutocratic world-view to the old aristocratic families, which in this manner are dragged into the whirlpool of luxury. In a chapter of my *Moderner Kapitalismus*, dealing with the formation of great wealth, I have stated that the enrichment of the middle-class money-lenders was due to the impoverishment of the nobility; this process of transferring feudal wealth to bourgeois fortunes had been going on in all European countries since the Crusades. We must now add that, most frequently, the reason for the impoverishment of the old families and their displacement by the *homines quos virtus aut fortuna e faece extulit* was the urge to equal the bourgeois parvenus in ostentatious display. This renunciation of the old aristocratic traditions led either to economic ruin or to the "disgraceful matrimonial alliances" with rich financiers which have been described in a previous chapter. The intermediate stage in this development, which interests us most here, is mainly the vulgarization of the noble families and their immersion in a spirit of materialism. The fact that the *subiti guadagni* of the Turcarets brought about this result—and there can be no doubt as to their responsibility for this condition although, as we have seen, the example of the court was a contributing factor—appears to me to be of especially far-reaching significance.

The pernicious tendency of the nobility to imitate the nouveaux riches in their pursuit of luxury is found in all countries and at all times whenever there is a sudden increase in bourgeois wealth.

Thus we hear that in Germany, even in the fifteenth century, "brutality and womanish finery became the characteristic of the knight." Extravagant expenditures on finery became one of the principal causes of the knights' perennial indebtedness. "It is the costliness of clothes that is destroying the nobles of our German lands!" exclaims a moralist of that period. "They want to strut like the rich merchants of the towns . . . but they have not their money," he adds. "Wherefore they have been borrowing money and are now in the usurious cluthes of the Jews and the Christian Jews and, hence, must part with their lands." Thus, a widow von Heudorf, we are told, sold the village of Göppingen-on-the-Ablach for a paltry sum so that she might purchase a blue velvet gown in which to go to a tournament.

In our times we are witnessing the final phase of the subjection of the nobility to the materialistic conceptions of the plebeian. We observe the last futile attempts of a few remaining aristocratic families to escape the materialistic trend of our period. It seems today almost like a fight against windmills when well-meaning spokesmen of the poor nobility warn their peers against the pitfalls of a luxury that has destroyed the old conception of noblesse as readily as a swarm of moths would consume a piece of woolen cloth.

In France, the process which was to dissolve the nobility apparently begins somewhat later. The duc de Sully, himself a nobleman of the old school, and perhaps a little inclined to take too pessimistic a view of his day, complains that, within his generation, the quickly made fortunes of the tax-farmers and financiers had begun to exercise their disastrous influence upon the ruling classes. His memorable words may be quoted here in full because they present in classic form one of the most important turning points in modern history:

> Nothing has contributed more towards perverting our ideas of probity, candour, and disinterestedness, or turning those virtues into ridicule; nothing has more strengthened that fatal propensity to luxury, which is natural to all men, but which is become with us a second nature, by that peculiarity of temper, which makes us fasten eagerly upon everything that can gratify our passions; and nothing in particular has so greatly degraded the French nobility as the rapid and dazzling fortunes of contractors and other men of business, by the opinion which they have circulated everywhere, and which is indeed but too well grounded, that in France this is almost the only method of arriving at the highest honours and the first employments of the State, and that then everything is forgot, and everything is allowable.[47]

It has been clearly demonstrated by the events which I have already mentioned in section 3 of chapter 1 of this book that the old aristocratic principles declined rapidly in all countries during the seventeenth and eighteenth centuries. What we have now to emphasize is the fact that the changed outlook of the nobility was bound to swell the great stream of luxury which we have been trying to trace to its source.

True, the nouveaux riches and the court may at first have induced the nobility to pursue luxury, but it was the nobility that gave the luxury of the age its characteristic quality. In contrast to our own era, the age had, therefore, an aristocratic character, its profiteers and plebian "moneybags" notwithstanding.

During the whole period with which we are concerned, i.e., from the Venetian conquest of Constantinople to the invention of the spinning rolls by Paul,[48] luxury, insofar as it has a uniform character, bears the hallmark of the courtly aristocratic tradition. The keynote was given by the court or the nobility (the character of which had not changed despite the infusion of plebian blood): at times, more specifically by the court, as in France during the seventeenth century; at others, by "society," as in Italy during the sixteenth and in England during the eighteenth century. But at all times, these two elements were the sole factors in the luxury civilization. In their own minds as well as in the minds of others, these circles, where all the luxury of the period blossomed forth, stood out sharply against the bourgeoisie, the "trash," even if it was a "trash" that possessed considerable wealth. In England, as late as the end of the eighteenth century, Mayfair and the city, cavalier and roundhead, were still definitely divided, if not in the old political sense, at least in the no less sharply defined social sense. Such is the opinion of all acute observers:

> Those in the city blame the people who live in the West end of the town for their luxury, idleness, effeminacy, and an attachment to French fashions; while the others speak of a citizen as a dull, fat animal, who places all his merits in his strong box.[49]

> When I consider this great city in its several Quarters and Divisions, I look upon it as an Aggregate of various Nations distinguished from each other by their respective Customs, Manners and Interests. The Courts of two countries do not so much differ from one another as the Court and City in their peculiar ways of Life and Conversation. In short, the inhabitants of St. James, notwithstanding they live under the same Laws and speak the same language, are a distinct People from those of Cheapside, who are likewise removed from those of the Temple on the one side and those of Smithfield

on the other, by several Climates and Degrees in their way of Thinking and Conversing together.[50]

Thus, if Chateaubriand, in speaking of his day, remarks that "the court and the city, the men of letters, the economists and the encyclopedists, the higher and the lesser nobility, financiers and bourgeois all resemble one another: witness the memoirs they have left us," this applies only to the "cream" of society. The "skimmed milk," as Goethe called the "middle class," did not count; the middle class, both in its upper and lower branches, was ignored. Their entire mode of living remained seignorial. Money, and all that was associated with money, was looked upon with contempt. To be concerned with money matters, to balance expenses and income, was considered vulgar and left to the care of stewards. What is the use of keeping help if one has to bother oneself about the household. Life holds no pleasure if one's time must be given up to petty duties. This and that are needed. The steward receives his instructions. It is then up to him to worry about from where the money is to come. Whether or not the steward pays the merchant is not a gentleman's concern. Only a person with the mentality of a shopkeeper thinks that bills are things to be paid; and to consider in making a purchase whether it is within one's means or not is in the manner of shopkeepers too.

This supreme contempt of an ordered economy is also characteristic of all speculators; it was the common ground on which *haute finance* and the old aristicracy met. Like the latter, the former is preeminently concerned with spending, with no overzealous regard for the income side of the ledger. Speculators are accustomed to having huge sums fall into their laps overnight and living recklessly into the new day. What they squander or lose during one night they always expect to recoup on the following day before noon. In the management of personal affairs *haute finance* is just as remote from the penny-pinching shopkeeper as is the feudal aristocracy. The notion of thrift is as little known to the one as to the other. These lower-middle-class views, which later spread to all ranks of the middle class, are foreign to the wealthy strata of the early capitalist era, that is to say, at least to those strata which accounted for luxury consumption in those days. It is this type of consumption which I designate as seigno-

rial[51] throughout this volume even when it is the practice of
Turcarets. A few examples will make my meaning clear.

Here you have the excellent Bassompière, almost a perfect
representative of his class.[52] He appears at a fête in a costume of
gold cloth, embroidered with palm leaves and covered with pearls,
the weight of which he himself puts at fifty pounds. This costume
cost the tidy sum of 14,000 écus, of which only 700 écus went for
labor. When it was ordered, the tailor demanded an advance of
4000 écus which Bassompière promptly—promised to pay. Leaving
his tailor, Bassompière went out to dine and to gamble (with 700
écus in his pocket). That night he won 5000 écus, out of which
(in what must have been a weak moment), he paid his tailor on
the following morning. He continued gambling during the following nights and won the balance of his tailor's bill and 11,000
écus to boot. Half of this sum (5500 écus) he spent for a diamond-
studded sword, and the remainder for his *menus plaisirs.*

Let us look at some figures on gamblers.[53] Orry de Fulvy
loses 600,000 livres in one night; Dupin de Chenonceaux, 700,000;
de la Haye (at the house of Mme de Genlis, against M de Féné-
lon!), 800,000. A son of Paris, la Montagne, and 80,000 écus of
his money are separated at a little game of quinze. Comte Jean du
Barry, the prototype of the eighteenth-century wastrel, is re-
lieved of 7000 louis at one sitting and boasts that his losses had
then reached the fifth million. In 1717 there were sixty-two gambling houses in Paris.

As far as this class of people was concerned, the value of
money was an unknown thing.[54] Maréchal Richelieu threw a filled
purse out of the window when his grandson, to whom he had
given it, returned it to him untouched. Let a streetcleaner have it
then! Prince de Conti, angered by his mistress who had returned
a diamond which she thought too small, pulverized the diamond
and sprinkled the dust over his answer to her. (The diamond was
valued at between 4000 and 5000 livres.) The same prince de
Conti finally did not have enough money to buy bread and wool
for his household, because he preferred to spend his yearly income
of 600,000 livres on luxuries. The Maréchal de Soubise spends
200,000 francs to provide one day's entertainment for the king at
his château. Madame de Matignon, who insists on having a new
coiffure every day, runs up a yearly bill of 24,000 livres at her
hairdresser's.

The debts incurred by these people reached gigantic heights. Mme de Guémenée owed her bootmaker 60,000 livres. The duc de Lauzun, after flinging away a fortune yielding an income of 100,000 écus, ran up debts amounting to two million livres.

The account books of the modiste, Rose Bertin, which were published by Emile Langlade, give us an interesting insight into the paying habits of the aristocracy in her days. When, several years after the outbreak of the French Revolution, she tried to collect her oustanding accounts, the following sums were due her:

Accounts	Years	Livres[54a]
Marquise de Bouille,	1774–86	6791
Comtesse de Salles,	1778–81	1148
Comte and Comtesse Duras,	1774–89	7386
Comte Aug. de Lamarck,	1774–75	1558
Chevalier de Saint Paul,	1778	1343

The clientele of Rose Bertin included, among others, the vicomtesse de Polastron, the princesse de Rochefort, and the marquise de Tonnerre, whose bills, amounting to 19,960, 10,904, and 10,946 livres, respectively, had been outstanding for years. The total owed to this famous dressmaker, who worked only for the elite, amounted to 490,000 francs.

The aristocracy also determined the path along which luxury traveled.

We have already noted the luxury in garments and robes at the courts; it is an extravagance more characteristic, however, of the seignorial mode of living. Nothing distinguished the cavalier from the roundhead as much as the elegance of his clothes, which, according to the prevailing fashion, were made of velvet and silk; they were profusely adorned with gold embroidery and lace and, consequently, were very costly.

As to the luxury in costumes during the fifteenth and sixteenth centuries, we possess accurate information in the form of the wardrobe inventories of, for instance, Valentina and Elisabetta Visconti, of Bianca Maria Sforza, and of Lucrezia Borgia. The latter had a trousseau which contained, among other items, fifty robes of brocade and velvet, enriched with embroidery and lace. A train of one hundred and fifty mules was required to carry her wardrobe when she left Rome.[55]

Works of art constitute a valuable source of information regarding luxury in dress at all periods. Other important sources of
information are descriptions of festivals, pageants, etc. Thus, for
instance, in the diary of Johann Burchard, to which I have referred previously, we find a description of the dazzling entry of
Prince Federigo of Naples into Rome in 1492: "The men, clothed
in gold brocade with costly jewels glittering on their chests and
adorning their berets and hats, were mounted on magnificent
steeds. The prince was attired in a gown of violet-colored velvet
and wore a necklace of pearls and precious stones worth 6000
ducats as well as a belt and sword estimated at the same value. The
bridle of his horse was richly encrusted with pearls and precious
stones, worth 3000 ducats, and all its trappings were heavily
gilded.[56]

The lavish adornment of costumes during the Renaissance
became even more elaborate during the baroque period; it reached
its highest refinement during the rococo period. We know, for
instance, that in seventeenth-century England elegant attire was
regarded as the very badge of distinction of the cavalier. The prevailing fashion of that period is notable for its exquisite elegance;
the high riding boots, dictated by fashion, were lined with costly
stuffs and fringed with lace. Even men's clothes were made for the
most part of heavy silk and velvet. Witness Van Dyck! Expenditures for clothes were indeed fabulous. In 1625, the duke of Buck-
ingham had a wardrobe of twenty-seven suits made of silk or
velvet, decorated with lace, pearls, etc.; each outfit had cost in the
neighborhood of 35,000 francs. The gala costume worn by him at
the wedding of Charles I was valued at 500,000 francs.[57]

Mme de Maintenon, in one of her letters to her brother,
makes mention of a French nobleman and his wife who spent one-
third of their entire income of 12,000 livres on clothes and nearly
one-half for toilet accessories and for coaches.[58]

Luxury in dress was carried to an even higher pitch during
the eighteenth century: it became overrefined. The average price
of a suit for a man of fashion ranged from 1200 to 1500 livres.
A person with any self-respect at all had at least six summer and
six winter suits. Habits for special occasions cost up to 15,000
livres; fine gray cloth, seventy to eighty livres a yard.[59]

Luxury in fine undergarments—the erotic luxury par excellence—also made its appearance at that time. The highly respected author of the *Complete English Tradesman*, Daniel Defoe, is outraged at the ordinary "beau," "our nicer gentleman," who wears shirts made of linen costing ten to twelve shillings a yard and changes his underwear twice daily. In olden days, he complains, people were content with shirts of plain Holland linen which cost half that much and, moreover, did not change them more often than perhaps twice a week. In the direction of the dandy of his day who had such exaggerated notions of cleanliness, he maliciously flings the following dart: "We may suppose their uncleaner bodies require it more than those of their ancestors."[60]

What gave luxury specific seignorial character were the expenditures made merely for the purpose of show and splendor, such as overelaborate costumes, gilded state coaches, and enormous staffs of liveried servants. The latter especially reveal seignorial traits, being a leftover from the feudal past and taking the place of the retainers of old. In addition, this setup of the household expresses the personal character of seignorial luxury, manifest in all older types of luxury. We know with what vehemence Adam Smith inveighed against his contemporaries for their vexatious custom of surrounding themselves with so many "unproductive hands" better to be employed at spinning yarn.

Extant descriptions of conditions then prevailing confirm the correctness of the facts which brought forth Adam Smith's censure. Defoe, to whom anything smacking of the seignorial manner was utterly obnoxious, notes that "very ordinary tradesmen" in London had at least two, and often more, maid servants, and some of them had footmen: he cites the case of a merchant's wife who employed as many as five maid servants and one man servant. The blue liveries of these tradesmen's domestics had become such a common sight that they were known as "tradesmen liveries." The "gentlemen" avoided clothing their servants in that color.[61] If this seignorial type of luxury had become such a commonplace among the plebians, it can easily be imagined to what extremes it must have been carried by the cavaliers. Archenholtz tells of an English lord who had as many as a hundred stable grooms.[62]

Still, the immense number of servants kept by some members of the high nobility is little short of staggering: the duc de Nevers had a staff of a hundred and forty-six servants, the comtesse de

Pontchartrain maintained a hundred and thirteen, and the duc de Choiseul no less than four hundred (of which fifty-four were in livery).[63] Mme de Sévigné always kept between thirty and forty servants.[64] Naturally, the parvenus sedulously aped this aristocratic habit. A landscape painter, who made a great deal of money by speculating in Mississippi stocks, employed ninety servants.[65] Mercier tells us quite casually that "in the house of a certain *fermier-général*, one could find twenty-four liveried servants, without counting the kitchen boys, the cooks, and the six chambermaids for Madame."[66] He further informs us that a Turcaret of his day always required the attendance of four servants when taking his chocolate.

The aristocratic nature of luxury during this entire period was manifest in the substance of that luxury and followed well-defined paths. This characterization refers not only to the negative aspect of luxury, i.e., its inaccessibility to the masses and its restriction to a select few, but also, one might say, to its positive aspect, inasmuch as this aristocratic character compelled even the most vulgar parvenu to conform to the tenets of good taste which, in its essence, is possessed only by the few. This luxury, always attentive to aesthetic principles and stylistic form, is intrinsically a luxury of the upper social stratum; the four styles distinguishing this entire period, namely, gothic, renaissance, baroque, and rococo, are styles expressing the will of ruling groups. "Styles" they are, indeed—in the most specific sense. In this respect, they contrast with the style of our own time, which is destitute of any distinctive mode of expression and bears the mark of the plebeian.

As early as the eighteenth century, however, something that we might call the "bourgeois" style came into being in England, and a plebeian element crept into contemporary social life. Richard Muther believed that this new note was already apparent in the portraits of Reynolds and Gainsborough and constituted the essential difference between England and France during that period. But it seems to me that the superlatively aristocratic character of those days finds its most telling expression in the works of these two painters. True, Gainsborough represented Mrs. Siddons "in street costume, a great hat upon her head, muff in hand, and no pearls, but a simple band of silk about her neck."[67] And yet, the difference between her and the wives of the city men of her day is as great as the difference that separates her from all the ladies of today. Who would say that his "Blue Boy" is not the very symbol of the sunset of that aristocratic civilization? Muther's thesis might, however, apply to Hogarth. In his works, indeed, after the short plebeian interlude of Dutch influence, the "coarse, ill-bred animal" found its first interpreter. Yet, these works were by no means an integral part of that section of society which was instrumental in developing luxury.

And what about the professional amiable companions of men's leisure hours—courtesans? We know that the keeping of mistresses was almost a commonplace in good society during the eighteenth century. "Who is the man without a mistress?" a philosopher of that time exclaims rather naively. Hence, when we consider the insane expenditures of these circles, we may assume without fear of contradiction that they were made to a large extent on the illicit love relations of men whose legitimate wives spent what was left.

We possess documentary evidence bearing on the prodigious extravagance of some of the famous courtesans of the eighteenth century.

Of *L'aimable Deschamps*, the attorney Carsillier, pleading in a court, said: "Her luxury amazes all Paris. The mines of Golconda have been exhausted for her. Wherever she sets her foot, money comes forth."

Many of the mistresses, and especially the mistresses of the great financiers, such as Mme Petitpas and Mme Dufresne, the mistresses of the enormously wealthy Montmartre, were notorious in Paris for their insolent display, their *luxe insolent*. The sums which ran through their fingers like so much water were indeed fabulous. The mistress of another captain of finance, Maison Rouge, an opera dancer, succeeds in wresting the following sums from her lover[68]: 210,000 livres for houses and furnishings, 150,000 livres for jewelry, and 50,000 écus for paintings and silver plate. The young Chauvelin contracts debts to the extent of 1,600,140 livres 19 s. 11 d. which he spends on the dancer, Mlle Minos. St. James, the treasurer of the king's navy, presents Mlle de Beauvoisin with jewelry and other valuables worth between 1,500,000 livres and 1,800,000 livres; in addition, he gives her a yearly allowance of 20,000 écus. Ten thousand livres (2000 écus) is the "normal" monthly allowance of a "high-grade" courtesan.[69]

But I should like to show even more clearly the intimate connection between the development of luxury during that period and the supremacy of the courtesan than is possible by general considerations and reference to the extravagant expenditures of individual representatives of the profession. It may be added here that some of the most insanely extravagant women of the period were the legitimate spouses of rich men. Yet, inasmuch as their mode of living followed the pattern of the courtesan, this era may still be designated as the period of the courtesan. I propose to go into greater detail and bring out the essential meaning of luxury. In this manner we shall not only learn a great deal more about the manifold possibilities for the display of luxury under the ancien régime, but we shall also arrive at a better understanding of the process whereby individual luxury expenditures or, to be more precise, luxury expenditures in their totality, were interwoven with the beginnings of capitalism in commerce and industry.

iv. *The Triumph of Woman*

I have previously indicated the characteristics common to every type of luxury during the era of early capitalism. I should now like to call attention to the fact that luxury underwent various changes in the course of the five or six centuries prior to the period under discussion, and I further propose to show how great a part women (by which I mean the type dealt with in the preceding chapters) played in bringing about these changes.

1. General Tendencies in the Development of Luxury

Before embarking on the following analyses, I must make one point clear: I refer to the luxury of a period unique in history—the period between the years 1200 and 1800. Any attempt, such as that of Wilhelm Roscher, to set up general epochs of luxury seems pointless. Even further from the mark are the theories of those blunderers who permit a misunderstood "historical materialism" to meddle with so delicate a problem as the phenomenon of luxury.

The following general tendencies in the development of luxury may be noted:

(a) *Domestication.* The luxury of the Middle Ages was largely public; even as private luxury, it made its appearance more often in public than in the home. After the seventeenth century, luxury became an affair of the home; women began to draw it within the confines of the domestic sphere.

During the Middle Ages, and even as late as the Renaissance, luxury took the characteristic form of display on such occasions as tournaments, pageants, processions, and public banquets. In becoming domesticated, luxury lost its transient character and assumed permanency.

(b) *Objectification.* We have seen that the luxury of the period under consideration still had a strongly personal character that found expression in the quantitative accumulation of things that signified wealth. We further noted that this feature betrayed the seignorial origin of luxury inasmuch as the strong emphasis on large trains of servants recalled the retinue that went with every lord. Undoubtedly, however, this personal character of luxury became less marked by the end of the Middle Ages. Formerly, luxury extended merely to providing feasts and entertainment for the large bodies of attendants attached to individual courts. Now, the maintenance of large staffs of servants was only the concomitant of the steadily growing use of objects in the display of luxury. It was again woman who was the guiding spirit in the movement toward objectification, as I wish to term this process. She could derive only scant satisfaction from the display of a resplendent retinue. Rich dresses, comfortable houses, precious jewels were more tangible. This change is exceedingly significant economically. Adam Smith would have said that this trend constituted a passing from "unproductive" to "productive" luxury since the former, i.e., personal luxury, was "productive" (in the capitalistic sense) because it gave employment to "productive" hands in a (capitalistic) enterprise. In point of fact, the objectification of luxury has been of fundamental significance for the genesis of capitalism.

(c) *Sensualization and Refinement.* This tendency went hand in hand with the tendency toward objectification and was advanced with remarkable energy by women. Under this heading come all developments tending to remove luxury further and further from ideal values (such as in art) and to make luxury subservient to the lower, animal instincts of man. The Goncourts have described this process in the following words, making particular reference to Madame Du Barry: "Her patronage of art extends down to the bronze-workers, wood-carvers, embroiderers, and even dressmakers," etc. With this characterization they seek to emphasize the difference between the Du Barry era and that of the Pompadour. It seems to me that this change, highly important economically, marks the end of the seventeenth and the beginning of the eighteenth century; that is to say, the triumph of the rococo over the baroque. It signifies the final and complete triumph of the female who deliberately uses her sex to secure a dominant role. The fact that this eminently feminine rococo style could dominate all domains of culture is sufficient proof of the correctness of the thesis advanced here. Every work of art and every object of the artcrafts of that period reflected and glorified the triumphant female. "Pierglasses and Lyonese cushions, blue silk beds with white muslin curtains, ... dainty silk petticoats, grey silk stockings, and pink silk clothes, ... coquettish dressing-gowns trimmed with swansdown, and ... ostrich feathers and Brussels lace. ..."—this ensemble of dainty objects was composed by Pater (the French painter) into the "symphonies of the salon," according to Richard Muther, the peerless declineator of the rococo.

The tendency to sensualize luxury is closely linked to the tendency toward refinement. The latter, in turn, means a greater expenditure of human labor on a specific object, provided the refinement is not restricted to the use of more costly materials. The result is a widening of the scope of capitalist industry and, because of the necessity of securing rare materials from foreign countries, also of capitalist commerce.

(d) *Increased Frequency of Luxury.* This tendency is expressed in the crowding together of many manifestations of luxury in a given period of time. Such luxury may consist in the use of a great variety of objects, or in the gratification of many desires and whims. It may also take another shape: former periodical gala festivities become permanent; celebrations observed only once a year become regularly recurring festivals; pageants held only on feast days are turned into daily masquerades; and the Lucullan feasts at kermises and the periodical drinking bouts become the dinners and suppers of everyday life. Finally, this, in my opinion, is the most important form of the compression: the rapid rate at which luxury goods are produced in order to be more readily available for those desiring them.

During the Middle Ages, leisurely production was the rule. Years, and even decades, were spent on one masterpiece, on one work of art; no one was in a great hurry to see it completed. Life was long because one lived within a whole. The individual who had commissioned the work might have long since turned to dust, but the church, the convent, the town, or the family would live to see its completion. How many generations helped to complete the famous Certosa of Pavia! Eight generations of the Sacchi family of Milan worked for three centuries on the incrustations and the inlaid woodwork of the altar panels. Every cathedral, convent, town hall, and castle of the Middle Ages bears witness to the extension of the individual's life span. The growth of all these structures was witnessed by a number of successive generations who felt sure that the line of their progeny would never end.

Once the individual had detached his own life from the eternally flowing life stream of the generations, the span of *his* life became the measure of his earthly pleasures. The individual himself wanted to experience as much of the diversity of life as possible. Kings, too, thought of themselves as individuals rather than as representatives of a dynasty. When they built a castle, they no longer had posterity in mind; they wanted to enjoy it themselves. Finally, when woman seized the reins of the world, the rate of producing the means for satisfying luxury demands was still further accelerated. Woman has little patience; a man in love has none.

A few instances will illustrate the profound change in the mode of life: Maria de' Medici had Luxembourg Palace built in the unprecedented brief period of five years.[70] Artisans worked day and night to complete the Palace of Versailles. In his memoirs, Colbert notes: "Pour Versailles, il y a deux ateliers de charpentiers, dont l'un travaille le jour et l'autre la nuit."[71] (Two shifts of carpenters worked on Versailles; one during the day and the other at night.)

The comte d'Artois had his château at Bagatelle completely rebuilt at one time, when he wanted to arrange a splendid fête for the queen. For this purpose he hired nine hundred artisans and laborers who worked feverishly day and night. Being unable to obtain all the building stones and the lime required, he had his *huissiers* stop and bring in all carts which carried these materials and passed in the neighborhood of the château.

These changes will assume even greater vividness if we picture in detail some of the more important domains of luxury. This method is particularly well suited to give us an understanding of the eminently economic significance which was attached to the quantitative alterations in the outward form of luxury.

2. Luxury in the Home

(a) *Table Luxury*. First, we shall turn to a form of domestic luxury that had its rise in the Italy of the fifteenth and sixteenth centuries: the luxury of the table. The "culinary art" became the sister of the other noble arts. Earlier times had only known the luxury of the gourmand. Now, eating became a refined enjoyment of dainty dishes, setting quality above quantity.

Like many other things, culinary luxury was brought from Italy to France where, during the sixteenth century and after, it became the object of fastidious cultivation. It is hardly possible to trace the development of this form of luxury without writing a long treatise on the preparation of food. Besides, such a treatise would hardly fit into the framework of this book. I should, however, like to raise a well-grounded question, similar to that asked in previous chapters, namely: Are we indebted to the courtesan for the refinement of the culinary art and, therefore, for the development of table luxury?

Viewed with respect to the interplay of human physiology and psychology, the closeness of the association of the culinary with the amatory art may be somewhat dubious. There is a tendency to bring eroticism and gourmandise into a certain antithetical relationship and to characterize the ages of man by: love of woman, love of distinction, and love of the well-appointed dinner table. Extreme nonerotics, such as Kant, have been known to be great gourmets. It seems to me, however, that without the pervasive refinement and sensualization of our tastes, which are due to the influence of women, this high development of the culinary art would never have taken place. Is the passionate gourmandise of confirmed old bachelors the result of a repression of the sexual impulse, the masculine equivalent of the old maid's love of cats? This point, too, stands in need of verification.

On one point, however, we already seem to have arrived at complete agreement: the connection between the consumption of sweets and feminine dominance. Even today we distinctly make out the physical boundary lines delimiting the sphere of predominant feminine influence. They coincide with the geographical boundries of the countries with good and indifferent cuisines, and dainty and coarse desserts. Italy, Austria, France, and Poland are unsurpassed in pastries; Northern Germany has its characteristic blancmange, and England the Albert cake.

This connection between feminism (old style) and sugar has been of the greatest importance for the history of economic development. Because of the predominant role of woman during early capitalism, sugar rapidly became a favorite food; and only because of the widespread use of sugar were such stimulants as cocoa, coffee, and tea adopted so readily all over Europe. Trade in these four commodities and the production of cocoa, coffee, and sugar in the overseas colonies as well as the processing of cocoa and the refining of raw sugar in Europe are outstanding factors in the development of capitalism.

The accuracy of these general conclusions is proved by the history of these popular foods and their common use in Europe. Insofar as this history coincides with that of sugar, we are well informed by the book of Edmund O. von Lippmann, from which we quote the following:

Sugar is first mentioned in the fourteenth century; it became a popular food in common use in Italy in the fifteenth century. Pancirollus writes: "There is today no great banquet at which a quantity of sugar in various forms is not served. Figures and groups, birds and quadrupeds, and the most beautiful fruits in natural colors are imitated in sugar. Rhubarb, nuts, and cinnamon and other spices are used, and candies— to the delight of the world. Nothing is served without sugar: it is used in cakes and wine; instead of plain water, one drinks sugared water; meats, fish, and eggs are prepared with sugar; in short, salt is not used more frequently than sugar."

Catherine de Médicis is instrumental in introducing the use of sugar among members of French society. It is said that,

among other luxuries, the retinue of this princess first introduced the consumption of cordials in Paris, which the French
later brought to a high state of perfection. One of the most
popular brands of that time was called "Oil of Venus" *(Huile
de Vénus)*, a mixture of alcohol, sugar, and saffron. Estienne
states, in his tract on agriculture, that "the consumption of
sugar has become very popular." La Bruyère Champier, the
personal physician of Francis I, states in 1560 that "sugar has
already become an indispensable food, naturally among the
upper social strata." He adds the remark, "because people of
good taste will not partake of any food unless it is covered with
powered sugar." In England in the sixteenth century, too, a
banquet was not complete if it did not include sweetmeats,
jellies, marmalades, candied lemon and orange rinds, glazed
ginger, as well as elaborate structures of spun sugar representing castles, ships, or figures.

Since the beginning of the seventeenth century, cocoa, coffee, and tea became indispensable in Europe, because of the
use of sugar. All of these beverages became popular in the
best circles, particularly at the courts. Coffee, for instance,
first became known in France and was introduced to court
society after Louis XIV had tasted some on the occasion of
receiving the ambassador of Sultan Mohammed IV in 1670.
In connection with these stimulating beverages, there came
into being a new type of luxury, particularly in the large
cities: the public coffeehouses, which will engage our attention later.[72]

(b) *Luxury in Residences.* The rise of this type of luxury is
closely connected with the previously discussed growth of the
metropolis. It is the city which has materially promoted the luxury of residences and interior decorations, for this type of luxury
became more and more popular from the end of the seventeenth
century. On the one hand, the city brought it about by the restriction of living space, which was natural because of the aggregation of large masses of people; on the other, by the restriction
of personal luxury which is another consequence of the transfer
of the aristocrat's residence to the city. These inner and outward
restrictions experienced by the rich in the city were followed, if

I may use the term, by an intensification of luxury, which, as we saw, became either materialized or refined. Culinary luxury, which perfected the technique of cooking, developed in the same manner as residential luxury in the metropolis. In place of the enormous, vacant castles, smaller city residences appeared; they were fitted, however, with innumerable costly articles. The palace replaced the castle.

But this urban mode of living, as we may call it, is then applied to country life; country houses equipped with urban elegance are beginning to appear, in other words, the "villas" which (just as in ancient times) are the direct consequence of city life. Luxury penetrates into the remotest parts of the country and subordinates it even in this respect to the city and its living conditions.

Reading the descriptions of the city and country homes of the well-to-do in France or England, for example, as they are handed down to us by the writers of the close of the seventeenth and the beginning of the eighteenth century, we are at first inclined to believe that they exaggerate. But, eventually, by discovering an ever-increasing number of identical writings, we become aware that the luxury display in the residences of that time must, indeed, have been tremendous, even from the point of view of our own sumptuous times. We think of the remnants of splendid furniture in quaint and rococo style as we see them on sale today in antique shops; we think of individual pieces of furniture of that time as we find them in art history books, and we remember that what we now see as individual pieces, pictorial or real, once stood assembled in the halls of the marquis and of the financial baron of the ancien régime. But we also think of the vast amounts which were spent by the Turcarets on their residences.

But what drove men toward the creation of such splendor? We need not wait long for an answer: it was in the residence that the fashionable of the ancien régime lived; here, woman painstakingly and wisely built a nest to which she could attract man. The history of furniture proves this beyond the shadow of a doubt.

So much is being said about the erotic trend during the time of the minnesingers; just where is this love life supposed to have been carried on? Perhaps in the woods, because the castles were certainly not ideal trysting places. At all events, the connotation of the term love life would then differ radically from the one to which we are accustomed. Gothic and erotic may form a rhyme but are nevertheless not homogeneous. No, even here it was again the Renaissance which created the external conditions for the fundamentally novel mode of living.

Everything which we today look upon as necessary to the elegant or comfortable furnishing of a home was first produced in Italy during the fifteenth and sixteenth centuries through the medium of the Renaissance which, by its very nature, was better qualified to meet the demands of daily life than the "one-sided, un-free" gothic style of decoration. "We read in the Novelists of soft, elastic beds, of costly carpets and bedroom furniture, of which we hear nothing in other countries. We often hear especially of the abundance and beauty of the linen."[73] The influence of the woman! Even more the influence of the mistress! The first modern residence, combining artistic display and comfort, was perhaps the country home of the rich Agostino Chigi; it was called Farnesina and was built for Morosina, the beautiful Venetian mistress of this financier. What a difference between the luxury of her home and that of the palace of Paul II in whose time Roman architecture began: "grace and joyous sensuousness had become necessities to the new generation" (Gregorovius), because it was under the domination of woman. It is in this Rome of the sixteenth century that modern home furnishings is born. We hear the following of the palace of Imperia, another mistress whom we have already mentioned: "the use of carpets, paintings, vases, knickknacks, selected books and beautiful renaissance furniture gave such splendor to her room that the noble Spanish Ambassador one day spat into the face of a servant because he could discover no other suitable place for this necessity."[74]

Generally speaking, the houses of mistresses during that time began to be looked upon as models in home furnishing, and as we shall see, they retained this distinction throughout the following centuries. For instance, the Venetian home of Angela Zaffetta was considered an attraction: "Angela resided in the regally furnished *palazzo* Loredan. The walls were covered with carpets from Flanders, with brocade and gilded leather; some rooms were even painted in fresco by the most famous painters. The floors were covered with Turkish carpets, and on the tables were spread gold-embroidered velvet covers. Furniture with carvings and incrustations filled the numerous rooms, and on the tables could be seen silver vessels, majolicas from Faenza, Cafaggiolo, and Urbino, as well as the most costly Venetian glassware. The owner, who was known for her good taste, had all through the house pictures, arms, well-bound books, mandolins, and valuable art objects."[75]

One might say that the baroque style perhaps is trying to free itself from the overpowering influence of woman. But even this masterful style falls under her domination: she adopts the mirror as an integral part of this style, and an enthusiastic poet makes the following observation of its initial use as home-decoration:

> *Dans leurs cabinets enchantés*
> *L'étoffe ne trouve plus place;*
> *Tous les murs de quatre côtés*
> *En sont de glaces incrustés;*
> *Chaque côté n'est qu'une glace.*
> *Pour voir partout leur bonne grâce*
> *Partout elles veulent avoir*
> *La perspective d'un miroir.*[76]

(In their enchanted chambers hangings no longer had a place; on all four sides, the room is full of mirrors reflecting their charms. They must everywhere see their beauty reflected; for all their graces they need this perspective of a mirror.)

Or they invent other allurements to increase the comforts of their living rooms and to entrap men there: they perfume their rooms and decorate them with flowers. One is under the wrong impression if one imagines the palace of Madame de Rambouillet to be cold and formal. A visitor, the amiable Mlle de Scudéry, describes it as follows: "Everything in her home is magnificent and even unique; the lamps are different from all others of their kind. The cabinets are filled with a thousand rare objects . . . the air in her palace is always perfumed; magnificent baskets, filled with flowers, create an atmosphere of eternal springtime in her room."

But it is always the bed which represents the most valuable

piece in the entire furnishings; Madame de Montespan presents M de Maine with a bed costing 40,000 livres "as well as three others equally magnificent."[77]

The extent to which luxury in residences can be advanced during a given period is always demonstrated by the furnishings of the home of the royal mistress during that period. Versailles represents the apex in this development during the baroque period, although besides the endeavor to please feminine desires, many other elements were here at work to create the greatest beauty ever produced through human skill. But the most perfect examples of amorous caprice are the private palaces of the royal mistresses, where luxury in residences was displayed in its highest form even during the baroque period. I am thinking, for example, of the palace of the duchess of Portsmouth (one of the last mistresses of Charles II) of which we are told by an eyewitness: "What aroused my curiosity was the beauty and opulence of this home, which was torn down several times in order to meet the wasteful demands of this woman, while her majesty, the queen, did not spend more for her household than some ladies of the aristocracy. . . . I saw there the latest products of French carpet weaving which, in design, workmanship and cleverness of reproduction, surpassed anything I have ever seen. . . . Then there was a cabinet with Japanese lacquered articles, as well as shades, clocks, silver vases, small tables, shelves, knickknacks for the mantelpiece, braziers—all of massive silver and in untold numbers—and, finally, some excellent pictures of his majesty."[78]

Thus we notice that the erotic rococo style is applied principally to the development of luxury in residences. The most outstanding example in this respect is Luciennes, the love nest which Louis XV built for Mme Du Barry, and of which the Goncourts exclaim: "Luciennes! Should we not speak of it as the palace of one of those funny sovereignties such as the books of the eighteenth century show us in those Turkisms in which, subjected to the whims of a favorite odalisque, the erratic good-pleasure of a capricious sultan holds sway?"[79]

Every man of rank, whose means were sufficient, created such a Luciennes on a modest scale for his mistress: a typical example is "Bagatelle," a small palace in the Bois de Boulogne, which the marshal d'Estrées, a grandee of Spain, gave to his wife at the beginning of the eighteenth century and which later became the property of Madame de Monconseil, the mistress of Stanislaus, king of Poland. The numerous homes of ordinary mistresses were called *petites maisons,* all of which were furnished in the most refined taste along identical, artistic lines.[80]

The unheard-of development of luxury in residences during the eighteenth century was looked upon by contemporaries as something extraordinary: "The rooms are furnished with exaggerated and somewhat common splendor," says Mercier, who concludes his description of the luxury in houses of that period with the following words: "The magnificence of the nation is displayed entirely within the houses."

Another contemporary, who finds himself in accord with Mercier, writes as follows: "Furnishings have become the objects of the greatest luxury and of the greatest expenditure. Every six years the houses are refurnished in order to enable one to profit by everything which elegance may have produced."

In England, luxury in residences was more strongly developed than in France, although perhaps it was lacking in the purely feminine aspect of the Parisian *petites maisons.* A competent observer paints the following picture of the houses of rich Englishmen:

No part of Europe exhibits such luxury and magnificence as the English display within the walls of their dwelling houses. The staircase, which is covered with the richest carpets, is supported by a balustrade of the finest Indian wood, curiously constructed and lighted by lamps containing crystal vases. The landing places are adorned with busts, pictures, and medallions; the wainscot and ceilings of the apartments are covered with the finest varnish and enriched with gold bas-reliefs and the most happy attempts in painting and sculpture. The chimneys are of Italian marble, on which flowers and figures, cut in the most exquisite style, form the chief ornaments; the locks of the doors are of steel, damasked with gold. Carpets, which often cost three hundred pounds a-piece and which one scruples to touch with his foot, cover all the rooms; the richest stuffs from the looms of Asia are employed as window curtains, and the clocks and watches with which the apartments are furnished astonish by their magnificence and the ingenious complication of their mechanism.[81]

This same observer renders us a similar account of the country houses of the rich, and the accuracy of these accounts is borne out by numerous other reports.

If we read the literature of the eighteenth century on the luxurious life of the rich, study the pictures of the palaces and furnishings, look in the streets of old Vienna, old London, and old Paris, and try to find the monumental private constructions dating back to the period prior to 1800, we cannot fail to realize the mighty grandeur which characterized luxury in residences during that time. Naturally, one would like to visualize this development in terms of statistics, but that is extremely difficult.

I have in front of me a collection of pictures of famous country houses[82] of the English nobility and gentry. The collection was assembled in 1779, in two good-sized volumes, and contains pictures and descriptions of eighty-four castles. These eighty-four castles appear very impressive, and their number alone certainly permits of at least some appraisal of the luxury displayed in them, particularly if we read the descriptions. As an example, I take the country seat of the earl of Oxford (Houghton in Norfolk): its construction was begun by Sir Robert Walpole in 1722 and completed in 1735. With its two wings it has a length of five hundred feet; the center structure is one hundred and sixty-five feet long. The salon is forty feet long, forty feet high, and thirty feet wide; its wall coverings are velvet with rose-flowered designs; the ceiling was painted by Kent; the mantelpiece, as well as the tables, are made of black and yellow marble; the hall is a room of forty feet in each dimension, and it has a stone gallery on three sides; the ceiling and frieze are painted by Altari. The drawing room measures thirty by thirty-two feet; it is decorated with yellow caffoy and with carvings by Gibbons, etc. Finally there is mention of a gallery, seventy-one feet long, twenty-one feet wide, twenty-one feet high, with wall coverings of damask made in Norwich.

Mercier gives us some information concerning the extent of building activities in Paris during the eighteenth century: "During the last decades," he says, "six hundred palaces have been built whose interiors seem to be the work of fairies, because our imagination cannot surpass luxury on such a scale." He says that the bankers, lawyers, and contractors *(entrepreneurs de bâtiment)* are the three types of people who make their fortune in the Paris of his time. Entirely new quarters composed only of sumptuous palaces are said to have arisen.[83]

These data likewise help us to form an accurate picture, providing always that we keep in mind the opulence with which, as we have seen, the individual houses were built and furnished.

3. Luxury in the City

For reasons already indicated, the large city intensifies the urge to luxury. The efficacy of these reasons is definitely confirmed by the most competent observers of that time, such as Montesquieu in France and Mandeville in England; it is in this way that the large city is directly responsible for an increased demand for luxury. The manner in which at that time the city with its luxury demands began to influence the mode of living of the people of the provinces, how it accustomed them to making luxury expenditures, and how it brought about a rise in their standard of living is vividly told by a country squire, Pierre de Cadet, who recorded this story in his household expense book:

> My grandfather insisted on going to Paris, where, in the course of one year, he spent 14,000 livres; on his return, his father told him that a pair of spectacles, which my grandfather presented him with, cost 14,000 livres. Although he had a carriage and four white horses at home, nevertheless, my grandfather arrived from Paris with a great fondness for led horses. . . . He brought with him from Paris a man servant of whom his father said jokingly that he did not dare to ask him for a drink, because the servant was better dressed than he.[84]

But the significance of the large city in relation to the development of luxury lies chiefly in the fact that it suggested new possibilities in gay and opulent living, creating thereby novel forms of luxury. The city is responsible for making available to large sections of the populace the enjoyment of festivities which heretofore had been the privilege only of members of the ruling court; and as a result the masses began to establish places for themselves where they could regularly enjoy their festivities. Following the demise of the duke of York, who had spent his last days with him, the prince of Monaco received an invitation from the king of England to visit that country. When he saw the many lights in the streets as well as in the show windows of the shops which were kept open until ten o'clock, he thought that the entire illumination had been arranged in his honor. This story beautifully reflects the basic transformation which was, however, only beginning to take place at that time, i.e., the replacement of the strictly private development of luxury by a collective type of development. It marks the beginning of a communal mode of living which is really only characteristic of the next economic period. At this point we make brief note of it and observe—and that is the reason why we mention it here—that the tremendous effect of the large city is primarily confined within the boundaries of the luxury demand and that only the highest strata of society are brought in contact with the change in conditions. Again it is the woman who plays a role of extreme importance in this development of urban luxury.

The salient points are as follows:

1. The theaters—principally the elegant opera houses, built first in Italy with great opulence and subsequently established in the other large cities of Europe: the S. Carlo Theater in Naples, erected in 1737, represents an epoch in the history of theater construction. Since 1673, the following have existed in Paris: the Opera, called the Académie Royale de Musique, which has given its performances in the Royal Palace since the death of Molière; the Comédie française, which opened its new building in the Rue St. Germain des Prés on April 18, 1689; and the Comédie italienne which performs in the Hotel de Bourgogne (with an interruption from 1697 to 1716).[85]

In the beginning, the court theaters are open only to invited guests, in addition to the court itself; but gradually they are open to anyone who pays the admission price. But even then the better theaters, for a long time, are the exclusive meeting places for the higher strata of society who thus are afforded a new opportunity to flirt and display themselves.[86]

Speaking of Paris, Capon says that the Royal Academy of Music and Dancing is nothing but a *maison publique pour gentilhommes*.

2. The public music halls and dance halls (as we might call them today)—which were first (it seems) erected in London with the greatest splendor, and whose elegance was admired by all Londoners and principally by strangers.

Defoe describes the Pantheon, the biggest and most outstanding of these buildings: "Nor should the Pantheon be forgotten, which in taste, magnificence and novelty of design and decoration may be pronounced superior to anything of the kind in Europe. Its principal room is truly magnificent: it is lighted by a central dome of a considerable magnitude . . . The circumjacent apartments are also finely ornamented with whatever the invention of modern luxury can suggest. . . ." In this Pantheon a concert was given regularly every fourteen days, "with a ball following, to which everyone is admitted who has purchased the required admission ticket."[87] Defoe particularly adds this remark since such an arrangement undoubtedly represented an innovation for his time. Next to the theaters and concert halls, there are:

3. The fine restaurants, the taverns—which also were still a specialty of London during the eighteenth century and which constituted a source of envy to Parisians.

Archenholtz gives us the following charming description of the London taverns: "In these taverns one dines as one pleases, in rooms with large or small company, with or without female companionship. But the latter must be provided by the guests themselves; it is also impossible to stay overnight since this is a custom exclusive with bagnios." These bagnios, another attraction of London, were really baths; "but in actuality they operate for the pleasure of mixed company. These houses are sumptuously, sometimes even royally, furnished. Everything which might possibly stimulate the senses is either available or else can be procured" (through the headwaiter). "Englishmen maintain their serious demeanor even at play, wherefore business in an establishment of this sort is conducted with a seriousness and decency difficult to imagine."

The expenditures in fashionable restaurants, and in the *salons particuliers* connected with them, were so enormous "that it justified the bon mot of the famous Beaumarchais who, familiar as he was with Parisian revelries, nevertheless professed astonishment at the debaucheries in London, claiming that the receipts for one evening in the London bagnios and taverns were greater than the total amount needed by the seven united provinces to maintain themselves for a period of six months."[88] (Archenholtz)

But neither was Paris without its fine restaurants during the eighteenth century: the "swankiest" were those of the Palais Royal, such as Beauvilliers, Huré, or the Taverne Anglaise.[89] The very location of such a restaurant in the Palais Royal, the meeting place of the "fast set," is indicative of its character.

4. The hotels, until the end of the eighteenth century, are likewise luxury hotels; thus, their number is limited.

The Savoy Hotel in London, which stood in the same place as the present well-known hotel of the same name, enjoyed a splendid reputation. What it meant to maintain such a hotel in an aristocratic world is indicated even today by the Hotel des Reservoirs in Versailles. Probably the oldest luxury hotel in Europe was the "Locanda Dell' Orso" in Rome, which had existed since the time of Sixtus IV.

But there was still another place where the growing city was responsible for bringing about a public display of luxury, accessible to all; and that was the place where luxury goods were purchased by the fashionable world, that is to say, by women of fashion, again principally by the demimonde. We must therefore mention:

5. The stores—upon which, from the middle of the eighteenth century, more and more care was lavished and which from that time on began to assume a more decorative appearance. It was a fact which caused worthy gentlemen like Daniel Defoe to shake their heads.[90]

In his *Complete English Tradesman*, he devotes an entire chapter to this nuisance "of fine shops and fine shows" which will seem incredible to a more rational posterity. As testimony to the folly to which his contemporaries were given in this respect, he, therefore, decides to describe a "pastry-cook's shop" and its equipment which actually cost three hundred pounds: "*Anno Domini* 1710: let the year be recorded!"

At that time the equipment of a pastry shop in London consisted of the following:

1) Sliding windows, made of mirrors, 12 to 16 inches in size;

2) All the walks in tiles; in the rear room a panel set with glazed tiles and decorated with landscape or figure paintings;

3) Two big column mirrors and one mantelpiece mirror, seven feet high, in the back room;

4) Two big chandeliers, one in the store, one in the back room;

5) Three big glass lanterns in the store and eight smaller ones;

6) Twenty-five wall fixtures, and one pair of big silver fixtures in the back room: value twenty-five pounds;

7) Six elegant, big silver platters for candy displays;

8) Twelve big centerpieces, three of them made of silver, for the display of small cakes, etc., used at parties;

9) Painting of ceiling, gilding of lanterns, window frames, and scroll work: fifty-five pounds.

From reliable sources I have learned that three hundred pounds was the amount needed for the above, plus a few decorative pieces, but not including small plates and Chinese dishes and cups.

In view of the composition of London society, it is easy to imagine what element formed a particularly important percentage of the clientele of these stores; it was the same element which, as we are told, filled the theaters: "If a chastity committee, such as existed in Vienna, could function in London, it would depopulate this city . . . innumerable food businesses, to which half the population owed their sustenance, even their existence, would be ruined and London would be turned into a desert. If further proof is desired, one only has to ask the owners of the thousands of small shops who their most frequent buyers and best customers are. The profit, which is reaped in one single night by this large class, is brought to the shopkeepers on the following day, because the personal tastes of these unfortunates are quite moderate; in fact, they are inclined to starve in order to spend their entire income in finery. Without them the theaters would be empty."[91]

After all, the fifty million francs which, according to Mercier, flowed yearly into the lap of these women had to go somewhere.[92]

As a fitting conclusion to this treatise, I wish to quote the dedication appearing in Godard d'Aucourt's *Mémoires turcs* (dedicated to Madame Duthé, the great actress and courtesan), which sums up the situation admirably:

> Indeed, my dear ladies, you are the true luxury, indispensable to every nation; you are the alluring bait by means of which strangers and their guineas are attracted: twenty modest maidens are of less value to the royal treasury than a single one among you.[93]

CHAPTER 5

Capitalism — The Child of Luxury

1. *Correct and Incorrect Formulation of the Problem*

THE PROBLEM to be developed is this: What is the role of luxury in the genesis of capitalism? Is luxury capable of contributing to the development of capitalism and, if so, through what factors? During the seventeenth and eighteenth centuries, these questions enlisted the serious attention of practical as well as theoretical economists. In a certain sense they constituted the nucleus around which were grouped all the other questions relating to political economy—somewhat as today all questions center in the controversy over an "agrarian or industrial state." At that time, of course, capitalism as such was not referred to by name. Instead, specific terms such as industry, manufacturing, or wealth were used. There was agreement, however, on fundamentals; on every hand it was recognized that luxury was responsible for the development of those economic forms which were then about to come into being, that is to say, the capitalistic economy. For this reason all friends of economic "progress" were also ardent advocates of luxury. Their only cause for anxiety lay in the fear that an excessive consumption of luxury goods might jeopardize the accumulation of capital, but like Adam Smith they comforted themselves with the thought that there would always be thrifty people in sufficient numbers to assure the necessary reproduction and accumulation of capital.

Governments adopted a benevolent attitude toward luxury. In countries where the capitalistic system advanced with rapid strides during the seventeenth century, the last sumptuary laws were annulled. The year 1621 marked the promulgations of dress regulations, which also contained clauses prohibiting the use of certain luxury articles and delicacies.[1] In France,[2] the last edict governing table luxury falls in the year 1629; as late as in 1644 and

1672 the excessive use of precious metals for luxury purposes was forbidden because of coinage considerations. The year 1636 witnessed a ban on beaver hats costing more than 50 livres; the final sumptuary laws to be promulgated in France were the dress regulations of 1708. Since then even the authorities have been convinced of the "necessity" of luxury (in the interest of capitalistic industry); the foremost authors of the period also joined forces with the advocates of luxury until the followers of Jean Jacques Rousseau launched a counter movement. The most appreciated factor in luxury was its effectiveness in creating new markets. "There is an absolute necessity for luxury," says Montesquieu.[3] (This is especially true of monarchies!) "Were the rich not so lavish, the poor would starve." In his second publication on "Nobility Engaged in Trade,"[4] the witty Abbé Coyer makes several excellent remarks on the significance of luxury in the early development of capitalism: "Luxury is akin to fire: it may be beneficial as well as destructive. In ruining the houses of the rich, it sustains our factories. In devouring the inheritance of the spendthrift, it feeds our workers. In diminishing the property of the few, it increases the prosperity of the many. Proscribe our stuffs from Lyons, our tapestries, our gold-cloth, our laces, our mirrors, our jewelry, our carriages, our elegant furniture, our table delicacies, and I see not only millions of arms drop in idleness, but I also hear an equal number of voices crying for bread. . . ."

One of the most outstanding among the numerous French works on luxury is the one written by the brilliant Jew Pinto, *Théorie du luxe ou traité dans lequel on entreprend d'établir que le luxe est un ressort non seulement utile, mais même indispensablement nécessaire à la prospérité des états*[5] (The Theory of Luxury or A Treatise in which an effort is made to establish the fact that luxury is useful, nay indispensable to the prosperity of nations). The motto of the book is a quotation from Voltaire: "*Le superflu, chose très nécessaire*" (The superfluous—a great necessity).

The same view, namely, that luxury, though an "evil" and a "vice," must be considered a boon to the collectivity because of its stimulating effect upon industry, was likewise current in England. "Prodigality is a vice that is prejudicial to the man but not to trade."[6] Even Hume,[7] in spite of his pronounced "ethical" tendencies, arrives at the conclusion that "good" luxury was good and that "bad" luxury, although "the source of many ills, was in general preferable to sloth and idleness, which would commonly succeed in its place." Finally, Bernard Mandeville, in his *Fable of the Bees*, virtually developed this conception into a system of social philosophy. He extols "luxury" in the following verses:

> *The root of evil, avarice*
> *That damn'd ill natur'd baneful vice,*
> *Was slave to prodigality,*
> *That noble sin; whilst luxury*
> *Employ'd a million of the poor,*
> *And odious pride a million more:*
> *Envy itself and vanity*
> *Were ministers of industry;*
> *Their darling folly, fickleness,*
> *In diet, furniture and dress,*
> *That strange ridic'lous vice, was made*
> *The very wheel that turned the trade.*[8]

Of particularly instructive value are the chapters devoted to a discussion of this subject in Defoe's *Complete English Tradesman*. It is a very droll egg dance which is staked here by our good non-conformist. Deep down in his heart, he despises luxury and vastly admires those Quakers who, though dealing in the trinkets of vanity, would not use these showy fineries themselves. Nevertheless, being a panegyrist of trade, he could not bring himself to condemn luxurious living, for he realized—and this is what interests us here—that luxury was the source of all growing wealth: "The extravagant pride of the age feeds trade and consequently the poor." Defoe supplies us with a great deal of information concerning the true interplay of luxury and capitalism, a subject which I shall discuss later on.

German authors, too, have discussed luxury at great length and recognized the significance of luxury for the development of capitalism. Schröder, for example, says: "I wish there were more splendor in our land . . . for the splendor of the rich serves to feed many of our workers and many of our poor. . . ."[9] In the light of the foregoing, one should think that present-day economists, inquiring into the origin of modern capitalism, would have sought to profit by these sagacious and learned observations. This, however, has not been the case. To be sure, a great deal has been said on the subject of luxury, and there has been much theorizing as to the part played by the market in capitalistic industry. But on the relationship between luxury and the market, no one had anything to say. Obviously, commentators on the question of luxury and the market found themselves in a *cul-de-sac*.

Time and again the problem of luxury has been approached with all the ethical fervor of the solid and thrifty bourgeois, and moralizing arguments have been brought into play for every phase of the question. Even Roscher's studies, the best perhaps of our time on the subject of luxury, are in the last analysis based upon ethical sentiments as to what constitutes good and bad in luxury. Such works as Baudrillart's *Geschichte des Luxus*, on the other hand, are merely compilations of source material.

With regard to the understanding of the function of the market in the development of capitalism, the writings of Marx have given rise to a very unfortunate theory. It has been stated that capitalism was greatly benefited by wider markets and, particularly, by the opening of colonial territories during the sixteenth century or, expressed on the basis of the somewhat more purposive orientation of the historical school of political economy (a viewpoint, incidentally, with which the majority of economic "historians" were soon in accord), that geographical expansion of the market, the "foreign market" or "export," "necessitated" the capitalistic organization. During the last generation this viewpoint found strong support in the following theory of Karl Bucher, outstanding investigator and truly productive thinker: handicraft = production for customers; capitalism = production for a group of unknown customers; handicraft = local market; capitalism = interlocal market.

This trend of thought, to which undoubtedly all economic historians have subscribed, I believe to be fallacious, for, as we have seen, it has brought research in this field to an impasse. In looking for the reasons underlying the transition to the capitalistic economy, the problem was attacked from an entirely wrong angle. Production for a definite circle of customers and production for distant markets do not in the least characterize the contrast between handicraft and capitalistic production. Capitalism very well may be associated with the strictest form of production for specific customers, e.g., custom tailoring; while, on the other hand, we know a great variety of flourishing handicrafts which, many centuries before they became capitalistic enterprises, sold their products in all the market places of the world.

The following discussions intend to lead the issue from the described impasse to a plane admitting of more fruitful inquiries. They pick up the thread at the point where the investigators of the eighteenth century have left off. These discussions will tend to bring out the decisive bearing of luxury upon capitalism prior to the close of its first stage. In following this line of thought, we must keep in mind several basic conceptions.

Luxury has contributed in many ways to the development of modern capitalism. For instance, it played a role of great importance in the transfer of the wealth of the aristocracy to the bourgeois classes, chiefly through indebtedness. In this connection, however, we are interested only in the effectiveness of luxury in creating markets, a function best understood in the following manner.

A capitalistic enterprise, in order to prosper, requires, as we know, a minimum outlet of exchange values. The size of this outlet depends upon two distinct factors: the rapidity of turnover and the exchange value of the commodities. The exchange value of the commodities in turn is determined by two factors: the exchange value of the simple units and the quantity involved.

Thus, the minimum outlet referred to is determined either by the limited sale of high-priced goods or by the more extensive sale of mass products: specialty sales—bulk sales. The increase in the value of an article can be brought about in two different ways: accumulation or refinement. Refinement, as we have seen, may assume various forms. Accumulation affects those goods which may be termed composite or complex, such as locomotives, ships, and hospitals. They represent an aggregation of ordinary goods, combined into a new greater entity which considerably enhances their value. Strictly speaking, the sale of such goods represents bulk selling in specialty form.

As far back as we are able to trace the history of European nations, we find concurrent demands for necessaries and luxuries. At first both were of modest proportions, so that for a long time both demands could be satisfied within the framework of the then existing groups, peasants, craftsmen, and the socage organization. As a rule, the demand for necessaries was satisfied by the resources of the village, the manor, or the town and its surrounding country. In other words, as far as articles in ordinary use were concerned both supply and demand had a local economic basis. Quality articles for select purposes, however, if they could not be supplied by the home production of the lord's estate or by importers, were furnished by artisans who had always worked for interlocal and international markets.

During the Middle Ages and the next centuries thereafter, economic development presented the following picture: The demand for ordinary goods remained essentially unchanged and, consequently, was of no importance as far as capitalism was concerned. Until the close of the era of capitalism, the demand for consumption goods on the part of the great masses of the population, as well as the demand for the instruments of labor (implements, tools, machinery) was as a rule supplied through home production or by artisans. This general rule had only two exceptions which will be discussed presently. The reason for this phenomenon is apparent. Populations were constant; concentration did not take place to any appreciable extent, nor was there any improvement in transportation facilities; hence, mass demand for any given commodity could not materialize. Furthermore, since the technique in production and transportation underwent no fundamental changes, there could be no increased demand for composite goods and, as a consequence, no market for production for sale on a capitalistic basis.

The two above-mentioned exceptions in which bulk sales of inferior or composite goods took place prior to the advent of full capitalism, i.e., before the eighteenth century, are: the colonies which also contributed to the development of markets for the capitalistic industry and, in particular, the modern armies. In the second volume of these "studies," I have called attention to the momentous importance of army contracts for the development of capitalism. Hence, we must now shed light upon the other aspect of the question and adduce evidence to support our contention that luxury, or rather the growth of the demand for luxury, played a prominent part in the rise of modern capitalism.

To say that I will prove the significance of increased luxury consumption for the development of capitalism means naturally, that, in accord with the scientific fashion of today, I shall use the historico-empirical method in substantiating my claim as to the relationship between the two complex phenomena. This is, of course, by no means an easy task, and the first attempt may be only in part successful. It is inherent in the nature of the work that the major responsibility of furnishing detailed proof will have to be borne by the coming generation of economic historians.

The difficulty of the task is intensified by the habitual carelessness of writers on economy. They speak of "economic rise," "expansion of production," "expansion of markets," and the like, leaving the reader in doubt as to whether handicraft or capitalism formed the basis of the economic system under discussion. In other words, one learns really nothing at all. At the present writing, in view of the scant printed material on the subject, it is impossible to add substantially to the literature which I am presenting in this volume.

II. *Luxury and Trade*

1. Wholesale Trade

It is not unlikely that trading in goods assumed capitalistic forms earlier than production of goods. I seriously question, however, the assumption that during the Middle Ages, trade was the principal factor responsible for the accumulation of wealth by the great houses of Italy, the South of France, Spain, and Southern Germany. Other factors, I believe, helped to elevate these few houses from among the mass of small traders to the level of wholesale establishments, although this does not altogether rule out the possibility that trading alone transformed these houses into capitalistic enterprises. But in such a case—and this is what interests us at present—it was undoubtedly trading in articles of luxury which brought about this development.

During the Middle Ages all trading of any importance (for which, therefore, capitalism was the only type of organization possible) centered around Italy. It consisted either in the export of Italian products (or the importation of raw materials or half-finished articles required in their production) or in the importation and distribution of oriental products.

Italian imports from Northern countries were mainly wool (for the Florentine luxury industry, which we shall later discuss in greater detail), furs and fine linens. The bulk of Italian exports probably had to be paid for in cash (principally with the yield of German silver mines).

On the other hand, Italy's exports to the North comprised: silk and silk products, the finest cloth, the finest glassware, cotton and cotton fabrics (which, as we shall see presently, even in modern times are still considered luxury goods), wines, and arms.

All merchandise of the Orient, bought either in Italy or via Italy, likewise served to supply the demand for luxury on the part of the well-to-do, with the possible exception of goods required by the Church, such as incense, although even in this instance it was a case of luxury consumption made possible through the concentration of wealth. I also include under luxury the demand for foreign medicines during the Middle Ages and even in more modern times (up to our epoch of humanitarianism and concern for the welfare of the masses). The populace at large and the ordinary citizen still cured themselves with herbs from their own forests and fields.

The following is a list[10] of merchandise compiled by Wilhelm Heyd for the Levantine trade (with the articles listed in the order of their usefulness):

1. Medicaments, which also served as spices for foods: aloe, agalloch (also used as perfume or as wood in cabinet work), balsam, costmary, galingale, gallnuts, ginger, camphor, cardamon, laudanum, manna, *succus bituminosus*, myrobalan, rhubarb, purging cassia, saffron (also as dye), scammony, tragacanth (also as dye), tutty and zedoary.

2. Spices, etc.: Principally pepper. But as late as the beginning of modern times, certainly throughout the entire Middle Ages, pepper was known as an article of luxury, used only in the kitchens of the rich and by potentates as a means of making presents to each other; cloves, which were twice and even three times as expensive as pepper; nutmeg, cinnamon; sugar, which, as late as the nineteenth century, was likewise looked upon as a delicacy of the rich.

3. Perfumes and fumigating material: gum-benjamin, mastic, musk, sandalwood, incense, and amber (out of which objects were also carved).

4. Dyestuffs: alum, Brazil-wood (Caesalpinia Sappan), madder, indigo, kermes, lacca; all materials used in delicate dyeing processes; mastic (for varnishes).

5. Raw materials for textiles: silks and the finest of Egyptian flax.

6. *Ornamental objects:* precious stones, corals, pearls, ivory, porcelain, glass, gold and silver thread.

7. *Dress materials:* silks, brocades, velvet, and the finest linen; wool and cotton materials, such as bocasine, buckram, camlet, all of which looked like silk and were equally expensive.

These materials were shipped partly from the Orient to Europe and partly also from Italy to the Orient as well as to the various European countries. A fair indication of the high quality which was demanded in merchandise during the Middle Ages can be obtained by examining the custom receipts, for example, those of the Customhouse at Como. Schulte[11] estimated that the value of the merchandise transported over the St. Gotthard Pass during the fifteenth century ranged from 320,000 to 518,000 librae.[12] The approximate weight of this merchandise is said to have been 25,000 hundredweights which would place the value of a hundredweight at roughly 50 florins and that of a pound at roughly one-half florin (approximately 4 marks in 1913).

In spite of the great discoveries of the fifteenth century, trading experienced very few changes, since even as late as the nineteenth century the exchange of goods between East and West and between Europe and America consisted chiefly of high-class luxury articles. Only the quantity increased, and a few new articles were added to the trade, principally tobacco, coffee, tea, and cocoa. But until the end of the period of early capitalism, the last-named articles (with the possible exception of tobacco) were still available only to the well-to-do; they must, then, continue to be regarded as luxury articles.

The following figures are a fair indication of the increase in the consumption of the most important luxury articles during the past centuries:

English tea imports by the East-Indies Company

Year	Pounds
1668	100

Year	Hundredweights
1710	1,420
1731	8,168
1761	26,192
1784	86,083

Let us assume that 50 percent of this merchandise remained in England and was consumed in that country. Let us next take as a basis for our calculations the population figures given by Finlaison:

Year	Millions
1700	5
1750	6
1800	9.187

We would then arrive at the following per capita consumption:

Year	Pounds
1700	0.01
1730	0.08
1760	0.2
1784	0.5

In 1906 the per capita consumption of tea in the United Kingdom amounted to six and one-half lbs., or to thirty to thirty-five lbs. per family, or the total consumption to 270 million lbs. The picture becomes still clearer on the basis of the following calculation: the use of tea in quantities approximating present-day English tea consumption would have been within the means of the following number of families:

Year	Approximate Number of Families
1668	3
1710	2,000
1730	12,000
1760	40,000
1780	140,000

In 1800 the European coffee consumption (according to Alexander von Humboldt) amounted to approximately 1,400,000 cwts; the population of Europe (according to Beloch), to approximately 120,000,000; therefore the per capita consumption of coffee was already at that time a little over one lb. At this rate of consumption, one is justified in numbering coffee among the mass commodities, particularly if one considers that in 1910 the per capita coffee consumption in Germany still amounted to only 6 lbs. a year.

Sugar consumption in Europe at that time—again according to Humboldt—was said to have been 4,500,000 cwts, i.e., three to four lbs. per person. In present-day Germany the average consumption of sugar per person is thirty-eight lbs. The fact that even in the eighteenth century, sugar was not as yet the customary means for sweetening is clearly demonstrated by the continued use of honey for that purpose. As late as 1750 honey was still being preferred in Germany as a means for sweetening, for the preserving of fruits and as an ingredient in the making of beer. It may safely be said that, as far as the rich Western European countries are concerned, it was around the middle of the eighteenth century that sugar ceased to be a commodity for the exclusive use of the well-to-do, but as to the rest of Europe this change did not take place until perhaps the nineteenth century.

There is yet another importation from India which retained the character of a luxury article; it was an article of very great commercial importance during the seventeenth and eighteenth centuries, but today it is worn by the wife of every postal clerk. This article is cotton, or rather the Indian cotton prints, as well as the other types of cotton materials which were shipped from Asia to Europe. It was toward the end of the seventeenth and during the beginning of the eighteenth century that Indian cottons became the fashion among the rich and threatened home industries with serious competition. This development especially jeopardized the existence of manufacturers of fine cloths and silks and confirms our assumption that the buyers were among the rich. Further support for this thesis is found in the efforts made by governments, for instance, that of France, to curb the importation of Indian cottons. (Indian cottons were sanctioned by Madame Pompadour but did not fully blossom into fashion until the days of Trianon.) After 1700 their use was forbidden. The prohibition, of course, was unsuccessful; we see the fashionable ladies dressed in cottons as they leave Paris for their country places. We are told of the following amusing episode.

The wife of Marshal de Villars was smuggling Indian cottons into the country. On July 17, 1715, Madame la marquise de Nesle appears publicly in the Tuileries gardens, dressed in a "robe de chambre brodée de fleurs de soie et façon des Indes sur une toile du même pays"—in an Indian cotton gown embroidered with silk flowers. The police, charged with the enforcement of dress regulations, are amazed and indignant. The police president hurriedly calls on Monsieur le Marquis and remonstrates. Monsieur promises to prevail upon Madame, "so that in the future. . . ."[13] (Unfortunately, the official document does not report the result of the domestic scene which followed.)

These prefatory remarks will enable us to interpret correctly the overseas importations to Europe during the seventeenth and eighteenth centuries. The picture is always the same, be it in England, Holland, or France. The Indian companies are importing: (1) spices; (2) medicines; (3) dyestuffs; (4) silks and silk materials; (5) cotton and cotton materials; (6) precious stones, porcelain, etc.; and, depending upon circumstances, (7) coffee, tobacco, sugar, tea, and cocoa. One list of such importations will be sufficient.

In 1776[14] French imports from the East-Indies were as follows:

	Francs
Coffee	3,248,000
Pepper and cinnamon	2,449,000
Muslins	12,000,000
Indian linen	10,183,000
Porcelain	200,000
Silk	1,382,000
Tea	3,399,000
Miscellaneous articles, such as silk materials, shells, raltan, saltpeter	3,380,000
	36,241,000

Payment for these goods was chiefly made with the silver and gold of American mines and also with home products, principally textile goods; among them there were undoubtedly already a number of inferior articles for the masses, mainly clothing for Negroes, Malays, and probably also for the middle-class population of the colonies settled by Europeans, such as those in North America (because the production of articles for trade was largely prohibited in these colonies). But this factor is inconsequential in the total evaluation of the overseas trade of that time. This trade springs from the consumption of luxury goods; it is still exclusively the private affair of the well-to-do, whose Paris expenditure for luxuries alone keeps it alive. If the imports, as we have seen, are luxury articles, then the nature of the export goods is utterly immaterial: after all, they are but an incidental form of payment. The trade itself would not exist without the importation of luxury articles because without them the people on the other side would, in turn, be unable to acquire European products (Countries where precious metals are mined must be excepted: according to the commercial statistics[15] compiled by Alexander von Humboldt, Mexico's imports from Spain in 1802 amounted to 20,390,859 piastres, while the value of her exported goods amounted only to 8,416,930 piastres; the balance was paid with Mexican silver).

There is one additional, very important branch of the international overseas trade which we must take into consideration, i.e., the slave trade, which, as we know, was conducted almost entirely along capitalistic lines. Of course, the objects themselves were not luxury articles (or were they?), but they did contribute directly to the production of luxury articles, as we shall realize presently.

We are in possession of a good deal of information concerning the scope of the slave trade, but part of this information is of a rather contradictory nature. The following data, supplied by Buxton, are the best known and probably the most authentic[16]:

Shipments from Africa:

Annual victims of Christian slave trade	400,000
Annual victims of Mohammedan slave trade	100,000
	500,000

Of the 400,000 victims of the Christian slave trade, 280,000 usually perish while being captured and transported and during the first year of their captivity, so that finally only 120,000 slaves remain. In view of the total demand for slaves at the beginning of the nineteenth century, this figure can hardly be called too high, and its accuracy is attested through the publication of official figures in modern times. We learn, for example, that from 1780 to 1789 an average number of 30,000 to 35,000 Negroes a year were brought into the French Antilles. If we assume that a total of between 240,000 and 260,000 slaves were kept in the French Antilles at that time, the yearly increase would have ranged from one-seventh to one-eighth. But if the total number of slaves eventually rose as high as 6,000,000 or 7,000,000, a yearly replacement figure of from 120,000 to 150,000 slaves would appear to be too low rather than too high.

It is not, however, of very great importance to determine the exact figures of the slave trade. For our purposes it is sufficient to establish the fact that the yearly figure ran into tens of thousands, and the total figure, for the entire period of slave traffic, ran into millions of human beings who (and this is the only fact that interests us here) were an excellent source of business.

We have no dependable data of any kind covering the expanded slave trade during the Middle Ages. But even then this traffic was extensively engaged in, to judge from the descriptions of the Arabian trade and from occasional reports, although the figures given appear fantastic. From these sources we learn that in 1310 the Sicilian fleet attacked the peaceful island of Gerba on the Tunisian coast and bore away 12,000 women and children into slavery; that in 1355 a Genoese admiral invaded and plundered Tripoli without the slightest provocation and enslaved 7000 men, women, and children.[17]

The nations which, without excluding others, played one after another the leading role in human traffic are the Jews,[18] Venetians,[19] Genoese, Portuguese, French, Dutch, and English. During the eighteenth century the monopoly in slave trading was held successively by the four last named. The following figures show how this trade, at its peak, was distributed among the various groups.

The number of Negroes taken by the various countries from the coast of Africa (from Cape Blanco to the Congo River[20]) is seen in the table below:

Countries of Trade	Number of Negroes
Great Britain	53,100
France	23,520
Holland	11,300
British-America	6,300
Portugal	1,700
Denmark	1,200

Bryan Edwards reports that in 1791 there were forty European trading centers on the coast of Africa: fourteen English, three French, fifteen Dutch, four Portuguese, four Danish. During that year the various countries exported the following:

Countries of Trade	Negroes Exported
Britain	38,000
France	20,000
Portugal	10,000
Holland	4,000
Denmark	2,000

Throughout the eighteenth century, when slave traffic reached its zenith, Great Britain undoubtedly was its center, and in Great Britain it pivoted around Liverpool. Of 192 English slave ships which set sail in 1771,[21] 107 left from Liverpool, 58 from London, 23 from Bristol, 4 from Lancaster. Postelthwayt has given us a list of all the slave ships owned by Liverpool merchants; at that time there were eighty-eight such ships, some carrying from 60 to 550 slaves, but most of them from three hundred to four hundred slaves.[22] The slave trade had developed rapidly in Liverpool. In 1729 the tradesmen of that city owned only one, thirty-ton sloop for this trade, while in 1751 as many as fifty-three vessels with a total displacement of 5334 tons sailed away from Morsey for the slave coast of Africa.

During the seventeenth and eighteenth centuries it was undoubtedly the overseas trade and principally the colonial trade which developed commercial capitalism; in comparison, the international European trade and, to a greater extent, the interlocal trade in the various countries fade into insignificance. Still, even in the latter, capitalistic structures had probably arisen in certain places. It is a point worth noting in this connection that this intra-European trade as well consisted chiefly in luxury goods. As far as I am able to determine, there were only two articles, outside the field of luxury, which were sold internationally and along capitalistic lines: grain and copper. The trade in these two articles was, in both cases, created by the demands of the modern armies.

If we wish to ascertain the type of merchandise shipped from one European country to another, we may consult, among many sources, a compilation by the Paris Chamber of Commerce of the year 1658, which lists the articles exported from France to Holland. As late as the beginning of the eighteenth century, the well-informed editor of the *Batavia Illustrata* declared this list still in keeping with actual facts, although, as we shall see later, a national luxury industry had already established itself in Holland. The following development is typical of those centuries which witnessed the strengthening of capitalism: one century after another begins to manufacture for itself the articles previously imported through traders from countries of advanced capitalism. First Italy, then France is the leading industrial country, then England, Holland, Germany, etc., follow.

The quotation referred to follows[23]:

France exports to Holland (not only for consumption in Holland itself, but also for re-export purposes):

Francs

1. In velvets, plush, satins, gold and silver stuffs, tafetas, and other silk stuffs of Tours and Lyon — 6,000,000 and above

2. In ribbons, silk and thread laces, buttons and tags made at Paris, Rouen, and the adjacent towns — 2,000,000

3. In castors and other sorts of hats made at Paris and Rouen — 1,500,000

4. In plumes, belts, umbrellas, masks, headdresses, looking glasses, gild frames, watches, and several kinds of toys and trinkets which the French term bijoux — 2,000,000

5. In gloves made at Paris, Clermont, Vendôme, and Rouen — 1,500,000

6. In woolen yarn spun in Picardy — 500,000

7. In paper of all sorts made in Poitou, Champagne, Limosin, Auvergne, and Normandy — 2,000,000

Francs

8. In pins and needles and in ivory, ebony, box, and horn combs made at Paris and in Normandy	500,000
9. In small iron and steel wares made at Auvergne	500,000
10. In sailcloth from Normandy and Brittany	5,000,000 and above
11. In chamber furniture of all kinds, beds, matresses, quilts, blankets, fringes, etc.	5,000,000 and above
12. In wines of several growths	9,000,000 and above
13. Brandy, vinegar, and syder	2,000,000 and above
14. In saffron, soap, honey, almonds, olives, capers, pruens, and other fruit	2,000,000
Total	39,500,000

Thus, all items were luxury articles with the exception of No. 10, and possibly No. 13, because brandy and cider may conceivably have been intended for the use of sailors and soldiers.

According to estimates by Moreau de Jonnés more than half of the value of French imports during the time of Louis XIV lay in articles supplied by Italy, England, and the Netherlands: silk materials, fine cloth, hangings, batiste, lace, cutlery, and mercury.[24]

2. Retail Trade

It is on the retail rather than on the wholesale trade that luxury has had profound, sustained, and predominant influence. Although during early capitalism there were a few important capitalistic branches of the wholesale trade not dealing in luxury articles (the copper trade in the sixteenth and the grain trade in the seventeenth century), I believe that, prior to the nineteenth century, not a single even moderately capitalistic retail business existed in which luxury articles were not offered for sale. An examination of the decades around 1700—when the tendency of the well-to-do to live extravagantly took a sudden flight, when Brazilian gold began to fill the pockets of speculators in Paris, Amsterdam, and London —discloses that intense desire on the part of the traders to satisfy the rich man's craving for luxuries shook them out of the easy-going ways characteristic of handicraftsmen and set them on the road toward capitalistic growth.

Perhaps we would grasp less readily the intimate, causal relationship between the development of luxury and the capitalistic retail trade, were it not for the fortunate preservation of a source rarely equalled in dependability and richness. This source permits us to trace in minute detail all the changes which took place in the English silk trade from the restoration period to approximately 1730. It is an account based on the experience of the well-informed author of the *Complete English Tradesman*,[25] a man who can justly say that none of his contemporaries fitted "by years and experience" to recount these episodes.

The dealer in silks, the mercer, is unquestionably the typical representative of the luxury trade in those centuries of arrogant wealth. The lady reigns supreme. All trade is molded to her fancies. The most precious luxury articles are sold to her because the silk trade comprises all gold and silver cloths, brocades, velvets, and perhaps lace.

The silk merchant of former days, as we find him in London even under the later Stuarts and in all likelihood a few decades thereafter (the major readjustments, I believe, probably only began to appear toward the end of the seventeenth century), was both a wholesale and a retail merchant; in other words, there were no independent retail silk merchants as yet: those who bought materials from the producers sold them by the yard directly to their customers. The merchant princes themselves, in earlier times, had followed the same practice. The Fuggers, for example, when almost at the height of their power and wealth, could be seen cutting silks and velvets. True enough, they were purveyors only to the royal households of gold cloth (at thirty-six florin per yard), or Florentine and Milanese damask (at eight to ten florin per yard), or silk velvet (at four florin per yard).[26] At any rate, they were merchant princes who dealt ordinarily in copper and with emperors. But fancy Herr Arnold or Herr Friedländer-Fould in person selling a few yards of ribbon to the former Kaiser William II.

Our London merchants of the time of the Great Fire, or twenty years later, were all in the city where, probably since the Plantagenets, they had been housed in narrow, somber Paternoster Row, for the purpose of selling their wares. "The spacious shops, backware houses, skylights, and other conveniences, made on purpose for their trade, are still to be seen," as we read in the fifth edition of the *Complete English Tradesman* (1745). Their stocks were "prodigiously great," and the traders sold them as their forefathers had undoubtedly sold their wares under the Plantagenets. The most select clientele, headed by the royal court, came to visit these shops in narrow Paternoster Row. The carriages stood in two lines: they drove in on one side and out on the other; traffic was regulated in this manner because the passage was too narrow to permit turning. The mercers themselves had employed two guards to maintain order. There were approximately fifty vaulted shops, housing the great merchants. The remaining buildings sheltered the satellites of this proud trade: the lacemen in the middle of Ivy Lane; the button shops at the end of the street near Cheapside; the crewel shops and the fringe shops nearby in Blowbladder Street.

All this underwent a radical change "as the gay humour came up" (but our writer fails to mention the exact time). He says: "There they sat, the great old mercers, about twenty years after the fire, and even in that time, as the gay humour came on. . . ." This would have been during the reign of Charles II since the Great Fire was in 1666—certainly an era to be termed gay. The number of retail mercers of that time grew at a tremendous rate: as Paternoster Row became too narrow, they began settling at the periphery of London: in Aldgate, Lombard Street, and Covent Garden, which soon received a name. Since the streets were much broader here, it was natural for the customers, who drove only in carriages, to prefer buying at the new stores, and even the members of the court no longer came into the city. Paternoster Row was deserted, and in little more than two years the old mercers were forced to abandon their vaulted stores and follow the stream of customers—to paraphrase our writer—much as fishermen move along with the fish to another locality. (Were they Jews, these new "outlaying mercers," who in this manner revolutionized the old silk trade? Were they Jews who had followed the wife of

Charles II or the prince of Orange to London? It can hardly be otherwise.) Another ten years, and Covent Garden found itself deserted; like swarming bees, the mercers searched for a new locality; finally "the swarm settled on Ludgate Hill" where it remained permanently. In the meantime the number of merceries, which had been fifty or sixty in 1663, had risen to between three hundred and four hundred.

At the same time, when the mercers left the locality where they had been for hundreds of years and spread widely over different parts of London, many other tradesmen and handicraftsmen also abandoned the old streets which they had occupied throughout the Middle Ages. Many of them, for example the linen-drapers, preeminently traders in luxury, "monstrously increased" in the same manner. As we have seen elsewhere, fine body linen became at about this time the luxury of the rich man and his beloved.

In other words, we learn from this account that, because of the rapidly increasing demand, the number of stores dealing in luxury articles rose considerably within a short time and the old localities were deserted. This development, however, opened the doors through which the modern commercial spirit penetrated the great halls of the retail trade; thus, it was only a question of time when the retail trade of the Middle Ages would be converted into capitalistic enterprises. On account of these changes—steady as well as sudden growth plus change in locality—the retail trade came under the influence of economic forces; soon competition between neighbors became inevitable, and new and effective methods of attracting customers had to be devised. It was this development which heralded the advent of the capitalistic spirit. We can learn how, during the next century, this competitive urge entrenched itself in the luxury establishments of the large cities— and nowhere else—by correctly interpreting the scant available data on the retail organizations of that period.

The following developments took place during the course of the next century, after the old mercers had departed from Paternoster Row:

1. Retail and wholesale trade became differentiated; only a small portion of the three hundred to four hundred mercers could remain wholesalers.

2. The shopkeepers began to equip their stores in a more elegant fashion, partly to attract new trade and partly to please their well-to-do customers by rendering their visits more agreeable. We are told definitely that this improvement in store appointments began among the "toymen,"—dealers in trinkets or novelties, as we might call them today; however, we must bear in mind that this merchandise represented only the finest in luxury articles; for instance, knickknacks. In a certain sense the luxury of the time culminated in these little trinkets. In French these costly trinkets are called "bijoux," which, at that time, signified not only ornaments in a narrower sense but also included *colifichets*, playthings and other trifles made of precious metals and exquisite in workmanship. These shops became the meeting places for the world of fashion, particularly the gentlemen who came to select presents for their lady-loves. It was here that they could purchase their *bijoux frivoles*, "which were   presented to respectable women who would not accept cash money" (*que l'on donne aux femmes honnetes qui n'acceptent de l'argent, mais bien des colifichets en or, parce qu'ils ont un air de décence!*), according to Mercier, who tells us of the "*Petit Dunkerque*,"[27] the fashionable luxury shop of his time, where the crowds of "*petits seigneurs*," particullarly during the first days of the year had to be held back. "There is nothing more sparkling than this shop" (*rien n'est plus brillant à l'oeil que cette boutique*), which Voltaire honored with a visit during his last stay in Paris. Mercier adds that "Voltaire smiled at all these luxurious creations; it seems to me that he detected a certain similarity between these glittering trinkets and his own style."

3. The form of the modern retail store, the commodity store, as I have called it,[28] where the merchandise is arranged according to use, is beginning to develop out of the old specialty store. To a certain degree the toyman, the *marchand bijoutier*, already represents this new principle; likewise, the inclusion of accessories for women's dressing tables reveals the tendency toward a regrouping of merchandise in the store. The mercer also seems about to become a clothing merchant: "He deals in silks, velvets, brocades, and an innumerable train of expensive trifles for the ornament of the fair sex."[29] As far as I can determine, however, the first commodity shop is the house furnishing store where everything is already assembled in one compact group, of course, only the very best of everything which serves to decorate a home. It seems that the upholstery shops in part changed over into such furniture establishments, in which were found: tables, chests, all tpyes of cabinet work *(tous les ouvrages d'ébénisterie)*, mirrors, chandeliers, etc., as well as beds and upholstery, draperies and tapestries, manufactured by them.[30] Again there were others who merely traded in these things; but even they concentrated all their wares within one single store. They sold paintings, etchings, candelabra, branched candlesticks, chandeliers, figures in bronze, marble, wood, and other materials, clocks and watches, cabinets, chests of drawers, tables, marble tables, and various articles and curios which are used for house decoration: *"marchandises et curiosités propres pour l'ornament des apartemens."*[31]

In the London of that time we encounter similar business houses: those of the cabinetmakers who sell in their stores a great variety of furnishings, which have only in part been manufactured by themselves. Many of their shops are so richly set out that "they look more like palaces and their stocks are of exceeding great value."[32] In addition, as in Paris, there are also furnishing stores conducted by upholsterers. Many of them are keepers of large shops and have always in stock a full line of ready-made goods.[33]

4. The impersonal relationship between tradesman and customer, typical of the entire subsequent capitalistic development, has its inception in these great luxury establishments; to my knowledge, the Petit Dunkerque is the first retail establishment to maintain a system of "fixed prices."[34]

5. In speaking of these great luxury establishments, I have arrived at the last and most important point. Obviously, the capitalistic basis upon which these enterprises rested had to expand as all these business principles enumerated were successively applied.

We are informed that the silk establishments in particular assumed considerable proportions at times. In the case of one Parisian retail store, Galpin, at the beginning of the eighteenth century, we find that in a single day it sold 80,000 livres worth of cloths.[35]

The *Complete English Tradesman* of 1727 speaks of a mercer who employed "a great many servants and journeymen" in his store. To a certain lady whom he served, and who spent two full hours with him without purchasing a single item, he displayed merchandise to the value of £3000. This author speaks of another mercer whose yearly turnover amounted to £40,000. The capital required during the middle of the eighteenth century to open a silk establishment was estimated by one authority to be between £500 to £2000; another authority claims it to be between £1000 to £10,000: "£10,000, unless wisely invested, represents only a small figure in this line."

The books from which I extract these data are two interesting and important sources[36] for determining the extent to which capital was concentrated within the individual branches of the London retail trade during the middle of the eighteenth century.

These books contain alphabetical lists of all the trades conducted in London at that time and also (as a guide for prospective apprentices or their parents) the minimum amounts required for anyone wishing to establish himself in a given trade.

Thus, we are able to furnish proof in support of our contention that luxury establishments are practically the only ones to make greater demands, requiring, as they do, investments in excess of—let us say—£500. A list of these establishments follows:

Establishments	*Investments in* £
Bookstore	500-5000
China-shop	500-2000
Druggist	500-2000
Grocer	500-2000
Laceman (edgings, galloons)	500-2000
Hosier's shop (woven materials, principally silk tricots)	500-5000
Nurseryman (flowers and shrubbery)	500-1000
Thread man	500-1000
Toyman	2000

The only merchants who do not deal directly in luxury articles (although in the last analysis they, too, were sustained by the well-to-do of the city) and whose establishments require initial investments of more than £ 500 are the coal, iron, and lumber merchants.

The outstanding significance of the luxury trade is clearly established through the fact that companies were formed only among the silk-dealers, linen-dealers, and goldsmiths–bankers.[37] Therefore, as a result of the increased consumption of luxury articles, capitalism asserts itself also (and principally) in the retail trade. The reasons are obvious; in the foregoing pages, they are implied. I shall enumerate them again at this point.

1. The type of merchandise makes necessary a capitalistic organization; the goods are of the highest value and the first to reach the markets in appreciable quantities.

2. The type of clientele acts as a stimulant in this capitalistic development; it demands the utmost in elegance and service. Furthermore (and this appears to have been a reason of great weight in those fortunate times since it is stressed by all trade counselors), this fashionable clientele either never pays in cash or never pays at all. Consequently, the merchant who deals in luxury articles is forced–if we accept all the other elements of the situation–to keep himself constantly supplied with a large amount of capital, because his turnover is so much less frequent (as a result of the credit system).

III. *Luxury and Agriculture*

1. In Europe

Capitalism received a direct impetus from agriculture when, as a result of the growing demand for wool, farmers during the Middle Ages began to discontinue the cultivation of certain sections of their land and turned them into sheep pastures. In southern Italy, Spain, and England, this trend subsequently became more prevalent. In England, the expansion of manorial sheep-farming at the expense of the old type of peasant farms is known to have been so widespread and rapid under the Tudors that it prompted Thomas More to say that sheep were devouring human beings. To my mind, current opinion overestimates the extent of the "fenced-off" areas, namely, the stretches of land converted exclusively into grazing grounds; a movement, however, in the direction of a large-scale capitalistic enterprise in agriculture was afloat and did not cease until the eighteenth century. As far as the genesis of modern capitalism is concerned, this movement has a twofold significance: first, it created forms of capitalistic organization, and second, it furthered the development of capitalist industry by diminishing the areas necessary for small, independent farmers to produce sufficient foodstuffs.

This entire trend must be attributed to luxury because the wool produced by the newly established sheep farms went into the making of very fine fabrics by the highly developed weaving industry in Flanders, Brabant, and Florence for the use of the wealthy, as will later be shown.

In other ways the influence of luxury upon agriculture resulted in the improvement and refinement of production, and this again increases the revenue and thereby the land values. Although it does not bring the owners to the establishment of capitalist estates, it does force them nevertheless, to attack their argicultural problems in a capitalist spirit which, by destroying the ancient forms of feudal agriculture, indirectly paves the way for the general capitalist development (as I endeavored to show in my *Modern Capitalism*).

Most of the technical and economic adjustments in European agriculture even into the nineteenth century were brought about by the increased desire for luxuries on the part of the well-to-do. Next to this influence of the demand for luxury upon agriculture, the influence of the mass demand (i.e., for grain) is undoubtedly of secondary importance. As indicated in the second volume of these studies, mass demand assumed revolutionary proportions in only one instance, namely, when the armies after the sixteenth century suddenly came forward with vast requirements. Otherwise, the grain production for the gradually increasing urban population was undoubtedly carried on within the framework of the feudal agriculture of the Middle Ages. Should exception be taken to my premise, and the supposition be made that the immense grain consumption of large cities like London, Paris, Amsterdam, Milan, and Venice constituted the stimulus to agriculture, I would reply that these cities, taken as a whole, represent an outgrowth of luxury. But I believe that arguments are not needed to show that the changes which agriculture experienced up until the eighteenth century are directly or indirectly to be attributed to luxury.

As a result of the rapid rise of the Italian towns toward the end of the Middle Ages, agriculture nearly everywhere in Italy assumed modern aspects: "Abundance of capital made it possible for the country fully to develop irrigation, drain swamps, and cultivate soil, as well as make other improvements. The wealth distributed among all classes of the population helped to increase and improve agricultural products. The prosperity of the textile business opened the way for a considerable expansion in the cultivation of various kinds of plants used in industry. . . ." These are the conclusions of one of the foremost authorities on the history of Italian agriculture.[38] His study of the muncipal laws, most of which contained sections dealing with agricultural matters, clearly reveals the capitalist spirit hovering over the acres and vineyards of the Italy of that time. These laws aim to protect property rights against the fraud and laziness of tenants or coloni, to enlarge the institution of field guards *(saltari)*, and to punish those who steal produce from the fields, etc.

Phenomena similar to those taking place in Italian agriculture can already be observed during the Middle Ages in Belgium, and –naturally–here and there in Germany, France, and England. Still, the effect of the urban capitalist development in these countries was not of sufficient force or duration to bring about a reformation of agrarian conditions as early as the Middle Ages.

In Spain, on the contrary, we may say that the only time when capitalist agriculture flourished was during the sixteenth century; it was brought about by a rapid and intensive increase in demand, particularly on the part of the conquistadores who had suddenly acquired wealth and also on the part of the merchants and financiers of the Spanish cities. Wine growing in southern Spain had assumed vast proportions. Cadiz and Seville alone exported 140,000 hundredweight of wine to America. "It was at this time that the gentlemen merchants of Seville thought of raising the fortunes of their establishments to even greater heights by taking into their own hands the cultivation of the articles in greatest demand. With the vast capital at their disposal, they had only to will, and, as if by magic, the Guadalquivir Valley as far as the

Sierra Morena was covered with fields of waving grain, with luxurious orchards, olive groves, and vineyards, the fruits of which would fill whole ships."[39]

The Cortes complained in the sixteenth century that the cultivation of the vine, being more profitable, was undermining the cultivation of grain. An attempt was made therefore, to prevent vineyards from encroaching upon grain acreage.[40]

The relationship between the "improvement in agriculture" and the increased demand for luxury articles can be clearly discerned in England during the seventeenth century and, more particularly, during the eighteenth century. Here what revolutionized agriculture was assuredly the growing importance of London as a center for the consumption of luxury goods. It is in England that we find the beginnings of modern, scientific agriculture, a natural phenomenon due to the peculiar position of London which was comparable to that of ancient Rome as described by Columella and his associates.

Speaking of rural England during the last quarter of the eighteenth century, writers like Arthur Young,[41] the editors of the eighth edition of Defoe in 1788,[42] and even as late an author as Eden,[43] still leave the impression that agriculture in England, as far as it developed along new lines, was governed exclusively by London. In the county reports (submitted at the direction of the Board of Trade toward the close of the eighteenth century), the capital was depicted likewise as the central sun, from which all the provinces received their light. Production for London inevitably engenders an agricultural advance; theoretically speaking, fixed spheres of intensity were being established about "the city." The most favored counties, where the "improvements of husbandry" are particularly praised, are the counties of Essex ("the whole face of the country like a garden"),[44] Sussex,[45] Kent,[46] Surrey,[47] Hertford,[48] Norfolk,[49] and Suffolk.[50] If a traveler encounters intensive agricultural activity at some distance from London, he is astounded to find it "so far from London."[51] Conversely, he is irritated when he finds areas in the vicinity of London where agriculture is conducted along old-fashioned and extensive lines without any attempt to profit by the advantageous location.[52]

Beginning at the periphery of London, the prices of most

agricultural products increase as one approaches the city.[53] The inhabitants of the provinces attribute the high cost of living there to the turnpike roads.[54] They say that expenses were increased by the roads which radiate from London and spread over the entire countryside,[55] or that the Londoners snapped away from them the best food products and left them second choice.[56]

But if we ask why London was able to exert such a decisive influence upon the price scale for agricultural products and, hence, upon the development of agricultural methods, the answer must be that, strictly speaking, it was not due to the revolutionizing effect of an increased population, because, after all, this population was not very large during the eighteenth century. If we accept the calculations of Petty and King, London around 1680 already boasted a population of approximately 700,000,[57] a figure which scarcely increased during the next hundred years.[58] In 1801, following a few decades which witnessed an unusual influx, the population mounted to 864,845. The appreciable increase in the demand for agricultural produce must rather be attributed to a refinement in taste on the part of the well-to-do. We arrive at the same conclusion if we examine the fluctuation in price of the various agricultural products during the eighteenth century; we find that there was no tendency to increase the price of grain in England, at least during the first half of the century, while in most of the other products, especially in meat, there is an advance.[59] And this hypothesis is thoroughly substantiated by the facts known to us concerning the growth of consumption itself. Above all, meat consumption in London must have been not only quite formidable during the eighteenth century, but it must have actually increased during that time. Even though too much importance is not to be attached to the figures submitted by Eden—for example,[60] he estimates the consumption of meat (excluding pork and veal) at approximately ninety pounds per capita toward the close of the century; that is to say, a level in no way reached by all capital cities even today, a level, furthermore, which in sixty years would have increased by fifty percent per capita if we assume a population increase of 100,000. Nevertheless, there was undoubtedly an extraordinarily large meat consumption. An apt illustration is the famous Smithfield cattle market,[61] the largest in the world, held twice a week, also the equally famous meat-market of Leaden Hall, where, according to a Spanish envoy,[62] enough meat was sold in one month to supply all of Spain for an entire year.

"Great meat markets for all sorts of fine meats," where fowl and game were sold also, are supposed to have existed in London during the middle of the eighteenth century "beside many street butchers" to serve families[63] more removed from a market.

Further proof is given us in the reports dealing with the extensive and in some respects, already highly developed English cattle-raising during the eighteenth century. All these accounts agree that opening up land to pasturage for the purpose of intensive cattle-raising contributed decisively to the advancement of agriculture, in Kent as well as in Norfolk, Essex, and Somersetshire. In many cases a far-reaching differentiation had already taken place as a matter of course between sheep-raising and cattle-raising but also with wider application in that the mountainsides like Devonshire took over cattle-raising proper and left the feeding to farmers of the fertile lowlands, like Somersetshire.[64]

The rapid perfecting of cattle-raising resulted in the amazing increase in the average weight of the individual head of cattle. At the Smithfield cattle market these weights were as follows:

Year	Pounds			
	Oxen	Calves	Sheep	Lambs
1710	370	50	28	18
1795	800	148	80	50

This same tendency toward specialization which allows us to draw conclusions concerning the refinement in consumption as well as the high technique of agricultural production can be observed likewise in relation to the other agricultural products. Reading the rural descriptions by Defoe, one is reminded vividly of similar descriptions by Roman writers on agriculture. Defoe speaks of sections specializing in beverages made of corn (barley or malt, respectively),[65] while others produce the hops needed in the making of these beverages.[66] Here it is oats;[67] there, potatoes[68] which form the principal produce. The best fowl comes from Dorking (Surrey),[69] the best cheese from Oxfordshire and Gloucestershire,[70] the best bacon from Wiltshire and Hamshire;[71] the regions along the Thames are the acknowledged producers of wood,[72] while in the immediate vicinity of London garden vegetables are grown.

The kitchen gardens extend as far as Gravesend, where the best asparagus is cultivated.[73]

2. In the Colonies

The increased demand for luxury goods had a totally different effect upon agriculture in the colonies: here it was directly responsible for the creation of large-scale capitalistic enterprises, perhaps the first of their kind.

To begin with, we have learned, by examining the type of merchandise which represented the colonial trade, that nearly all the European colonies were engaged in the production of high-class luxury articles since the materials themselves were largely produced in colonial agriculture. The articles which chiefly concern us at this time are: sugar, cocoa, cotton (a luxury article until the middle of the eighteenth century), and coffee, all of which were produced in the American colonies; also spices, the principal product of the East Indian colonies. Tobacco (with the exception of the finer grades) is excluded since it was consumed likewise by the lower classes. "In the colonies everyone works for the luxury trade," as one author correctly remarked at the beginning of the eighteenth century.[74]

Except for spice colonies of the Netherlands, where the natives were used in a system of forced production, the colonies of Europe produced all the enumerated luxury goods on large plantations run along entirely capitalistic lines. It has been said, perhaps justly, that here, far removed from the traditions of European culture, the first purely capitalistic structures came into being. Of course, the conception of capitalism must then be taken in a wider sense; we also must include in the category of capitalistic enterprises the organization founded upon forced labor, at least if this forced labor is performed by slaves who have been bought. After all, it is well known that business in the colonies of Europe was based upon slavery. But all the other requisites of a capitalistic enterprise were most certainly in evidence: the profit motive, economic rationalism, great size, the social distinction between producer and worker. Knapp reminds us that emergence of a class of manual laborers, who are that and nothing more, can be witnessed in the institution of Negro slavery "in all its nakedness and blackness."

During the Middle Ages a capitalistic character already was displayed by the colonial plantations of the Italian cities in the Aegean Sea. The fertile islands (Crete, Chios, Cyprus) yielded wine, cotton, indigo, gum mastic, olives, mulberry trees, figs, gum opium, colocynth, carobs, and, principally, sugar. For example, in the Limassol region the patrician Cornaro family owned an extensive sugar plantation which Ghistele termed the staple of the entire island of Cyprus. When the Italian Casola traveled through this region in 1494, the plantation employed four hundred persons.

In the American colonies everything began to run on a gigantic scale, and after a short period red slaves gave place to black slaves.

J. E. Cairnes, one of the best theorists on the subject of slavery, has stated the reasons why Negro slavery and large-scale production have always gone hand in hand. This is a system consistently encountered in the English West Indian colonies, in Cuba, in Brazil, and in the southern states of North America; Henry Clay tells us how the rich planters bought out their poorer neighbors, expanded their own plantations, and increased the number of their slaves. The few wealthy owners able to maintain themselves on the basis of a small margin of profit and to allow their burnt fields to lie for a time uncultivated, thus, are driving away the many independent owners.[75] The figures we have on the expansion of individual plantations confirm these general statements.

According to Labat, who was a keen observer, a plantation in the French Antilles around the year 1700 was estimated at 350,000 to 400,000 francs.[76] Alexander von Humboldt describes[77] a sugar plantation of 650 hectares of land, which employed three hundred Negroes and cost 2,000,000 francs. Another plantation with two hundred slaves is valued at 35,000 pounds.[78] In 1791 there were 792 plantations in French Haiti; 341 of this number were valued at 180,000 francs each, while the individual price of the remaining 451 amounted to 230,000 francs. These plantations exported a minimum of 75,000,000 kilos of sugar, amounting to more than 100,000,000 francs per year. The entire island was in the hands of a small number of plantation owners then called *les gros habitants;* they formed a solid group that dominated the island.[79]

The best way to obtain a clear picture of the expansion as well as of the collective importance of the plantations, is to ascertain the number of slaves employed on them. This information is not difficult to secure as there are fairly accurate statistics on the slave population, at least for the nineteenth century and, in part, even for the eighteenth century. The use of slaves in forced labor reached its high point only shortly before the abolition of slavery, when the production of luxury goods no longer constituted the principal output of the plantations and when the cotton slaves were already engaged in the manufacture of stuffs for European consumption. But the necessary deductions can easily be made.

In 1778 there were 663,899 Negro slaves[80] in the English West Indian colonies.

In some colonies, for which we have more accurate figures,[81] it can be shown that the development of slavery proceeded as follows (I am quoting the first authentic figure as well as that denoting the high point):

	Year	Slaves
Martinique	1700	14,566
	1831	86,299
Guadaloupe	1700	6,725
	1831	99,039
French Guiana	1695	1,047
	1831	19,102
Bourbon	1776	26,175
	1834	70,425
Jamaica	1658	1,400
	1817	343,145
Barbados	1822	69,870
	1829	81,500
Antigua	1774	37,808 (high point)
Mauritius	1776	25,154
	1826	63,432
Cuba	1774	44,333
	1827	286,942
Puerto Rico	1778	6,530
	1836	41,818

Around 1830 the total number of slaves in all slave trading countries amounted to 6,822,759.

That the pretty little damsels of Paris and London were able to mobilize this vast black army to satisfy their whims is an intriging thought.

iv. *Luxury and Industry*

1. The Importance of Luxury Industries

It is within the field of industrial production that the influence of luxury is most clearly noticeable; here the most obtuse mind will be able to grasp the relationship between the development of the demand for luxury goods and the development of capitalism.

If we are able to determine, merely on the basis of the most superficial experience, that numerous industries were created in order to meet the demand for luxury goods, in other words, that many industries had to be called "luxury industries," it is impossible, upon closer scrutiny, to evade the question as to whether the concept of the luxury industry is not a very nebulous one and whether it is not of primary importance to work out a practical definition of that concept.

It will be said that luxury industries are those engaged in the manufacture of luxury goods: costly garments, elegant furnishings, jewelry, etc. But on second thought, what are luxury goods? As examples we can undoubtedly cite the goods just mentioned which have the common characteristic of answering directly the demand for luxury and which may be designated as custom-made, consumption goods of primary rank. Consequently, the enterprises manufacturing these goods may, without hesitation, be considered luxury industries. But must we not likewise regard as luxury industries the mills engaged in the weaving of brocades and velvets? And yet, such a mill does not directly manufacture individual consumption goods, but the means of producing them, for instance, the material for clothes, in other words goods of secondary rank. But if silk-weaving is a luxury industry (and to say otherwise is to do violence to the accepted meaning of the term—to separate the inseparable), is it not logical to call a silkmill also a luxury industry since it manufactures the raw material for silk fabrics—luxury articles of tertiary rank, as it were.

But are we to apply the term "luxury article" to the loom used for the silk-weaving and "luxury industry" to the manufacture of silk looms? Or does the picture change as soon as one deals with the instruments of labor? Is the sawmill to be called a luxury industry because it serves cabinet manufacturing by cutting the wood, i.e., secondary goods in the cabinet-making process? I do not think so. I believe that the name luxury industry should not be applied to the iron foundry which produced the iron pipes for the fountains of Versailles, although the pipes were a distinct necessity in the construction of this munificent display of luxury.

Naturally, there is some connection between this type of industry and the development of luxury, and if we wish to appraise the significance of this cultural phenomenon with all its implications, we must likewise take into consideration these spheres of influence. After all, if there were no luxury, there would be none of these industries which participate more or less directly in meeting the demand for luxury goods. A very large proportion of the early capitalistic industries, then, was brought into being in a roundabout way through luxury. At times this route was extremely circuitous. Since the glass industry as well as other luxury industries had exhausted the supply of timber, coal came to be more and more in demand for fuel purposes, and this demand increased in direct proportion to the number of people who settled in the large cities which owed their existence to luxury. In this manner one of the greatest industries of the epoch of early capitalism sprang up: the coal industry of Newcastle.

But when I speak of how luxury transformed industrial production, I do not refer to the industries brought about indirectly by luxury. I have in mind rather the luxury industry in its primary sense, which, I feel, divorces itself clearly from the other industries in order to form a category all its own. But it is impossible to restrict the concept of—let us say—direct, true luxury industry to perhaps those industries which manufacture primary-rank, luxury goods because, as we have pointed out above, this would mean the exclusion of "luxury industries," unquestionably recognized as such: brocade-weaving and gold lace-making. In my opinion it is the nature of the manufactured article which essentially determines the concept of the luxury industry. Whether or not this article is of high value decides whether or not the industry in which it was produced is a luxury industry. A silk-mill, therefore, although it manufactures luxury goods of tertiary rank, is a luxury industry, while a sawmill, delivering a luxury article of secondary rank, cannot lay claim to this title. If luxury is responsible for bringing about capitalism in industries manufacturing low-priced goods, i.e., goods of low intrinsic value, it is selling always in volume which has made capitalism possible—but, of course, these volume sales take place by the grace of luxury.

We are interested here only in the true luxury industries. But even if we consider these industries alone, we find that the sphere of influence of luxury and its significance for the development of the capitalistic industrial system are enormous. Unfortunately, we may never visualize quantitatively this significance, nor shall we ever be able to determine in figures the part which luxury has played in the transition from industrial production to the capitalistic organization. Even today, with our highly developed occupational and industrial statistics, this would be an impossible task. The reason lies in the fact that the various categories of the luxury industry, or even of the quality industry, are never appraised on the basis of figures or size. We find the classification "cloth-weaving," but no statistics tell us whether fine or coarse cloth is involved; and this is one of many instances. Therefore, whenever we possess figures dealing with the entire range of individual industries, it is impossible for us to ascertain the volume of the luxury goods produced by these industrial fields. On the other hand, in dealing with pure luxury industries we are able to compile estimates such as the manufacturing of Gobelins, gold lace, jewelry, etc. In contradistinction to these "pure" luxury industries, we can apply the term "mixed" industries to all those engaged in the production of coarse as well as luxury goods.

Consequently, if it is impossible even today to determine the percentage of industrial workers engaged in luxury industries, in Germany, for example, how much less possible would it be to obtain similar figures for the past centuries, concerning which no general industrial statistics of any sort are available.

If, nevertheless, we wish to estimate the part that the luxury demand played in the development of industrial capitalism, we must proceed, as in all similar cases, in a roundabout way along monographic-inductive lines. Above all, we must discover the basic characteristics which mark these recognized and acknowledged manifestations of industrial life as capitalistic luxury industries. We shall then be able to prove something like the following: (1) that some luxury industries have undergone a great, in fact, a radical expansion, the significance of which we are able to grasp by way of several examples; (2) that pure luxury industries become an early prey to capitalism; (3) that, within the scope of distinct industrial groups, those industrial branches which produce luxury goods are seized upon by capitalism sooner than others; (4) and that the organizations of full capitalism and of large-scale industrialism are first developed in luxury industries.

For the sake of greater clarity, we shall discuss separately the pure luxury industries and the mixed industries.

2. The Pure Luxury Industries

a) The Silk Industry. Even our "historians" know that the silk industry assumed a role of overwhelming importance in the industrial life of the European nations during early capitalism; in other words, it is a well-established historical fact, not requiring lengthy proof. There are two figures which will illuminate the picture at this point: during the period from 1770 to 1784, according to statistics in the *Encyclopédie méthodique*, the value of the silk production of Lyon amounted to approximately 60,000,000 francs a year. The value of all imports into France from 1779 to 1781 amounted to approximately 208,216,269 francs, while the exports are estimated at 235,236,260 francs. Consequently, the total value of the export trade is 443,452,529 francs. Thus, the value of silk goods produced in Lyon alone represented between one-eighth and one-seventh of this total. Since the value of goods passing the German border in 1911 amounted to 19,161,000,000 marks, the above-named production figure of 60,000,000 francs would have corresponded to 2,400,000,000 to 2,700,000,000 marks before the war. As a comparison we might cite the following figures: according to the production figures of the German Ministry of the Interior, the total value of pig iron produced in Germany in 1908 amounted to 657,152,000 marks, of cotton yarn, to 644,-464,000 marks; and of coal extracted (in 1910), to 1,535,258,000 marks. Thus, the pig iron, cotton yarn, and coal combined would be as important to the economic picture of a modern nation as the silk industry of Lyon was to the national economy of France during the eighteenth century. It must also be remembered that, 130 years ago, export played a comparatively larger role in the industrial life of a nation than it does today. Silk goods produced in Berlin amounted to 3,000,000 to 4,000,000 thalers at the time when the total value of all products manufactured in Berlin was approximately 6,000,000 thalers (in 1783: 6,098,226 thalers, according to Nicolai).

What interests us here is the fact that this standard industry was one of the first to submit to capitalistic organization at that time, so that we may well look upon it as having set a milestone in the history of industrial capitalism. As a matter of fact, for all forms of capitalism the silk industry at a very early period offers characteristic examples. It constitutes perhaps the first medium for for the development of home industries; for the first time it also shows us manufacturing and the factory in perfect form; the silk-mills of the fourteenth century, we may say, are the cradle of society's large-scale enterprises.

It is impossible to determine how the extensive silk industry was conducted in the Levantine colonies by the Italians, principally the Genoese and the Venetians. Slavery or serfdom probably was the basis of their industrial system.

In European countries, on the other hand, the capitalistic silk industry (both spinning and weaving) is usually first launched in the form of home industry and at a very early time.

The statutes of March 27, 1324, tell us that in Paris, as early as the beginning of the fourteenth century, the women engaged in silk-spinning and twining (the *filaresses*, as they were called) assumed the position of hired workers in relation to their employers, the mercers, who bought the raw silk and sold it again for sewing, embroidering, or weaving, after it had been spun, twined, and finished.[82] We find that as early as the fourteenth century the silk industry of Venice[83] is already organized as the output system, and during the fifteenth century the same condition prevails in Genoa (statutes of 1432)[84] and the remaining centers of the Italian silk industry, such as Lucca, Florence, and Milan. When silk manufacturing was established in Lyon during the sixteenth century, it likewise began as a home industry; the first statute of 1554 already contains provisions concerning the tampering with raw materials,[85] and the edict of January 28, 1554, speaks of men "who put out work and conduct their business without themselves sitting the whole day before their looms."[86] We know that, subsequently, the home production of silk became also the standard system of other countries.

But in addition to the jobbing system, the silk industry very soon developed the compact and large-scale social enterprise in the form of manufacturing or (principally) the factory. Indeed, it is quite possible that the first concrete example of a factory founded on a capitalistic basis during the Middle Ages was in the field of silk manufacturing. Of course, a great deal of caution must be used in interpreting the reports of the early centuries, concerning industrial enterprises. As a rule, when these reports speak of manufacturing or even factories, they do not mean the form of organization but the industry as such. Even when a definite person is referred to as having established a silk factory employing five hundred workers, one still does not know whether it is a large-scale industrial organization or a system of home industry.

In any case, we definitely can prove the existence of large-scale industrial enterprises in the silk industry during the earliest times; however, as far as silk-weaving is concerned, this would not apply before the sixteenth century. To my knowledge, the earliest silk-weaving enterprise was that of Raoulet Viard, one of the founders of the Lyonese silk industry, who set up forty-six looms in one house. Large-scale production, with the immediate establishment of factories, occurred much earlier in the silk-spinning industry. Alidosi tells us that silkmills boasting 4000 spindles and driven by water power were in existence as early as the first half of the fourteenth century. He states that on June 23, 1341, a permit is said to have been issued to one Bolognino di Barghesano from Luca for the establishment of such a mechanically operated mill, where "one single machine performs the work of four thousand spinners." We give here the text of this important account:

> There are (certain) great machines, which, moved by the waters of the Reno, swiftly spin and throw 4000 threads of silk, performing in an instant the work of 4000 spinners. The

water makes the silk durable and beautiful. They produce 180,000 pounds of silk every year, that is to say, 100,000 pounds of foreign and 80,000 pounds of our own, with double thread silk, of which there is an abundance. The oldest record that I have found of this is that of June 3, 1341, that the city granted a license to Bolognino di Barghesano da Luca, living in Bologna, in the quarter of Santa Lucia, to construct a silk-mill in the quarter of San Biagio above the moat near the walls of the city. And in 1345 it was decreed that Giovanni Oreto of the quarter of San Colombano could have water for a silk mill in the suburb Polecino.[87]

For the year 1371 Alidosi lists (on page 38) thirteen silk-spinning mills which belong to the community and are leased to entrepreneurs.

This silk-spindle and silk-twisting machine of Bologna was famous. J. J. Becher[88] states that "in Bologna, Italy, they have invented a spinning machine which unwinds as well as throws the silk. But this instrument is very large, expensive, and cumbersome. It has thousands of parts, cogs, and wheels, wherefore it is frequently out of order. The Italians hold it in such esteem and secrecy that to display it to anyone is punishable by hanging. In Munich I have seen an imitation of this Italian-made machine, but, by reason of its great cost and its many parts, I did not value it very highly."

On the basis of the foregoing account it is doubtful whether this big, silk-spinning machine was utilized at all outside of Italy. Possibly the organization of the silk-spinning industry on a large-scale basis in other countries did not take place until the seventeenth century, when the invention of the above-mentioned Johann Joachim Becher was applied practically. Becher tells us that his machine was put to use in a factory which had been built for this purpose by the city of Harlem. The factory was 300 feet long and was erected at a cost of 40,000 guldens. In 1676 Becher went to the Netherlands. At the beginning of the year we hear of big "silk factories" which were opened at Utrecht and were supposed to have employed five hundred workers; it is most likely that they were silk-spinning mills. Moreover, the invention by Becher signified a return from producing goods by power-driven machines to production by hand-operated machines because his "machine was not subjected to break-downs and could be easily operated, so that one worker could unwind a thousand strands at a time, whereas the machine at Bologna had to rely upon water power."

In short, large-scale silk-spinning enterprises have been in existence since the fourteenth century in Italy, certainly also since the seventeenth century in the northern countries. In England these enterprises were called "silkmills." Were they driven, therefore, by water power? During his travels Defoe[89] encounters in Sheffield a silkmill of this kind copied after the one in Stockport; it was five stories high, ninety yards long, and employed two hundred workers.

b) The Lace Industry. This luxury industry has been of great importance for certain countries and regions. In 1669, 17,300 male and female workers were engaged[90] in the lace industry in France. During the eighteenth century, in the kingdom of Saxony, entire communities supported themselves by lace-making. It is fortunate for us that the county administrator, C. L. Ziegler of Hanover, traveled from Chemnitz to Zwönitz on June 18, 1775, to ascend the Schneeberg and that he wrote an account of the journey[91] to his friend, Johann Beckmann, professor of economics at Göttingen. From this letter we learn of the lace-making industry in the Erzgebirge. We know that in each house "there were as many lace-making cushions on the table as there were women in the house." Five-year-old children, we are told, "already begin to make lace with the aid of two bobbins, and the toy of a three-year-old girl is a lace-making cushion with four bobbins."

Although during the eighteenth century these laces probably no longer constituted a luxury article available solely to the well-to-do, the fact remains that the delicate, handmade laces, which had been produced in Brabant as well as in France since the time of Colbert, could be sold only to the higher strata of society.

The organization in all instances was the same: the lace-workers were engaged by merchants who were called *Spitzenherren* in the Erzgebirge; at times (as in France) they had under their direction women contractors, who, in turn, employed four or five workers.

The lace industry developed very unique forms of industrial organization, such as I have never known to exist in any other industry. In France, regular boardinghouses were established where the workers lived, ate, and undoubtedly also received instruction. A series of expense accounts give us information concerning such boarding establishments.[92]

In 1699 a certain Clément de Gouffreville submitted estimates for a *Manufacture de dentelles* to be erected in St. Denis:

	Livres
Thread, annually	6,000
20 Beds for the teachers	1,000
200 Beds for the apprentices and workers	6,000
400 Sets of linen for the afore-going	1,600
40 Sets of linen for the beds of the teachers	400
Table service	500
Table linen	500
Salary of teachers at 200 livres each	4,000
Board for the apprentices at 100 livres each	20,000

c) Mirror manufacture is conducted entirely on a large-scale capitalistic basis. In France in the year 1704 two enterprises were competing with each other: the firm of Dombes in Tour la Ville and the firm of St. Gobain in Paris. The latter had been acquired two years previously by Antoine Dagincourt, a rich Parisian, for the sum of 990,000 livres.[93] The mirror-manufacturing plant in the Faubourg St. Antoine employed five hundred workers. Mercier describes the furnishing of this establishment where four hundred workers were engaged in one grindery.[94]

d) The porcelain industry is the outstanding luxury industry of the eighteenth century. Porcelain factories, more or less under control of the state, were established in the following cities: Meissen, 1709; Vienna, 1718; Höchst, 1720; Vincennes, 1740; Sèvres, since 1756; Capo di Monte, near Naples, 1743; Fürstenberg, 1744; Berlin, 1750; Frankenthal, 1755; Nymphenburg and Ludwigsburg, 1758; Copenhagen, 1772. In addition, however, private establishments abounded.[95] The porcelain manufactories soon grew into large-scope enterprises; at that time only a few of this type were known.

In 1798 the Berlin porcelain factory already employed four

hundred workers.[96] The personnel of the Meissen plant grew as follows: 26 in 1719, 49 in 1730, 218 in 1740, 337 in 1745, and 378 in 1750.[97]

e) Other Industries. To present an account as detailed as the foregoing of the other luxury industries would be to little purpose. The reader would be bored, because the picture is always the same. Not a single true luxury industry is known to me which did not later in the course of the eighteenth assume capitalistic and, frequently, also large-scale form, if it had not originally been established along these lines. There are many examples:

The glass industry (since Murano) and the sugar industry. In the eighteenth century, Cambden demanded from £1000 to £5000 capital to establish a confectionary store in London.

The goldsmith industry as well as other work in gold. François Thomas Germain, the famous goldsmith, who succeeded his father in the Louvre in 1748, had a business with liabilities of 2,400,000 francs; the minimum capital required of London goldsmiths was £500 to £3000; in Berlin the largest enterprises of the eighteenth century were the business of those gold and silversmiths who manufactured laces, sashes, tassels, etc.; they employed 813 workers in 1784, 1013 in 1799, and 1151 in 1801.

The embroidery industry. In Berlin in 1744, a Frenchman erected a factory which employed seventy-seven workers and produced many "articles of silk and rich materials for men's and women's wear." The manufacture of artificial flowers: in 1776 the first factory of this type was opened in Berlin; in 1784 it produced goods to the value of 24,000 thalers and employed 140 women.

3. Mixed Industries

Most of all, luxury industries, as we have seen, are dominated by capitalism and, frequently, also by large-scale enterprises which, in these cases examined, had developed side by side with the old handicraft system. But in order to determine the close connection between luxury industries and capitalism and to gauge the importance of the increased demand for luxury goods in the growth of capitalism, we must review those luxury industries which have sprung up within the framework of the old handicrafts and acquired a distinct and separate character. We notice, from the standpoint of economic history, it is the most important realization brought home to us—that branches of handicraft yielding to capitalistic organization always supply demands for luxury goods. In other words, even during early capitalism, most handicrafts underwent a process of differentiation; artistic work of high quality became distinct from the ordinary, rough work produced by craftsmen and created enterprises of its own. Whereas these businesses assumed a capitalistic aspect, the rough work continued to be produced by craftsmen until finally, in our own times, capitalistic organization has extended its dominance over this field. Even contemporaries realized this contrast, as a beautiful and characteristic passage in Mercier clearly reveals:

> Artisans appear to be the happiest of people. Using their industry and skill, they keep in their place, and this is wise and very rare indeed. They are neither ambitious nor vain. They work only for their upkeep and entertainment. They are civil and courteous towards every one because they are dependent upon all classes. The life of the artisan is well ordered. It might be said that, having dedicated themselves to occupations more useful than the luxury arts, they are recompensed by a peaceful conscience and a tranquil life. A carpenter has an air of uprightness that a minature painter does not possess.[98]

We apply the term "mixed" to these industries because, as contrasted with the pure luxury industries, they answer the demand for luxury as well as for coarse goods. Again it is unnecessary to make a complete survey of all the industries in question. The most important ones will suffice to prove the correctness of my trend of thought.

a) The Wool Industry. It goes without saying that, next to the silk industry, the wool industry was the most important during the early period of capitalism. Naturally, the wool industry produced fabrics for the poor and rich alike. But whenever we encounter a "flourishing wool industry," the pride of a country and of its cities and responsible for their wealth, it is always an industry engaged in the production of rich and costly fabrics. It is a "luxury industry," which at a very early stage was organized on a capitalistic or even on a large-scale industrial basis (until army contracts brought into being a large-size, capitalistic, weaving industry producing in bulk). In other words, to the extent that the wool industry participates in the development of modern capitalism, it represents a luxury industry.

The Florentine wool industry perhaps constitutes the earliest large-scale industry organized strictly on a capitalistic basis. That the splendor and the might of Florence were rooted in the wool and the silk industries, insofar as the latter did not rest on purely financial transactions, is common knowledge. The excellent investigations of Alfred Doren[99] have established clearly that these industries were founded on a capitalistic basis as early as the thirteenth century. Even the first statute of the Calimala guild of the year 1300 reveals that home industry was firmly established.

But this home industry was undoubtedly also a luxury industry in the narrow sense of the word. The history of the Calimala guild (which, as we know, involved a refining process) is obscure. One thing is certain: The Florentine trade did not reach its height until it had become possible, through the application of a series of refining processes (dyeing and finishing), so to improve the coarse, northern fabric that it would meet the most exacting whims of the rising Oriental and Occidental luxury trade. The demands and requirements of the Mohammedan world had become known; the extremely fine fabrics of the sultanate of Algarve had been imported. In this manner the secrets of that technically superior production of luxury articles gradually penetrated, and we learned to give to the coarse fabric of the northern countries the fine blend and the lustrous colors, which from that time on began to distinguish the Florentine product from all others.[100] "In Florence," wrote Goro Dati during the middle of the fifteenth century, "they know how to make smoother and finer fabrics than elsewhere." Because, then, of the quality of its output, the Florentine wool industry as a whole rose above that of other countries and cities. In Florence itself a distinction was made between coarse and fine fabrics, since naturally in the output of the entire industry there were bound to be inferior products also. During the fourteenth century even a local division existed between the low grade and the fine materials; this is found in the contrast between the quarters of Garbo and San Martino. It is particularly interesting to observe that the Garbo quarter, where the coarse bulk merchandise was manufactured, was the place where the small master craftsmen, organized in guilds, lived, while in the San Martino quarter, where the luxury industry proper was located, capitalistic business had the upper hand. At least, that is the conclusion which I draw from the continuous quarrels between the Garbo and the San Martino quarters.[101]

We know very little about the Spanish wool industry. According to conventional reports, it "flourished" during the sixteenth century. Nevertheless, we know enough about it to say that (1) it was a luxury industry (to the extent that it did "flourish") and (2) it was organized along capitalistic lines (as far as it was engaged in the production of luxury goods). Guicciardini tells us no more than this:

> Today they have begun in some places to pay attention to the making of woolens, and in some parts of Spain they are already producing woolens, brocades and cloth of gold in great quantity, as in Valencia, Toledo, and Seville.[102]

In a sixteenth century report describing a procession in Segovia we find the following instructive passage:

> In the second group were the wool and the cloth manufacturers, whom the people erroneously call merchants. Actually, they are like fathers of families, who in and outside their houses employ a great number of people; some as many as two hundred, others as many as three hundred. By means of hired labor they manufacture vast quantities of the finest cloth....[103]

In France, during the seventeenth century, fine cloths were woven chiefly at Rouen, Sédan, Elbœuf, and Reims.[104] But it is here also that capitalistic organization developed to an unusual degree as early as the seventeenth and eighteenth centuries. Of course, the home manufacturing system at Sédan attained only moderate proportions: of four privileged *entrepreneurs de fabrique*, two used 104 looms each; another, 65; and another, 50 looms. Of twenty-one nonprivileged operators, forty looms were used by one; over thirty were used by each of four others, etc.[105] I have in mind, however, the establishments of the brothers Van Robais, which represent large-scale plants of considerable size.

Accurate statistical information[106] permits us to determine even the most minute details regarding the organization of these enterprises. We see that there are twenty-two separate processes before the wool is turned into a finished product. We find no less than 1692 workers engaged in one establishment; of these, 822 are wheelspinners and two hundred are weavers, working at one hundred looms. In addition to this luxury industry there was an extensive wool-weaving craft, engaged in the production of ordinary goods.

The English wool industry was the most famous of the eighteenth century. In popular language, "wool is eminently the foundation of the English riches."[107] In 1738 a million and a half people were engaged in the English wool industry. This figure is, of course, wrong. Nevertheless, in 1700, exported woolen articles were worth £3,000,000, while in 1815 their value had mounted to £9,381,426.[108]

Among these woolens there were naturally coarse as well as fine materials. It is understood that the English wool industry was not, in its entirety, a luxury industry. Later, particularly when America became a large consumer of English woolen goods (of the £9,000,000 worth of goods in 1815 more than £4,000,000 were exported to the United States), the coarse materials for the middle class and the masses were probably more abundant. Still, it must be said that this wool industry was also a luxury industry to a very large extent. Throughout the eighteenth century, fine English cloth and fancy English materials were in particular demand by the well-to-do of the entire world. To give only one example, in North Germany, Poland, and Russia in the eighteenth century the upper classes preferred to wear English woolens, "in all which countries the nobility, gentry, and principal burghers are clothed with English cloth, druggets, serges, stuffs, etc., and consume a very great quantity. The great quantity of British goods exported to all these parts and places will be judged by this, that the late czar himself and all his court, with all the chief of his people from St. Petersburg to Moscow and down to Astracan, have entered now, within these few years, into the general use of English manufactures and are all clothed with them to the infinite increase of our trade thither."[109]

The question now arises: Is it possible to trace the difference between the coarse and finer grades of weaving in the English wool industry to different manufacturing methods and economic setups? As far as I am able to determine, this question has not been asked as yet, although it seems to me the most important in a problem of vast range.

If, in view of the foregoing, I venture to answer the question in the affirmative, I do so reservedly. The facts upon which we must base our judgment are as follows: we know that, at the end of the epoch of early capitalism, two different systems of organization existed side by side in the English wool industry: the capitalistic home industry and the handicrafts.[110] The former, known also as the West-English system, predominated in Western England, in the great weaving district of the East (in Norfolk, etc.), and also in the South. In the Northern part (in Yorkshire), however, the handicrafts continued to hold sway. The North and the other districts are principally known as the regions of carded yarn and of worsted yarn. The very fine cloths, flannels, etc., were fashioned from the worsted yarns. Were the luxury goods, then, manufactured by capitalistic organization and the less valuable and coarse material produced by handicraft?

Attention might also be called to the weaving industry which in the sixteenth century was already organized on a manufacturing basis. In a description of the enterprises of Jack of Newbury,[111] mention was made of "200 looms in a big, long hall." At that time such establishments were by no means a rare occurrence.

It is obvious that the wool industry, with its large-scale organization, was a luxury industry. The goods manufactured by John Winchcombe, "Jack of Newbury," were known throughout Europe. In Western England where capitalism had already taken root, enterprises of this type were found: for instance, the Malmesbury convent in Newbury, which a rich cloth manufacturer by the name of Stump had leased for the purpose of setting up looms; Circencester, where a large-size fulling mill was built; the abbey of Osney near Oxford, which Stump had also intended to lease, are all located in the industrial wool district of Western England. We learn too that, during the sixteenth century, woven goods, previously imported from Italy, were being produced by rich entrepreneurs of Norwich. These were high-grade luxury goods.[112]

b) The Linen Industry appears to me to be entirely problematical. There can be no doubt that in Silesia, Westphalia, and Ireland it was to a large extent a luxury industry. During the eighteenth century it provided the dandies of London with fine shirts at 10 or 12 shillings per yard; it furnished costly batiste and gauzes; it supplied the sumptuous table covers which we still admire today in our museums. But it also supplied wearing apparel in great quantity for the Negro. In Ireland, especially, a great deal of low-priced linen was produced: the linen to which the Linen Board of Ireland awarded a prize in 1747–48 had a fixed value of not less than 6 and not more than 10 shillings per yard.

But I am unable to determine the relationship between the quality of the product and the form of the industry. We know that, at the end of the eighteenth century, handicraft and home industry in the great linen export establishments coexisted. But where was the dividing line between luxury goods and bulk goods? This question merits a doctor's dissertation.

c) The Tailoring Industry. During the eighteenth century certain establishments of the tailoring trade are reorganized as capitalistic undertakings. They cater to the fine trade, namely, the trade able to pay good prices; in other words, they are enterprises manufacturing luxury goods.

Strange to say, in the field of men's tailoring it is the ready-to-wear trade which during the eighteenth century is first reorganized along capitalistic lines. Today there is no longer evidence of this tendency. In the eighteenth century the manufacture of ready-to-wear luxury apparel does not appear to have been in any way taboo. The ready-to-wear luxury trade flourished in England as well as in France. The one reference which proves its existence during the eighteenth century, appears in the *Allgemeine Schatzkammer der Kauffmannschaft* and reads as follows:

> Clothes are today appearing in the open market to an extent greater almost than is warranted by the demand in Germany, with the result that not only is money being sent to France by many German gentlemen for high-grade . . . clothes, but Frenchmen themselves are also sending to our markets whole cases and barrels full of apparel. . . .[113]

The other source is an advertisement inserted by one Darti-galongue among the *Affiches, Annonces et Avis divers* of April 4, 1770:

> M Dartigalongue, master and merchant tailor of Paris, has had for a long time a shop for ready-made clothing of all kinds, in all sizes, and of the latest fashion. By reason of his large staff of workers, Master Dartigalongue can supply almost instantly the needs of those wishing to be promptly served if their taste is not suited by the stock on display. Livery of every sort is furnished at the lowest prices, out-of-town and foreign orders will be filled, but customers writing in are requested to prepay the postage on their letters.

The tenor of the advertisement seems to indicate that it is a question of apparel for the "better" clientele. Undoubtedly, liveries in use at that time also belonged to the category of expensive clothing.

A. Franklin, however, who discovered this advertisement, is wrong in believing[114] that M Dartigalongue is the "first dealer in ready-to-wear apparel," unless he means the "first dealer known by name." We have evidence to show that the ready-to-wear apparel business existed much earlier; even the above-mentioned reference dates back to 1741.

In London, as early as the seventeenth century, we find tailors who sell ready-made apparel in the better sections of the city. The practice must have originated around the middle of the century, that is, probably again during that eventful period when the silk mercers were seen to move about the city "like a drove of swarming bees." In 1681[115] we find a complaint about this innovation: "Many remember when there were no new garments sold in London (in shops) as now they are." The "accustomed tailor," or working craftsman, objected to "taylers being salesmen," paying high rents for shops in fashionable neighborhoods, giving long credit to their aristocratic clients, and each employing in his own workshops dozens or even scores of journeymen (therefore, selling luxury apparel).

But the field in which tailoring on a capitalistic basis could best develop was, nevertheless, (as today) fine custom tailoring.

The description of the business of a custom tailor in London, given us by R. Campbell,[116] would fit equally well any similar establishment of our time: exacting customers who mostly buy on credit; high investments for expensive materials and trimmings, amounting to more than the wages; high-class workmanship in cutting and sewing. "The earnings of the cutter are high, for besides his cabbage he has generally a guinea a week and the drink money given by the gentlemen on whom he waits to fit on their cloaks." Good cutters are in demand. The other tailors are "as numerous as locusts" and commonly "as poor as rats"; being "out of business about three or four months in the year," they lead decidedly proletarian lives. It might be pointed out that the tailors' guild is the first known.[117]

Ladies' dressmaking and millinery were large-scale enterprises of great importance even during the eighteenth century: the frequently mentioned tailoress of Marie Antoinette went bankrupt to the extent of 3,000,000 francs.[118]

d) The Leatherworker. In shoemaking, as in tailoring, fine custom work is the first to arrive at higher forms of organization. In Paris during the eighteenth century we encounter "the shopmaster" (as described by Kanter in speaking of the city of Breslau),[119] who works solely for the fashionable trade: "This shoemaker wears a black coat, a well-powdered wig, and his waistcoat is made of silk; he has the bearing of a public official," and, yet, he personally takes the fit for the shoes of the countess. "His colleagues have pitch on their fingers; they wear damaged wigs and dirty linen; but they work for the common people; they do not fit the small feet of beautiful marchionesses."[120]

The saddler, who is also a luxury harnessmaker, is "a very considerable and useful tradesman." It requires a large stock of ready money to deal considerably, "as the materials he uses are high-priced, and the gentry are no more solicitous about paying their saddler than any other tradesmen."[121] At that period of the eighteenth century the saddler is on the way to becoming a manufacturer; he employs numerous craftsmen who, however, "still work for their own account." Within the French tanning industry at the beginning of the eighteenth century we encounter the "manufacture" of the following kinds of leather, the preparation of which subsequently became a capitalistic enterprise: Hungarian leather, English calf, morocco, buffalo, and chamois.[122]

In the eighteenth century conditions were similar in Berlin.[123] About the middle of the century the manufacture of fine leathers, such as Saffian, Cordovan, and Danish was introduced in Berlin by French immigrants, partly in the form of large-scale enterprises which at times proceeded to add to their activities the preparation of leather ("Danish gloves").

e) Hat-making. "Every man, from king to peasant, needs a hat. This renders the hat-makers indispensable craftsmen for the state. Most hat-makers, particularly in small cities, manufacture only cheap and inferior hats for the lowest classes. Since high personages, state officials as well as the rich and well-to-do, consider such hats beneath their dignity and demand fine hats, it can be seen readily that the latter likewise were manufactured in the country itself. . . ."[124]

As a consequence, "fine hat factories" were first established in the French cities of Paris, Marseilles, Lyon, Rouen, Candébec, etc. As early as the close of the seventeenth century we learn of a famous hat-maker in Rouen who employed nineteen helpers and took twelve of them with him to Rotterdam.[125] Later such factories came into existence in England, where all the cardinals' hats, for example, were manufactured (at 5 to 6 guineas each!). Finally they appeared in Germany, in Erlangen, and in Berlin. In Berlin, up to the close of the eighteenth century, the hat-making business bears the unmistakable stamp of handicraft, which, as far as the manufacture of the lower grades is concerned, was maintained until the middle of the seventeenth century. But in 1782 a hat factory was established, employing thirty-seven workers and producing "hats of excellent quality and fineness" to the value of 21,800 thalers (while the total production of the entire hat-makers' guild, comprising 133 members, amounted to only 45,240 thalers for the same year).[126]

f) The Building Industry. Under the popes of the Renaissance the construction of big palaces and churches was already proceeding along capitalistic lines. For instance, Beltramo di Martino from Varese in Como, a builder under Nicholas V, employed a whole army of workers and owned large brickkilns and limekilns in Rome; his annual bills against the papal treasury amounted to approximately 30,000 ducats. For many overworked contractors it was no longer possible to supervise personally all buildings they had under construction. They appointed a foreman or representative *(soprastante)* to take their place; Filarete estimated in his contract that each group of eighty-five masons required one foreman.[127]

It is not surprising, then, that during the building of the French royal palaces in the seventeenth century we encounter contractors operating with large capital resources. From the construction accounts, whose importance I have already indicated and whose full worth appears only at this point, we are able to determine the number of individual craftsmen who participated in the construction as well as the exact amounts they received for their activities. With the aid of these facts it is then easily possible to ascertain the volume of business contracted for and the development of this business during the course of several years, etc. The picture we get from the building industry in Paris at the close of the seventeenth and the beginning of the eighteenth century is about as follows: masonry and carpentry (always, of course, in connection with gigantic construction projects) are already completely organized on a basis of full capitalism.

In both industries we constantly encounter the same firms, represented usually by two partners and plainly labeled *entrepreneurs du bastiment neuf du Louvre, entrepreneurs des ouvrages de charpenterie du bastiment du Louvre*, etc. In 1664 we find the large contracting firms, Jacques Mazières and Pierre Bergeron, received in one year 861,330 livres; in another, 610,600 livres, during the construction of the Louvre; and in Versailles, for masonry, 200,965 livres. Poncelet Cliquim and Paul Charpentier received between 100,000 and 150,000 francs. To these firms were added a half dozen others during the following years.

Besides these two principal building trades, roofing likewise is in the process of assuming a capitalistic form. In 1664, a certain Ch. Yvon, I find, performed work in the Louvre, in St. Germain, and in Versailles, for which he received 49,900 livres. Of about the same caliber is the firm of Jean Pillart of Claude Fresneau, calling themselves *maistres couvreurs, entrepreneurs des ouvrages de couverture, et plomberie*. (Master roofers, contractors for roofing and plumbing).

The remaining building trades, such as paneling, locksmithing, glazier's work, etc., present the aspect of handicrafts at the beginning of our epoch. It is a situation in which obviously well-to-do masters perform the work with the aid of a half dozen assistants and apprentices, ten or twenty frequently being engaged in the construction of one building, with a total yearly account ranging from a few thousand livres (the top figure is that for panelling), unless we assume that the four carpenters who received 63,000 livres in 1666 and the other four who received 59,000 livres and 16,317 livres, respectively, constituted a single firm. A few locksmiths, on the other hand, particularly in later years, established small capitalistic businesses. It looks almost as if business became "concentrated" from the middle of the seventeenth to the beginning of the eighteenth century (probably under the influence of the strong building activity initiated by the king and his noblemen). In 1715 the bill of a locksmith, by the name of François Cafin, amounted to 51,578 livres; that would indicate an enterprise consisting of at least from twelve to fifteen or more helpers, even if the foregoing amounts covered the only subsisting contracts.

Mercier, in describing the organization of the building industry in Paris at the close of the eighteenth century, shows that the great luxury constructions have aspects of fully developed capitalism.[128] At this point, Mercier does not specifically mention that these construction projects are luxury undertakings, but his earlier reports tell us to what extent the building history of the Paris of that time was dominated by the sumptuous constructions of the rich financiers.

g) During the era of early capitalism, the carpenter's, upholsterer's, and saddler's trades gave up some of their activities and combined to form the carriage-making trade, a new luxury industry conducted along capitalistic lines. At the middle of the eighteenth century coach-making reached the halfway mark on the road to a complete manufacturing system.

The art of coach-making has reached the utmost perfection (in London).[129] The coach-maker's proper business is to make the body of the coach and all the carriage except the wheels; his trade is compounded of the carpenter, the tailor, and the shoemaker; he finishes his work by the assistance of the carver, the wheeler, the foundryman (casting the brasses for the body, etc.), the leather currier, the blacksmith, and the harness-maker.

But even in this half-finished form carriage-making at that time required "a great stock of ready money," which again in no small measure was due to long credit terms extended to the fashionable clientele. As a matter of fact, carriage-builders dealt "with none but nobility and quality" among whom often enough were some who never paid.

Furthermore, the carriage industry in England was just then beginning to expand considerably, "our nobility and gentry even now taking pride in driving themselves."[130] Where a few dozen carriage-makers existed a generation ago (ten or twelve within the citadel and not quite as many in the other parts of London), they now occupy[131] whole streets and have united in a guild.

h) Cabinetmaking has always had a tendency to break down trade barriers as soon as it began to manufacture luxury articles. Therefore, we find very early—for instance during the sixteenth century in Augsburg—that luxury carpentry, which does "elegant work," presents a certain contrast to the "common handcraft." While a master usually was allowed to employ only one or, since 1549, two assistants, a special dispensation was requested[132] in cases where a large "fashionable contract" was to be filled.

During the seventeenth century, luxury cabinetmaking began to take on large-scale industrial forms. At first this industry did not develop within the capitalistic framework but was subsidized by the state. As everyone knows, the *Manufacture royale des Gobelins*, brought to flower by Colbert,[133] may be held up as a model for all artistic furniture manufacture, even to the *Vereinigte Werkstätten* of the present day.

This manufacturing plant produced everything needed in appointing the royal palaces, in other words, not only furniture of ebony, tortoise shell, and variegated woods with carvings and incrustations but also tapestries and carpets, chandeliers and candelabra in bronze and crystal, silver and gold services set with precious stones, etc.

This is not the place to speak of the marvelous products of the Louis XIV period turned out in these workshops by a tremendous staff of workers (in the carpet section alone 250 workers were engaged) under the direction of eminent artists. Lebrun for a long time was its director; Baudonin Yvard, van der Meulen, Bapt. Monnoyer, and others were engaged as painters; the brothers Anguier and Coysevox Tuby as sculptors; Audran, Rousselet, and Leclerc as copper etchers. (Nevertheless, it would be a worthwhile task for men of talent to write the history of the organization of industrial or applied arts). Suffice it to say that here a very great luxury consumption resulted in an industrial revolution of equally great proportions which in turn was bound to be of vast importance in the development of modern capitalism. For, cabinetmaking enterprises were established after the pattern of the *Manufacture royale des Gobelins* whenever there was a centralized demand for luxury furniture. In France, the famous enterprise of Charles Boule probably represents the first example of a finished cabinetmaking factory. Boule, with his four sons, organized the work and manufactured at first only for the royal court but later also for fashionable society outside of the court. He produced furniture of all kinds in bronze and wood, such as clock casings, desks, dressing tables, kitchen cupboards, chandeliers, chests, guéridons, etc. His work was in demand from 1672 to 1732; in 1720 (the time of the South Sea Bubble) the value of the pieces already begun in his work shops (in the Louvre) amounted to 80,000 livres.[134]

The famous English furniture-makers, Sheraton and Chippendale,[135] conducted their business on a very large scale.

During the eighteenth century we find that luxury furniture manufacturing in Germany likewise is organized already along capitalistic and large-scale industrial lines and that this luxury industry is the only one thus organized, because the production of ordinary handmade furniture was carried on well into the nineteenth century. One of the earliest capitalistic cabinetmaking enterprises in Germany is that located at Mayence. This developed as a luxury enterprise in conjunction with the splendor-loving electoral court.[136]

In the same manner numerous other trades grew and expanded.

The lace-makers in Berlin at the close of the eighteenth century present a flourishing trade: 259 masters employ 248 helpers and 170 apprentices. "But the rich work requiring the use of gold and silver thread was given out by the gold and silver industry to be finished as home work by the lace-makers."[137]

Ordinary pomade, during the eighteenth century, is manufactured by the barbers; two factories, on the other hand, produce makeup and "hair-growing pomade."[138]

The soap-makers lived tranquil and content until one fine day luxury soaps were devised. "The factory system begins with the appearance of luxury soaps." During the eighteenth century the field of production was divided sharply between handicraft and capitalistic enterprise; while the former produced ordinary soaps, the latter was engaged in the production of the finer grades, the Marseilles soaps, etc.[139] In 1760 Marseilles itself, a manufacturing center of luxury soap, had thirty-eight soap factories with a total of 170 vats and 1000 workers.[140]

The elegant "soap boiler" in London required an initial capital of from £2000 to £3000.[141]

But—enough of examples. In concluding, it is better for us to ascertain the reasons underlying this largely uniform development of industrial production.

4. The Revolutionizing Force of the Consumption of Luxury Goods

What is the factor which, in advance of technique, has been responsible for the development of trades along capitalistic lines? What is the reason why in one instance handicraft is maintained while in another it is replaced by capitalism?

As I have pointed out above, the prevailing opinion gives this answer: geographical expansion of markets caused capitalism to dominate industrial activities. In my opinion, however, the organization of industrial production is influenced to a far greater extent by increase in the consumption of luxury goods. In numerous cases (although not in all) increase in consumption opens the door to capitalism, permitting it to invade the sanctuary of trade. My arguments, I believe, confirm this theory.

But if it were said: "You deceive yourself. Those trades, which you rightly designate as luxury industries and which were indeed the first to succumb to capitalism, submit to its rule, not because they are luxury industries, but because they are export industries (after all, they do have that characteristic in common)," I would answer: "You are mistaken, my friend. You are doubly mistaken."

1. All luxury industries with capitalistic organization are, by no means, export industries. I call attention to the furniture and carriage industries, carpet manufacturing, luxury tailoring, and the shoemaking industry. They all represent "local" production and, in most cases, even "customer production" in the strictest sense.

2. All export trades are by no means of a capitalistic nature. Throughout the entire Middle Ages innumerable trades sold their goods interlocally and internationally. Export handicrafts of this type have maintained themselves to modern times; even at the beginning of the nineteenth century the wool-weaving of Yorkshire and the linen-weaving of Silesia, both of which produced for the world market, were still operated strictly as handicrafts.

Thus, the geographical expansion of markets cannot be the decisive cause, which in other trades is responsible for the establishment of capitalism.

The following is my defense of the theory that increase in the consumption of luxury goods is the deciding factor; in other words, that the enumerated trades fall under capitalistic rule because they are luxury industries.

The reasons which make a luxury industry more adaptable to capitalistic organization lie in:

1. The Nature of the Production Process. In most cases a luxury article demands a valuable raw material which frequently must be obtained from distant sources. As a result, an advantage accrues to the rich and commercially trained entrepreneur: when the *filaresses* of Paris during the thirteenth century already are spinning silk as wage earners for the mercer, who then sells this silk in the city, while centuries later independent farmers are still processing flax and cotton, what other reason can there be for the system of home industry than the fact that the mercer alone is in the position to acquire valuable raw materials?

Furthermore, the process by which a luxury article is manufactured, frequently is more costly than the one used in the production of ordinary goods. This, of course, no longer holds true. We refer to the early textile industry (dyeing and finishing), the production of glass and procelain, the making of hooked rugs, the weaving or toy industries, in short, to most of the processes of the luxury industries. Again, the man with capital is favored. But the process used in the production of luxury goods is not only more costly; in most cases it is also more of an art process and more complicated. It demands more knowledge, a wider outlook, and a greater managerial talent; consequently, the most capable and (in this sense) the best minds are brought to the fore: with their qualifications they are the only ones capable of filling the newly created positions demanding leadership and organizing ability. Frequently, however, the high standards of luxury goods are attained only if the manufacturing process, by means of team work and specialization, likewise is advanced to a higher level. For example, capitalistic, custom tailoring produces quality merchandise only because it makes the high-grade work of talented cutters available to the average cutter. But a differentiation of high-grade workmanship is not possible except on a broader basis of production such as the capitalistic organization alone creates.

2. The Nature of Sales. I will not stress the opinion which we have already met with and which was current during the old régime, namely, that the lordly nonchalance of fashionable customers in the payment of their bills resulted in frequent losses to the manufacturer of luxury goods and that, in consequence, he required unusually large capital resources.

What seems important to me, however, is the fact that the trade in luxury goods undoubtedly is far more subject to fluctuations than the trade in articles designed for mass consumption. The history of all luxury industries has taught us that there are frequent changes in the whims of the rich, whose tastes during the epoch of early capitalism are beginning to be influenced by "fashion." On the one hand, these capricious changes often result in the curtailment of sales and, on the other, great resourcefulness is demanded of the manufacturer if he is to continue to adapt his production to the constantly varying demands. Capitalistic organization is now, however, in a far better position than handicraft to maintain itself under adverse fluctuations and to profit by favorable market conditions.

3. In addition to these "intrinsic" reasons, there is the historical reason that all luxury industries during the European Middle Ages were artificially created either by the ruling princes or by enterprising foreigners. The foreigner (as I shall demonstrate elsewhere in detail) plays the leading role in the development of modern industry. Beginning with the Humiliati, founders of the Florentine cloth industry, to the French emigrants, fathers of the

Berlin industry, there is an uninterrupted flow of migrating industrialists and of industrial enterprises founded by them. What they established were nearly always luxury industries, whose development, incidentally, was also a matter of great concern to the ruling princes.

But all these industries which were deliberately created by foreigners immediately assume a rational aspect. They are founded mostly outside the confines of the guilds and, frequently, in opposition to the deep-rooted interests of local craftsmen. When these interests were set up, no consideration was shown to old traditions; suitability is the only motivating factor, and it is principally for these reasons that they form the basis for the development of the new and economically higher industrial system.

4. But the most important prerequisite to the maintenance of this industrial system was still a suitable market. Since (this is the final reason) the other possibility for large sales, i.e., volume sales of inferior or composite goods, did not occur until much later, the luxury industries were the only enterprises offering opportunity for investment of capital.

Luxury, then, itself a legitimate child of illicit love—as we have seen—gave birth to capitalism.

NOTES

CHAPTER I
Sources and Literature

1. *See* Section I of this chapter.
2. *See* Section II of this chapter.
3. *See* Section III of this chapter.

I. The Court

4. Laude, *op.cit.*, i, p. 128.
5. M Duc de Sully, *Mémoires* . . . ; English tr. by Sir Walter Scott, *Memoirs of the Duke of Sully* (London, 1856), II, pp. 222–23.
6. L. S. Mercier, *Tableau de Paris* (Amsterdam, 1783–88), I, pp. 21 *et seq.*
7. Th. Starkey, "England in the Reign of Henry VIII," in William Denton, *England in the Fifteenth Century* (London, 1888), p. 259.

II. Middle-Class Wealth

8. Reprinted in German and thoroughly annotated by J. Goldstein, *Berufsgliederung und Reichtum* (Stuttgart, 1897).
9. Cf. the schedule in M. Postlethwayt, *Universal Dictionary of Trade and Commerce* (n.p., 1758), 2, pp. 746–47.
10. *The Present State of Great Britain and Ireland*, ed. by Bolton (London, 1745), p. 157.
11. From a "Livre de raison," cited in C. de Ribbe, *Les Familles*, . . . (Paris, 1874), 2, p. 125.
12. Turcaret, the figure of the newly rich financier, created by Lesage (1688–1747) in the comedy of the same name presented in Paris in 1709. (Translator's note.)
13. Henri Thirion, *La Vie privée des financiers au XVIIIᵉ siècle* (Paris, 1895).
14. L. S. Mercier, *op.cit.*, X, p. 248.

III. The New Nobility

15. Gneist, *op.cit.*, p. 7.
16. W. Harrison, "Description of England," 1577 ed., vol. 3, chapter 4, cited in H. de B. Gibbins, *Industry in England* (London, 1906), p. 323. The explanations given there do not clarify the origin of the gentry. William Camden, *Britannia*, . . . (London, 1590), says quite generally: "Gentlemen belong to a certain class of noblemen who have risen above the masses by reason of higher birth and by their outstanding qualities and fortunes."
17. Daniel Defoe, *The Complete English Tradesman* (London, 1745), 1, p. 322.
18. *Ibid.*, 1, pp. 224 *et seq.*
19. *Ibid.*, 1, p. 324.
20. Postlethwayt, *op.cit.*, Guy Miege, *op.cit.*, p. 156.
21. Charles R. Dodd, *op.cit.*, p. 251.
22. Daniel Defoe, *op.cit.*, 1, pp. 323-24.
23. Daniel Defoe, *op.cit.*, XXIV.
24. B. Laffemas, *Traité du commerce de la vie du loyal marchand* (Paris, 1601); G. Fagniez, *L'Économie sociale de la France sous Henry IV* (Paris, 1897), p. 253.
25. Cf. Jacob Strieder, *Zur Genesis des modernen Kapitals* (Bonn, 1903), p. 40, and bibliography. Cf. also Rudolf Hapke, "Die Entstehung der grossen bürgerlichen Vermögen im Mittelalter," in *Schmoller's Jahrbuch* (Leipzig, 1906), 29, pp. 245 *et seq.*
26. Cf. H. Sieveking, "Die kapitalistische Entwicklung in den italienischen Städten des Mittelalters," in *Vierteljahrschriften für Social- und Wirtschaftsgeschichte* (Berlin-Stuttgart-Leipzig, 1909), No. 7, p. 73.
27. B. Thorpe, ed., *Ancient Laws and Institutions of England* (London, 1840), 1, p. 193. Editor's note: "It is possible that craeft (craft) may here as at the present day signify a vessel."
28. Cf. numerous instances in H. Pigeonneau, *Histoire du commerce de la France* (Paris, 1885–89), 1, pp. 397 *et seq.*, and G. d'Avenel, *Histoire économique de la propriété*, . . . (Paris, 1894), 1, pp. 144 *et seq.*
29. Instances are given in E. Levasseur, *Histoire des classes ouvrières*, . . . (Paris, 1900), 2, pp. 175, 200.
30. Ch. Normand, *La Bourgeoisie française au XVIIIe siècle* (Paris, 1908), pp. 9 *et seq.*, 21 *et seq.*, 64 *et seq.*
31. G. d'Avenel, *op.cit.*, 1, pp. 144 *et seq.*, 208 *et seq.*
32. Sully, *op.cit.*; English tr., *op.cit.*, II, pp. 222–23.
33. L. S. Mercier, *op.cit.*, 2, p. 201.

CHAPTER 2

Sources and Literature

1. Marie d'Aulnoy, *La Cour et la ville de Madrid* (Paris, 1874).

I. The Cities in the Sixteenth, Seventeenth,
and Eighteenth Centuries

2. The figures are taken from the painstaking inquiry by F. Beloch, "Die Entwicklung der Grosstädte in Europa," published in *Comptes rendus du VIIIe Congrès International d'Hygiène et de Démographie,* pp. 55 *et seq.* The census figures of Dublin have been taken from A. Moreau de Jonnès, *Statistique de la Grande-Bretagne, . . .* (Paris, 1837), 1, p. 88. The last figure for London is that of the census of 1801; the figures given for Berlin are those in the compilation of Normann, cited by H.G.R. Mirabeau, *De la Monarchie prussienne* (London, 1788), 1, pp. 395 *et seq.*

3. The edict is cited in T. Rymer's *Foedera, . . .* (London, 1726–35), 16, p. 448.

II. Origin and Inner Structure of the Cities

4. Daniel Defoe, *A Tour Through the Islands of Great Britain, . . .* (London, 1778), 2, p. 253.

5. H.G.R. Mirabeau, *op.cit.*

6. W.E.J. Berg, *De Refugiés in de Nederlande, . . .* (Amsterdam, 1845), 1, pp. 269, *et seq.*

7. E. Gerland, "Kreta als venetianische Kolonie" (1204–1669), in *Historisches Jahrbuch* (München, 1899), 20, p. 22.

8. Cf. the descriptions of Venice in H. Simonsfeld, *Der Fondaco dei Tedeschi in Venedig, . . .* (Stuttgart, 1887), 2, pp. 265 *et seq.*

9. F. Gregorovius, *Geschichte der Stadt Rom im Mittelalter* (Stuttgart, 1859–72), 7, p. 236; English tr. by Annie Hamilton, *City of Rome in the Middle Ages* (London, 1900), 7, p. 247, note.

10. *Ibid.,* 8, p. 287; English tr., 8, p. 302.

11. Ludwig Pastor, *Geschichte der Päpste, . . .* (Freiburg, i.B., 1901), 1, pp. 78 *et seq.*

12. "Conservación de monarquías y discursos." Discurso XIV, cited in L. Ranke, *Fürsten und Völker von Südeuropa* (Berlin 1837–45), 1, p. 458. Cf. K. Haebler, *Wirtschaftliche Blüte Spaniens, . . .* (Leipzig, 1888), pp. 53, 153, 155, and *passim.*

13. Cf. the interesting description of Madrid in her Golden Age, based on good sources, which W. F. von Gleichen-Russwurm gives in *Das galante Europa, . . .* (Stuttgart, 1910), p. 19.

14. The descriptions in E. Gothein, *op.cit.,* pp. 317 *et seq.,* pp. 342 *et seq.,* make pleasant reading. Cf. J. Burckhardt, *Die Cultur der Renais-*

sance (Leipzig, 1878), 2, pp. 106, 166; English tr. by S.G.C. Middlemore, *The Civilization of the Renaissance* (London, 1909), p. 371. Hippolyte a Collibus, *Incrementa urbium, . . .* (Helmestadii, 1665), 1, p. 207.

15. A. L. Lavoisier, "Essai sur la population de la ville de Paris, sur sa richesse et ses consommations," in *Mélanges d'école politique,* ed. Daire (Paris, 1847), 1, pp. 601 *et seq.*

16. V. R. Mirabeau, *op.cit.* (Avignon, 1756), 2, p. 408.

17. F. Quesnay, "Fermiers," in *Encyclopédie,* ed. Oncken (Frankfort and Paris, 1888), p. 189. Authors speak of the unnaturally large size of Paris as early as the sixteenth century. Cf. V. R. Mirabeau, *op.cit.,* 2, p. 408. The same applies to London in the seventeenth century. John Graunt, *Natural and Political Observations, . . .* (London, 1662), *passim.*

18. V. R. Mirabeau, *op.cit.,* 2, p. 442.

19. *Ibid.,* p. 412. Cf. H. Taine, *Les Origines de la France contemporaine* (Paris, 1885), 1, p. 52, for figures on the enormous incomes of the high church and secular dignitaries. Strangely enough, the authority from whom Taine derives his information on the absenteeism of the French nobility and its gathering in Paris is none other than Arthur Young who speaks of French conditions as if conditions in England were different.

20. L. S. Mercier, *op.cit.,* 1, pp. 67–68.

21. *Ibid.,* Chapter XC.

22. *Ibid.,* Chapter XCI.

23. *Ibid.,* 2, pp. 39 *et seq.,* 44 *et seq.*

24. T. Rymer, *op.cit.,* 19, p. 374.

25. E. Chamberlayne, *Angliae Notitia: The Present State of England* (London, 1687), p. 200.

26. David Hume, *Essays* (London, 1882), 3, p. 364.

27. "Artificial Fire" (1644). Ms. in the British Museum, cited in W. Cunningham, *The Growth of English Industry and Commerce* (Cambridge, 1907), 2, p. 319.

28. Guy Miege, *The Present State of Great Britain and Ireland,* ed. by Bolton (London, 1745), p. 101.

29. Daniel Defoe, *A Tour, . . .* 2, pp. 135–36.

30. See the figures in J. Goldstein, *Berufsgliederung und Reichtum* (Stuttgart, 1897), p. 143, quoting Chalmers and Price Williams.

31. *Op.cit.,* p. 236.

III. Theories of the City in the Eighteenth Century

32. Richard Cantillon, *Essai sur la nature du commerce en général* (London, 1755), pp. 17 *et seq;* English tr. by Henry Higgs (London, 1931), pp. 16–17.

33. In: *Oeuvres économiques et philosophiques*, ed. Oncken (Frankfort and Paris, 1888), pp. 250 *et seq.*
34. *Ibid.*, p. 297.
35. *Ibid.*, p. 298.
36. *Ibid.*, p. 302.
37. Cantillon, *op.cit.*
38. "De l'Homme," *Oeuvres*, 2, p. 360.
39. H.G.R. Mirabeau, *op.cit.*, pp. 403 *et seq.*
40. C. Beccaria, *Economia pubblica* (1771) Paragraph 30. Custodi, P.M. 11, pp. 58–59. See also p. 86, where the author deals with the origin of luxury industries in the great cities.
41. Gaetano Filangieri, *Leggi politiche e leggi economiche* (1780). Custodi, P.M. 32, pp. 185–86.
42. Sir James Stuart, *Inquiry*, . . . (London, 1767), 1, p. 48.

CHAPTER 3

1. The Triumph of Illicit Love

1. Ludovico Valeriani and Urbano Lampredi, *Poeti del primo secolo,* . . . (Firenze, 1816), 2 vols.
2. Alwin Schultz, *Das höfische Leben zur Zeit der Minnesinger* (Leipzig, 1889), 2, p. 423.
3. For an interesting description see Joseph Kirchner, *Die Darstellung des ersten Menschenpaars in der bildenden Kunst,* . . . (Stuttgart, 1903).
4. Lorenzo Valla, *Opera,* . . . (Basel, 1590). (*De Voluptate*, lib. 1, c. XXII.)
5. Aug. Firenzuola, "Discorso delle bellezze delle donne," cited in: J. Burckhardt, *Die Cultur der Renaissance* (Leipzig, 1878), 2, p. 64; English translation by S.G.C. Middlemore, *The Civilization of the Renaissance* (London, 1909), p. 345; and in R. Günther, *Kulturgeschichte der Liebe* (Berlin, 1899), pp. 298 *et seq.* In view of such evidence it is strange that Burckhardt, (*op.cit.*, p. 63; English tr., *op.cit.*, p. 344), should have said: "Whether the fifteenth century has left any written account of its ideal of beauty, I am not able to say." Evidently, when writing this book the quoted passages must have slipped his mind.
6. Lorenzo Valla, *op.cit.*, p. 668.
7. Francesco Colonna, *Poliphili Hypnerotomachia,* . . . (Venice, 1499).
8. Pietro Bembo, *Gli Asolani* (Venice, 1575), p. 134.
9. *Ibid.*, pp. 189–90.

10. Life somewhat better might content him
    But for the gleam of heavenly light, which Thou hast lent him:
    He calls it Reason—thence his power's increased,
    To be far beastlier than any beast.
    —From the Prologue to Goethe's *Faust*.
11. Love has thrust me in the furnace
    Love has thrust me in the furnace
    He has plunged me in the furnace of love.
    —From Frederick Ozanam, *The Franciscan Poets in Italy in the Thirteenth Century* (London, 1914), p. 85.
12. Lorenzo Valla, *op.cit.*, libl. i, c. xxxviii.
13. F. Gregorovius, *Lucrezia Borgia* (Stuttgart, 1875), 1, p. 96.
14. These passages are in the famous fifth chapter of the third book of the Essays. Were such views entirely new then? Or better, was it the first time that such views were integrated into a system? (After all, since the decline of the minnesingers people did live in accordance with them). This seems rather unlikely when we think of many a decision of the *Minnehöfe*. Cf. K. Weinhold, *Die Deutschen Frauen in dem Mittelalter* (Wien, 1897).

II. The Courtesan

15. I shall give here the original passage because it so admirably reflects the spirit of the time, and because to my knowledge, it has never before been cited:

    Quae tunc pestis incipiens nunc adeo certa est, ut adolescens cui non feliciter adulterium successerit, quamvis dives, quamvis formosus ac nobilis, coaevorum iudicio inter miseros habeatur, quasi abiectus ac repulsus non pudicitia sed contemptu; et quasi dilectio castitatis convicium sit amantis. Hinc ille iuvenum fervor et sollicitudo improba, tanquam non de libidine sed de gloria sit certamen: hinc labores, hinc suspiria, hinc repentinae repulsae amarissimae: saepe tamen successus amarior.

    Epistolae de rebus familiaribus et variae, ed. by Joseph Fracassetti (Florence, 1862), 2, liber nonus, epistola IV, p. 10.
16. Heinrich Laube, *Französische Lustschlösser* (Mannheim, 1840).
17. Extract from the periodical "Gli studi in Italia" (1882), in F. Gregorovius, *op.cit.*, 7, p. 722.
18. E.J.F. Barbier, "Journal historique, . . . ," 4, p. 496, in R. Günther, *op.cit.*, p. 397.
19. See the long list of mistresses of the farmer-general in: Paul Ginisty, *Mlle Duthé et son temps* (Paris, 1909), p. 11.

CHAPTER 4

I. Definition and Nature of Luxury

1. This development will be dealt with in greater detail in another volume in which the genesis of the capitalist spirit will be traced.
2. L. S. Mercier, *Tableau de Paris* (1783), Chapter 573, VII, pp. 97–98.
3. Daniel Defoe, *The Complete English Tradesman* (London, 1745), Chapter 50.
4. Remarks by Senator Stephan Garczynski in his book "Anatomie der Republik Polen," quoted by R. Roepell, *Polen um die Mitte des 18. Jahrhunderts* (Gotha, 1876), p. 17. Taken from W. Naudé, *Die Getreidehandelspolitik der Europäischen Staaten* (Berlin, 1896), p. 386.

II. The Courts

5. *Sonnets of Petrarch*, tr. by Joseph Auslander (New York, 1931), Sonnets CVI–CVII, pp. 106–7. (Translator's note)
6. L'Abbé J. F. André, *Histoire de la papauté à Avignon* (2d ed.; Avignon, 1887), p. 300.
7. G. Milanesi, ed., *Conviti (I due sontuosissimi) fatti a Papa Clemente V nel 1308 descritti da Anonimo fiorentino* (Florence, 1868).
8. E. Müntz, "L'Argent et le luxe à la cour pontificale d'Avignon," in *Revue des Questions Historiques* (Paris, 1899), LXVI, pp. 5–44 and 378–406. E. Müntz and Maurice Faucon, "Inventaire des objets précieux vendus à Avignon 1358," *Revue archéologique* (Paris, 1882), pp. 217–25. Thomas Okey, *The Story of Avignon* (London, 1911), with bibliography. Charles Martin, *Le Château et les papes d'Avignon* (Aix-en-Provence, 1899). To my knowledge there exist no trustworthy and accurate accounts of the secular life at the courts of Avignon.
9. Leo Koenig, *Die päpstliche Kammer unter Clemens V. und Johann XXII* (Vienna, 1894), pp. 56 *et seq.*
10. F. Gregorovius, *Geschichte der Stadt Rom im Mittelalter;* English tr. by Annie Hamilton, *History of the City of Rome in the Middle Ages* (London, 1900), VII, p. 255.
11. Read the description of the festivals, *ibid.*, p. 249.
12. Matteo Palmieri, "De temporib. suis ad A. 1478," *ibid.*, p. 254.
13. Johann Burchard, *Diarum sive Rerum Urbanarum Commentarii* [1483–1506] (Paris, 1884), II, p. 17.
14. F. Gregorovius, English tr., *op.cit.*, VIII, part I, pp. 180 *et seq.*

15. Reference to this publication in William Roscoe's *The Life and Pontificate of Leo the Tenth* (Philadelphia, 1805), I, p. 244, and Appendix XXIX.

16. Sources in F. Gregorovius, *op.cit.*, VII, pp. 360–61. The revenue from taxes in the duchy of Este in 1592 amounted to 690,993 l. 19 s. 8 d. *(marchesane)*, according to Pietro Sitta, *Saggio sulle istituzioni finanziarie del ducato estense nei secoli XV e XVI* (Ferrara, 1891), p. 126.

17. Niccolo Tommaseo, "Relations des ambassadeurs vénétiens sur les affaires de France au XVI siècle," *Collection de documents inédits sur l'histoire de France*, Series III (Paris, 1838), I, p. 285. Concerning the expenditures for luxury by the older Valois, see Henri Baudrillart, *Histoire du luxe privé et public depuis l'antiquité jusqu'à nos jours* (Paris, 1881), III, p. 273.

18. Niccolo Tommaseo, *op.cit.*, II, p. 529.

19. Report of Matteo Dandolo in Eugenio Alberi, *Relazioni degli ambasciatori Veneti al senato* (Florence, 1860), IV, pp. 42–43.

20. Value $3,750,000. (Translator's note)

21. (Fr. Forbonnais), *Recherches et considérations sur les finances de France, depuis l'année 1595 jusqu'à l'année 1721* (Basle, 1758), I, pp. 119 et seq.

22. *Ibid.*, II, p. 41.

23. J. Guiffrey, "Comptes des Batiments du roi sous le règne de Louis XIV." 5 vols., *Collection de documents inédits*, Series III (Paris, 1881–1901).

24. *Ibid.*, V, pp. 953–54. (Translator's note)

25. *Ibid.*, I, pp. 1392–93; II, pp. 1316–17. (Translator's note)

26. *Ibid.*, V, pp. 953–54. (Translator's note)

27. *Ibid.*, I, pp. 1390–91. (Translator's note)

28. J. Guiffrey, *Inventaire général du mobilier de la couronne sous Louis XIV (1663–1715)* (Paris, 1885), 2 vols.

29. The marc weighs 7.86 oz. troy. (Translator's note)

30. J. Guiffrey, "Comptes des Bâtiments," *op.cit.*, I, Chapter 42, pp. 370–71.

31. An account of the luxury in dress is given in *Le Mercure galant*, (December, 1697), cited in Alfred Franklin, *La Vie privée d'autrefois: Les Magasins de nouveautés* (Paris, 1894), pp. 227 et seq.

32. Marc' Antonio Giustiniani, *Diarium Europaeum* (October 24, 1666), cited in Leopold von Ranke, *Französische Geschichte* (Leipzig, 1868–70), III, p. 177.

33. *Archives Nationales* (Series) O¹, 3792–94, cited in Emile Lan-glade's instructive book, *La Marchande de modes de Marie Antoi-nette: Rose Bertin* (Paris, 1911), pp. 29, 122.

34. "État des dépenses de Mme la Marquise de Pompadour du 9 sep-tembre 1745 au 15 avril 1769, jour de sa mort," published by M Luc Leroy, cited in H. Baudrillart, *op.cit.*, IV, p. 327.

35. Bibliothèque Nationale, Nos. 8157–58. Edmond and Jules de Gon-court, *Madame Du Barry* (London, 1914), pp. 141–42 and pp. 275–77. (Translator's note)

36. Equivalent to about thirty million dollars. (Translator's note)

37. Marie d'Aulnoy, *La Cour et la ville de Madrid*, ed. by Mme B. Carey (Paris, 1874), App. Note C.

38. Interesting description of the luxurious life at the court of William of Orange, before he became king of England, by Wilhelm Ernst Berg, *De Refugies in de Nederlande* (Amsterdam, 1845), I, pp. 269 *et seq.*

39. All figures concerning the expenditures of the English kings are taken from John Sinclair's *The History of the Public Revenue of the British Empire* (3d ed.; London, 1803), I and II.

III. The Cavaliers and the Parvenus as Imitators of the Court

40. Willy Doenges, *Meissner Porzellan* (Berlin, 1907), pp. 76 *et seq.*, 126.

41. Saint-Simon, duc de, *Memoirs of the Duke of Saint-Simon*, English tr. by Francis Arkwright (London, 1918), V, p. 278.

42. Danto, *Inferno*, Canto XIII, 118–22. English tr. by Henry W. Long-fellow (Boston, 1871), p. 51; cf. also Anton von Kostanecki, *Dantes Philosophie des Eigentums* (Berlin, 1912), pp. 8 *et seq.*

43. H. Baudrillart, *op.cit.*, IV, p. 68.

44. This charming expression will be found in William Camden, *Bri-tannia* (London, 1590), p. 106.

45. Taken from Pierre César de Cadenet de Charleval, *Livre de Raison*, begun in 1728, continued in 1763 by François de Charleval and con-cluded by his son; cited by Charles de Ribbe, *Les Familles*, . . . (Paris, 1874), II, p. 114. The Smithsonian Institute in Washington possesses an especially valuable collection of English household bud-gets between the years 1650 and 1750. The owner of this collection, James Orchard Halliwell, gives us some extracts which he has com-piled and presented to the Smithsonian Institute in his book, *Some Account of a Collection of Several Thousand Bills, Accounts, and Inventories, Illustrating the History of Prices Between the years 1650 and 1750*, Brixton Hill, 1852.

46. A few examples of incomes during the eighteenth century are given in Section 2 of Chapter 1.

47. M Duc de Sully, *Mémoires*, . . . ; English tr. by Sir Walter Scott, *Memoirs of the Duke of Sully* (London, 1856), II, p. 221.

48. Three rolls of Paul: Invention of a spinning contrivance by Lewis Paul of Birmingham 1738. (Translator's note)

49. Johann Wilhelm von Archenholtz, *England und Italien* (Leipzig, 1785), I, p. 130; the part on England, tr. into English as *A Picture of England* (London, 1789), I, p. 125.

50. *The Spectator* (June 12, 1712), No. 403.

51. "Seignorial" is used here in the sense of display and ostentation.

52. H. A. Frégier, *Histoire de l'administration de la police de Paris* (Paris, 1850), II, p. 34.

53. Henri Thirion, *La Vie privée des financiers au XVIIIᵉ siècle* (Paris, 1895), p. 292. Add. material in Humbert de Gallier, *Les moeurs et la vie,* . . . , pp. 85 *et seq.*

54. Sources in Hippolyte A. Taine, *Les Origines de la France contemporaine*, I, p. 168.

54a. E. Langlade, *op.cit.*, pp. 263 *et seq.*

55. Polifilo, "La guarderoba di Lucrezia Borgia," in *Dall' archivo di stato di Modena* (1903).

56. Johann Burchard, *op.cit.*, II, p. 16. (Translator's note)

57. Hermann Weiss, *Kostümkunde* (Stuttgart, 1872), Part II, p. 1028.

58. Letter of Mme de Maintenon to her brother, September 25, 1679. Cf. Aimé Houze de l'Aulnont, *La Finance d'un bourgeois de Lille au XVIIᵉ siècle* (Paris, 1889), pp. 51, 116.

59. E. J. F. Barbier, *Journal historique et anecdotique du règne de Louis XV* (Paris, 1847–56), I, p. 42; II, p. 435.

60. Daniel Defoe, *Complete English Tradesman* (1745), II, p. 328.

61. *Ibid.*, (ed. 1727), pp. 115, 116, 141.

62. J. W. Archenholtz, *England und Italien*, III, p. 141.

63. Charles de Ribbe, *Une Grande dame dans son ménage au temps de Louis XIV d'après le journal de la comtesse de Rochefort* (Paris, 1889), p. 137.

64. *Lettres de Madame de Sévigné, de sa famille et de ses amis* (Paris, 1862), recueillies et annotées par M. Monmerque.

65. Duhautchamp, *Histoire du système des finances sous la minorité de Louis XV pendant les années 1719 and 1720* (La Haye, 1739). Oscar de Vallée, *Les Manieurs d'argent* (Paris, 1857), p. 121.

66. L. S. Mercier, *op.cit.*, II, p. 123.

67. Richard Muther, *The History of Painting*, English tr. by George Kriehn (New York, 1907), II, p. 737. (Translator's note)

68. H. Thirion, *op.cit.*, p. 124.

IV. The Triumph of Woman

69. Many figures are cited in Humbert de Gallier, *Les Moeurs et la vie,* ..., pp. 96 *et seq.* An important source is Pierre Manuel, *La Police de Paris dévoilée* (Paris, 1794).

70. Wilhelm Lubke, *Geschichte der Renaissance in Frankreich* (Stuttgart, 1868), p. 287.

71. Pierre Clément (ed.), *Lettres, instructions et mémoires de Colbert* (Paris, 1868), V, p. 300.

72. Edmund O. von Lippmann, *Geschichte des Zuckers, seine Darstellung und Verwendung, seit den ältesten Zeiten bis zum Beginne der Rübenzuckerfabrikation* (Leipzig, 1890), pp. 434, 437–38, 595.

73. Jakob Burckhardt, *Die Cultur der Renaissance* (Leipzig, 1877–78), II, p. 117; English tr. by S.G.C. Middlemore (London, 1909), p. 377.

74. Ferdinand Gregorovius, *Geschichte der Stadt Rom im Mittelalter* (Stuttgart, 1894); tr. from the 4th German edition into English by Annie Hamilton (London, 1894–1912), VIII, Part I, Chapter 4, p. 307.

75. Kazimierz Chledowski, *Rom; die Menschen der Renaissance* (Munich, 1912), p. 377. Further descriptions of similar dwellings will be found in this book.

76. Regnier Desmarets, cited in Edward Fournier, *Le Vieux neuf* (Paris, 1859), II, p. 147.

77. *Lettres de Madame de Sévigné, op.cit.* (November 26, 1694), X, p. 216.

78. John Evelyn, *Memoirs,* ed. by William Bray (London, 1871), p. 450.

79. Edmond and Jules Goncourt, *Madame Du Barry;* English tr. *op.cit.,* p. 139.

80. Read the descriptions of the chambres à coucher by H. Thirion, *op.cit.,* pp. 438 *et seq.,* 352 *et seq.*

81. J. W. von Archenholtz, *op.cit.,* p. 136; English tr., *A Picture of England,* p. 130.

82. William Watts, *The Seats of the Nobility and Gentry in a Collection of the Most Interesting and Picturesque Views Engraved* (London, 1779).

83. Read the interesting passage in L. S. Mercier, *op.cit.* (1783), I, Chapter 89, p. 166; I, Chapter 88, p. 162.

84. Cited by Charles de Ribbe, *Une Grande dame,* ..., p. 167.

85. Antoine de Léris, *Dictionnaire portatif historique et littéraire des théâtres* (Paris, 1763), XX *et seq.* Cf. Albert du Casse, *Histoire anecdotique de l'ancien théâtre en France* (Paris, 1864). Chiefly of literary interest.

86. For England of the seventeenth century: *The Character of a Town Gallant.* Extracts cited by Albert Savine, *La Cour galante de Charles II* (Paris, 1908).
87. Defoe-Richardson, *A Tour Through the Islands of Great Britain* (London, 1778), II, pp. 92–93.
88. J. W. von Archenholtz, *op.cit.*, II, p. 230; English tr., *op.cit.*, I, Chapter X, pp. 387–88.
89. Henri d'Almarás, *Les Plaisirs du Palais Royal*, p. 11.
90. Daniel Defoe, *Complete English Tradesman* (1727), p. 259.
91. J. W. von Archenholtz, *op.cit.*, II, pp. 231 *et seq.;* English tr., *op.cit.*, I, Chapter X, p. 390.
92. L. S. Mercier, *op.cit.*, III, pp. 109 *et seq.*
93. Paul Ginisty (ed.), *Mademoiselle Duthé et son temps* (Paris, 1909), p. 40.

CHAPTER 5

I. Correct and Incorrect Formulation of the Problem

1. Exact statements found in Adam Anderson's *Origin of Commerce* (Dublin, 1790), II, p. 387.
2. "Lois Somtuaires," in *Encyclopédie*, or in *Dictionnaire raisonné des sciences, des arts et des métiers* (Berne and Lausanne, 1780), XX, p. 301. The most informative article on the subject.
3. Montesquieu, *De l'Esprit des lois* (Geneva, 1748), Book VII, Chapter IV; English tr. by Thomas Nugent, *The Spirit of Laws* (London, 1902).
4. Gabriel F. Coyer, *Développement et défense du système de la noblesse commerçante* (Amsterdam, 1757), I, p. 52.
5. (1771), 2 vols.
6. Nicholas Barbon, *A Discourse of Trade* (London, 1690), p. 62, in W. Cunningham, *The Growth of English Industry and Commerce* (Cambridge, 1907), II, p. 392, with additional relevant passages.
7. David Hume, "Of refinement in the arts," in *Essays* (1793), II, pp. 19 *et seq;* also (1882), I, Part I, p. 309.
8. Bernard Mandeville, *The Fable of the Bees: or Private Vices, Publick Benefits* (6th ed.; 1732), p. 10 (Notes I-N); also (Edinburgh, 1772), I, p. 13.
9. Wilhelm Freiherr von Schröder, *Fürstliche Schatz- und Rentkammer nebst seinem nothwendigen Unterricht vom Goldmacher* (Leipzig, 1744), p. 172.

II. Luxury and Trade

10. Wilhelm Heyd, *Geschichte des Levantehandels im Mittelalter* (Stuttgart, 1879), II, pp. 550 *et seq.*

11. Aloys Schulte, *Geschichte des mittelalterlichen Handels und Verkehrs zwischen Westdeutschland und Italien mit Ausschluss von Venedig* (Leipzig, 1900), I, pp. 720 *et seq.*

12. One libra had 53 solidi and equalled 1 Milanese gold florin.

13. Germain Martin, *La Grande industrie sous le règne de Louis XIV* (Paris, 1899), pp. 288 *et seq.*

14. Table in Jean A. Chaptal de Chanteloup, *De l'Industrie françoise* (Paris, 1819), I, p. 130.

15. Alexander de Humboldt, *Essai politique sur le royaume de la Nouvelle-Espagne* (Paris, 1811), IV, pp. 366 *et seq;* also English tr. by John Black (London, 1811), IV, Book V, Chapter XII, p. 33.

16. Thomas Buxton, *The African Slave Trade* (New York, 1840), p. 171.

17. Otto Langer, *Sklaverei in Europa während der letzten Jahrhunderte des Mittelalters* (Bautzén, 1891), p. 16.

18. Ign. Schipper, *Anfänge des Kapitalismus bei den abendländischen Juden im früheren Mittelalter (bis zum Ausg. des XII. Jahrhunderts)* (Vienna, 1907), pp. 19 *et seq.* Georg Caro, *Sozial- und Wirtschaftsgeschichte der Juden im Mittelalter und der Neuzeit* (Frankfurt am Main, 1924), I, pp. 137 *et seq;* also Wilhelm Heyd, *op.cit.*, II, pp. 542 *et seq.*

19. Corroborative passages in Reinhard Heynen, *Zur Entstehung des kapitalismus in Venedig* (Stuttgart and Berlin, 1905), pp. 32 *et seq.*

20. Adam Anderson, *op.cit.*, IV, p. 130 (according to a "French author").

21. Bryan Edwards, *The History Civil and Commercial of the British Colonies in the West Indies,* II, p. 65; also (Dublin, 1793), II, p. 54.

22. Malachy Postlethwayt, *Dictionary of Commerce* (London, 1758), I, pp. 709 *et seq.*; see chapter entitled "England."

23. Onslow Burrish, *Batavia Illustrata or a View of the Policy, and Commerce of the United Provinces: Particularly of Holland* (London, 1728), pp. 354 *et seq.*

24. Alexandre Moreau de Jonnés, *État économique et social de la France, depuis Henri IV jusq'à Louis XIV, 1589 à 1715* (Paris, 1867), p. 349.

25. Daniel Defoe, *Complete English Tradesman* (5th ed.; London, 1745), Chapter LI.

26. *Zeitschrift der historischen gesellschaft für Schwaben und Neuberg,* VI, pp. 38–39.

27. Mercier, *Tableau de Paris* (Amsterdam, 1783), Chapter DLV.
28. In connection with the entire presentation of the subject, my book *Moderner Kapitalismus*, in which I have shown the trends of modern retail merchandising, may be consulted.
29. R. Campbell, *The London Tradesman* (London, 1745), p. 47; (1747), p. 197.
30. Article "Tapisserie," in the *Encyclopédie méthodique* (Paris, 1791), II, pp. 219 *et seq.*
31. Jacques Savary, *Dictionnaire universal de commerce* (1748), II, p. 407.
32. *A General Description of All Trades Digested in Alphabetical Order* (London, 1747), p. 49.
33. *Ibid.*, p. 215.
34. L. S. Mercier, *op.cit.*, VII, p. 73.
35. *Les Correspondants de la marquise de Balleroy*, published by Count E. de Barthélemy in Humbert de Gallier's, *Les Moeurs et la vie privée d'autrefois* (Paris, 1911), p. 57.
36. *A General Description of All Trades, . . .* (1747). R. Campbell, *The London Tradesman, Being a Compendious View of All the Trades, Professions, Arts, . . .* (1747).
37. Daniel Defoe, *Complete English Tradesman* (5th ed.; 1745), I, p. 215; (1727), Letter XVII, p. 226.

III. Luxury and Agriculture

38. C. Bertagnolli, *Delle vicende dell 'agricoltura in Italia* (Florence, 1881), pp. 226 *et seq.*
39. Konrad Haebler, "Die Wirtschaftliche Blüte Spaniens im 16. Jahrhundert und ihr Verfall," in *Historische Untersuchungen* (Berlin, 1888), IX, p. 35.
40. Corroborating texts in M. J. Bonn's, *Spaniens Niedergang der Preisrevolution des 16. Jahrhunderts* (Stuttgart, 1896), p. 113.
41. A. Young, *A Six Weeks Tour Through the Southern Counties of England and Wales* (2nd ed.; 1769).
42. Daniel Defoe. *A Tour Through the Islands of Great Britain, ...*
43. Sir F. M. Eden, *State of the Poor, or an History of the Labouring Classes in England from the Conquest to the Present Period* (London, 1797), 3 vols.
44. Daniel Defoe, *A Tour, . . .* , I, p. 101.
45. Arthur Young, *op.cit.*, pp. 78 *et seq.*
46. Daniel Defoe, *A Tour, . . .* , I, pp. 139, 160.
47. *Ibid.*, I, pp. 199, 206.
48. *Ibid.*, II, p. 137.

49. *Ibid.*, I, p. 65; also Arthur Young, *op.cit.*, pp. 21 *et seq.*

50. Arthur Young, *A Six Weeks Tour*, . . . , pp. 49 *et seq.*

51. Daniel Defoe, *A Tour*, . . . , III, p. 10, meaning Lincolnshire.

52. Arthur Young, *A Six Weeks Tour*, . . . , pp. 200 *et seq.*, meaning the countryside around Salisbury.

53. *Ibid.*, *op.cit.*, pp. 308 *et seq.*

54. *Ibid.*, p. 317.

55. W. Hasbach, "Die englischen Landarbeiter in den letzten hundert Jahren und die Einhegungen," in *Schriften des Vereins für Sozialpolitik* (Leipzig, 1894), LIX, p. 10.

56. Daniel Defoe, *A Tour*, . . . , I, p. 182.

57. According to Sir William Petty, *Several Essays in Political Arithmetick* (London, 1699), there were 670,000. Cf. Essay No. 1 (1699).

58. Daniel Defoe, *A Tour*, . . . , III, p. 265.

59. As compiled by W. Hasbach, *Die englischen Landarbeiter*, . . . , LIX, p. 116 *et seq;* also LIX, p. 123.

60. Sir F. M. Eden, *op.cit.*, I, p. 334.

61. Daniel Defoe, *A Tour*, . . . , II, p. 111.

62. *Ibid.*, II, p. 112.

63. Miege and Bolton, *op.cit.*, (10th ed.; 1745), Chapter IX, p. 102.

64. Daniel Defoe, *A Tour*, . . . , I, p. 324.

65. The regions near Surrey, Berks, Oxford, but in particular North Wiltshire, where the barley produced in the countryside for the London market—there was a special market for malt in Queenhith—was processed into malt in the towns of Abingdon, Farringdon, and others; also Daniel Defoe, *A Tour*, . . . , II, p. 113.

66. Near Henningham in Suffolk, according to Arthur Young, *A Six Weeks Tour*, . . . , p. 69; but in particular around Farnham, Surrey, where the cultivation of wheat, once in a flourishing state, had to give way to hops; also Daniel Defoe, *op.cit.*, I, p. 196; also Arthur Young, *op.cit.*, p. 217.

67. Croyden in Surrey was the greatest oat market of London; see also Daniel Defoe, *op.cit.*, I, p. 217.

68. Parts of Essex; also Arthur Young, *op.cit.*, p. 266.

69. Daniel Defoe, *A Tour*, . . . , I, p. 209.

70. *Ibid.*, II, pp. 32, 181.

71. *Ibid.*, II, p. 32.

72. In particular the regions, rich in forests, of Berkshire and Buckinghamshire; also Daniel Defoe, *op.cit.*, II, pp. 32, 55.

73. *Ibid.*, I, p. 120.

74. Jean Francois Mélon, *Essai politique sur le commerce* (Amsterdam, 1734). *Coll. des Economistes*, p. 696.

75. J. E. Cairnes, *The Slave Power* (New York, 1863), p. 76.
76. Jean Baptiste Labat, *Nouveau voyage aux isles de l'Amérique* (The Hague, 1724).
77. Alexander Humboldt, *Essai politique sur le royaume de la Nouvelle-Espagne*, III, p. 179; also (Paris, 1811), IV, Chapter 10, p. 178.
78. Albert Hüne, *Darstellung aller Veränderungen des Neger-sklaven-handels* (Göttingen, 1820).
79. Heinrich Handelmann, *Geschichte der Insel Hayti* (Kiel, 1856), pp. 28–29.
80. Adam Anderson, *Origin of Commerce*, IV, p. 690.
81. Moreau de Jonnés, *Recherches statistiques sur l'esclavage colonial* (Paris, 1842), p. 17 *et seq.*
82. E. Pariset, *Histoire de la fabrique Lyonnaise* (Lyon, 1901), p. 15.
83. R. Broglio d'Ajano, *Die venetianische seidenindustrie* (Stuttgart, 1893), p. 2.
84. Heinrich Sieveking, "Die Genueser Seidenindustrie im 15, und 16. Jahrhundert," *Schmollers Jahrbuch* (Leipzig, 1897), XXI, pp. 101 *et seq.*, 103.
85. E. Pariset, *op.cit.*, p. 35.
86. Justin Godart, *L'Ouvrier en soie* (Lyon, 1899), p. 89.
87. Giovanni Niccoló Pasquali Alidosi, *Instruttione delle cose notabili della cittá di Bologna & altre particolari* (Bologna, 1621), p. 37.
88. Johann Joachim Becher, *Närrische Weissheit und weise Narrheit* (Frankfurt, 1683), pp. 19 *et seq.*, 234.
89. Daniel Defoe, *A Tour, . . .* , III, p. 104.
90. Alexandre Moreau de Jonnès, *État économique . . .* , p. 337.
91. Johann Beckmann, *Beyträge zur Oekonomie, Technologie, Polizei und Cameralwissenschaft* (Göttingen, 1779), pp. 108 *et seq.*
92. Taken and reported from the National Archives by Germain Martin, in his book *La Grande industrie sous le règne de Louis XIV*, pp. 85 *et seq.*
93. *Ibid.*, p. 301.
94. L. S. Mercier, *op.cit.*, IX, p. 186.
95. G. Martin, *op.cit.*, pp. 197 *et seq.*
96. Otto Wiedfeldt, "Statistische Studien zur Entwickelungsgeschichte der Berliner Industrie von 1720 bis 1890," in Gustav Schmoller, *Staats- und socialwissenschaftliche Forschungen* (Leipzig, 1898), XVI, p. 322.
97. Victor Böhmert, "Urkundliche Geschichte und Statistik der Meissner Porzellanmanufactur von 1710 bis 1880, mit besonderer Rücksicht auf die Betriebs-, Lohn- und Kassenverhältnisse," *Zeitschrift des K. Sächsischen Bureaus* (Dresden, 1880), XXVI, pp. 44 *et seq.*

98. L. S. Mercier, *op.cit.* (1788), XI, pp. 41–42.
99. Alfred Doren, *Die florentiner Wollentuchindustrie, vom 14. bis zum 16. Jahrhundert* (Stuttgart, 1901), p. 23.
100. *Ibid.*, p. 22.
101. *Ibid.*, pp. 86 *et seq.*
102. Francesco Guicciardini, *Opere inedite* (Firenze, 1863), in K. Haebler, *Die wirtschaftliche Blüte Spaniens*, . . . , p. 47.
103. Diego de Colmenares, *Historia de la insigne ciudad de Segovia, compendio de la historia de Castilla* (Madrid, 1640), in M. J. Bonn, *Spaniens Niedergang*, . . . , p. 120.
104. G. Martin, *op.cit.*, p. 17.
105. *Encyclopédie Méthodique*, Manufacture, No. III, p. 60.
106. The original documents are for the main part reprinted in E. Levasseur's *Histoire des classes ouvrières* (1904), II, p. 563.
107. Jos. Child.
108. G. R. Porter, *The Progress of the Nation* (London, 1912), p. 324.
109. Daniel Defoe, *Complete English Tradesman* (1841), p. 203.
110. The main source from which later students drew their information is the *Report of the Committee of the House of Commons on the Woolen Manufacture of England* (1806).
111. Sources in N. J. Ashley, *Englische Wirtschaftsgeschichte* (Leipzig), II, p. 270.
112. 1 and 2 P. and M. c. 14, cited in W. Cunningham, *The Growth of English Industry and Commerce* (Cambridge, 1890), p. 467.
113. *Allgemeine Schatzkammer der Kauffmannschaft* (1741), pp. 1213–14.
114. A. Franklin, *op.cit.*, p. 265.
115. *The Trade of England Revived* (London, 1681), p. 36, cited in S. and B. Webb, *The History of Trade Unionism* (London, 1920), p. 31.
116. R. Campbell, *op.cit.*, (1741), pp. 47, 192.
117. S. and B. Webb, *op.cit.*, p. 26.
118. Emile Langlade, *op.cit.*
119. H. Kanter, "Die Schuhmacherei in Breslau," *Schriften des Vereins für Sozial-Politik* (Leipzig, 1895), LXV, p. 26.
120. L. S. Mercier, *op.cit.* (1788), XI, pp. 12 *et seq.*
121. R. Campbell, *op.cit.*, pp. 233 *et seq.*
122. Jacques Savary, *op.cit.*, II, p. 790 *et seq.*
123. O. W. Wiedfeldt, *op.cit.*, p. 364.
124. Carl Julius Bergius, *Cam. Magaz.*, III, p. 236.
125. *Négociations du Comte d'Avaux*, V, p. 267, in Chr. Weiss, *Histoire des réfugiés protestants de France*, II, p. 131.

126. O. Wiedfeldt, *op.cit.*, p. 209.
127. E. Muentz, *Les Arts à la cour des papes*, I, No. 3, p. 84. Cf. Jacob Burckhardt, *Geschichte der Renaissance in Italien* (Stuttgart, 1891), I, pp. 19–20.
128. L. S. Mercier, *op.cit.*, VIII, Chapter 636, pp. 110 *et seq.*
129. R. Campbell, *op.cit.*, pp. 229 *et seq.*
130. *A General Description of All Trades*, p. 65.
131. Daniel Defoe, *Complete English Tradesman*, II, p. 337.
132. Arthur Cohen, "Das Schreinereigewerbe in Augsburg," *Schriften des Vereins für Sozial-Politik* (Leipzig, 1895), LXIV, p. 500.
133. Emile Levasseur, *Histoire des classes ouvrières* (1904), II, pp. 568 *et seq.*
134. Emile Levasseur, *op.cit.*, II, pp. 569 *et seq.*
135. R. Clouston, *English Furniture and Furniture Makers of the 18th Century* (London, 1906), pp. 302 *et seq.*, 10 *et seq.*
136. Richard Hirsch, "Die Moebelschreinerei in Mainz," *Schriften des Vereins für Sozial-Politik* (Leipzig, 1895), LXIV, pp. 296, 312.
137. O. Wiedfeldt, *op.cit.*, p. 188.
138. *Ibid.*, p. 390.
139. O. Wiedfeldt, *op.cit.*, p. 386.
140. Germain Martin, *La Grande industrie en France sous le règne de Louis XIV* (Paris, 1900), pp. 144–45.
141. *A General Description of All Trades*, p. 196.

* Persons are grouped under Artists, Mistresses and courtesans, Rulers
and popes, and Various persons.